Collins Illustrated Guide to
JAPAN

Alan Booth

Photography by Ken Straiton

COLLINS
8 Grafton Street, London W1
1988

(Preceding page) Tokyo skyline. **Pachinko** *is pinball. The blue-bordered sign advertises liquor, the yellow sign a shop that sells jeans.*

William Collins Sons & Co. Ltd
London • Glasgow • Sydney • Auckland
Toronto • Johannesburg

British Library Cataloguing in Publication Data

Collins Illustrated Guide to Japan — (Asian Guides Series)
1. Japan — Description and Travel — Guide books
I. Series
915.92'0448   DS805.2

ISBN 0-00-217951-2

First published 1988
© The Guide Book Company Ltd 1988

Editor: David Price
Picture Editor: Ingrid Morejohn

Photographs by Ken Straiton / Pacific Press Service, with additional contributions
by Mike Yamashita / Pacific Press Service (220),
and Wayne Brothers (201)

Artwork: Unity Design Studio
Maps: Bai Yiliang

Printed in Hong Kong

Contents

Introduction	10

Tokyo and the Kanto Region — 20
- Tokyo: History, Size, Crowds, Chaos, Character — 20
- Historical Tokyo — 28
- Institutional Tokyo — 40
- Fluid Tokyo — 45
- Tokyo's Islands — 50
- The Rest of the Kanto Region — 51

Nara, Kyoto and the Kinki Region — 62
- The Ancient Capitals, their History, their Primacy — 62
- Nara — 66
- In Nara Prefecture — 78
- Kyoto — 81
- Kyoto: The Skin — 82
- Kyoto: The Bones — 91
- Festive Kyoto — 98
- In Kyoto Prefecture — 99
- The Rest of the Kinki Region — 101

The Tohoku Region — 113
- Homely Wilds — 113

The Chubu Region — 134
- The Belly and the Back — 134
- The Pacific Belly — 135
- The Japan Sea Back — 146

Hiroshima and the Chugoku Region — 157
- The Politics of Peace — 157
- In Hiroshima Prefecture — 160
- The Rest of the Chugoku Region — 162

The Inland Sea and Shikoku — 170
- This Side of Paradise — 170
- An Unbridgeable Remoteness? — 174

Kyushu — 183
- Pioneers and Persecutors — 183

Okinawa and the Southern Islands — 207
- Invasion, Disruption, JALPAK — 207

Hokkaido — 214
- The New Frontier — 214

Helpful Information — 223
- Getting Around Japan — 223
- Getting, and Not Getting Around Tokyo — 226
- Accommodation in Japan — 227
- Eating Out — 230
- Drinking Out — 231
- Hot Springs — 232
- Language and Names — 234
- The Calendar, the Years and Public Holidays — 235

Sources of Information	238
Further Reading	239
General Index	241
Index of People Mentioned	248
About the Author	256

Special Topics

Japanese Theatre	39
Religion in Japan	75
Tohoku's Four Great Summer Festivals	121
Japanese Music	132
Lavatories, Baths and Other Headaches	190
Arts, Martial and Polite	199

Maps

Japan	9
Central Tokyo	18-19
Kanto Region	52
Kyoto	83
Kinki Region	100
Tohoku Region	112
Chubu Region	136
Chugoku Region	156
Shikoku Region	172
Kyushu Region	182
Okinawa Region	206
Hokkaido Region	216

Introduction

More thorough nonsense must be spoken and written about Japan than about any comparably developed nation.

On the congested Washington metro a newly returned traveller remarks to his fellow passengers, 'If you think this is crowded, you should see the subways in Tokyo. There they employ attendants to push people on and off trains because Japanese commuters are too polite to push each other'. And a guide to Japan published recently for the American business community informs its readers that Japanese office workers begin each working day with a tea ceremony.

As with all the most misleading myths, there is a tiny grain of truth in both these extraordinary statements, sufficient to throw the credulous completely off balance. During Tokyo rush hours, white-gloved station employees can indeed be seen pushing people onto jam-packed trains, but social decorum is not among their reasons. And it is true that a male office worker arriving at his desk in the morning will probably be served a small cup of green tea by a female office worker who thereby discharges the main part of her job; but this has as little to do with the tea ceremony as an office outing to the pub has to do with a royal garden party.

One of the difficulties of coming to grips with Japan is that myths about Japanese quaintness die so very hard. Ever since the 'discovery' of Japan by the West, Western visitors have gone out of their way to emphasize as many of the unfamiliar aspects of Japanese life as they could, partly because by doing so they made their own stay there sound all the more intrepid. And ever since the discovery by Japanese government and business circles that Western trade negotiators and others are willing to be fobbed off with such lines as 'You can't understand the way we do things because you are not Japanese', the mythmaking fraternity has multiplied to plague proportions.

Of course the foreign visitor to Japan wants to see unfamiliar things; if he didn't he would have gone to Brighton. His delight in the vertical neon signs of Ginza is genuine, and made possible by the fact that he can't read them. A British poet's enthusiastic comparison of Japanese conversation to the twittering of birds is tolerated because neither he nor his readers can understand a single word that is being said. Where the foreign traveller in Japan is concerned, ignorance is the best guarantee of bliss.

The most difficult myths to dispel are those concocted by the Japanese themselves: for example, the curious and universally credited myth that Japan is a small country. Of Japan's four main islands, the largest, Honshu, is slightly larger than all of Great Britain; Hokkaido is about the size of Austria; Kyushu is exactly the size of Denmark; and Shikoku is a little smaller than Wales. The climate and vegetation of northern Hokkaido are subarctic, while those of southern Kyushu are subtropical (in fact, Japan's southernmost island, Iriomote, lies a bare one degree north of the Tropic of Cancer). If this is a small country, then most of the other countries in the world must be classified as microscopic.

Or there is the equally pervasive belief in Japan's 'uniqueness', a quality taken for granted whenever Japanese people attempt to define their country and the ways in which it differs from everyone else's. For example: 'Japan has four seasons. Japan is unique. Therefore no other country has four seasons.' Or: 'The Japanese language is subtle and poetic. Japan is unique. Therefore all other languages are crude and merely "logical".' These and similar articles of faith can be encountered at all levels of the social spectrum —in unthinking youths for whom they are reinforced nightly by television quiz shows, as well as in educated 'opinion makers' who write books 'proving' the Japanese to be totally unlike all other human beings. This class of literature is called *nihonjinron* (literally, 'Japanese People Discussions'), examples of which regularly rank among the nation's best sellers.

Naturally enough, these facts of Japanese life can exert a somewhat negative influence on the long-term foreign resident or the Japanese specialist who takes his field of study seriously. But the short-term visitor is more likely to find them enchanting than otherwise. They are ideal subjects with which he can regale fellow passengers on congested Washington trains and, if you don't understand a word of it, *nihonjinron* must sound disarmingly like the twittering of birds.

From 1639 to 1854 Japan maintained a policy of national seclusion (*sakoku*—literally 'closed country'), when Japanese citizens were forcibly prevented from travelling abroad and foreigners who found their way to Japan were either sent packing or beheaded. Within the country a strict military dictatorship ensured social conformity at all levels, the price of peace and unity being a conspicuous absence of personal freedoms. For example, the authorities operated a series of barrier gates on all of the main feudal highways at which tolls were collected, thus seriously discouraging travel between regions, particularly among the impecunious. Most people born into the peasant or farming classes spent their entire lives within a few miles of the place where they were born, with the possible exception—once and once only—of a pilgrimage to the Grand Shrine at Ise.

This de facto restriction of movement had two main results, both of which can still be strongly felt. The first was an almost mystical attachment to one's 'home country' (*furusato*—a word that has no real equivalent in English, implying both the place where a person was actually born and the place to which he feels the strongest spiritual ties). Regional identity is still an

A permanent market under the elevated tracks near Ueno station, Tokyo.

important fact of life in modern Japan and, for all the official stress upon homogeneity and the never-ending litany of 'We Japanese', local diversity—whether of dialect, diet, music, produce or custom—is a major and continuing source of pride.

The second result was that travel to distant parts of the country obtained an aura of romance which has hardly diminished in modern times. The great feudal highways, particularly the Tokaido which ran from Edo (Tokyo) to Kyoto and Osaka, were among the best-loved settings for stories, plays and legends. The *michiyuki* (literally, 'Going Along the Road') was an essential scene in most popular Kabuki and puppet plays, and usually depicted the flight of a pair of doomed lovers down some impossibly picturesque thoroughfare, strewn with cherry blossoms and overshadowed by the pristine cone of Mount Fuji. Recently this aura of romance found its way into the slogans used in two campaigns mounted by the national railways to persuade people to spend their holidays exploring distant parts of the country. The slogans were 'Discover Japan' and 'Exotic Japan' (both, incidentally, couched in English so as to imbue them with the same degree of dreamy unreality as was conveyed by the cherry blossoms and Fuji's cone).

With postwar affluence has come a large-scale boom in leisure travel, and domestic tourism is one of the most flourishing industries in the nation. For the foreign visitor, this state of affairs has both advantages and disadvantages. The chief advantage is that, with an infrastructure so comprehensively and efficiently developed, he will rarely experience any difficulty in obtaining information about, and then reaching, a chosen destination, and his problem once there will hardly ever be lack of accommodation but rather a plethora out of which to choose. The disadvantage is that, unless he is unusually fortunate, he is likely to find himself viewing some spot noted for its tranquillity and remoteness in the company of half the population of Osaka.

What is the best time of year to visit Japan? Skiing and other winter sports now form a sizeable chunk of the booming tourist industry, and the most reliable months for these are January and February. The most popular resorts do not yet employ white-gloved attendants to push skiers in and out of chair lifts but, at weekends and during holidays, congestion falls not far short of rush-hour density. Local festivals provide a colourful reason for visiting provincial cities, and the thickest concentration of these occurs in August, during the Buddhist observance of *O-Bon,* sometimes called the 'Festival of the Dead', when the spirits of departed ancestors are thought to return to the homes of their families, who dance and provide other diversions to entertain them. Family members who have moved to the great cities often go back to the towns and villages where they were born to celebrate O-Bon, making mid-August the peak travel period of the year. Between August 8 and 18 (or thereabouts, depending on the distribution of weekends) long-distance trains carry up to twice their normal capacity of passengers and seats on domestic

flights are usually unavailable unless booked well in advance. Beaches near major cities are so popular with bathers on August Sundays that, almost without fail, the Monday morning papers report between 20 and 30 drownings.

New Year is, for most people, a family celebration, but increasing numbers of 'nuclear families', not tied to home by the presence of older relatives, seize the opportunity to spend a few days away, often at a hotspring resort. Hotels and inns at the more popular tourist destinations may receive New Year reservations up to a year in advance, dooming spur-of-the-moment plans by foreign visitors to likely frustration. This is even truer of the week beginning 29 April and ending 5 May, known as 'Golden Week' because it contains no fewer than three national holidays: 29 April (The Emperor's Birthday), 3 May (Constitution Day) and 5 May (The Boys' Festival, now more equably known as Children's Day). It is becoming the custom for people to take the whole week off work and make it the high point of their travelling year, though whether this custom will survive the death of the present emperor and the celebration of his successor's birthday on a different date remains to be seen. Nowadays, too, more and more Japanese people are using the leisure time available at New Year, Golden Week and O-Bon for taking trips abroad, so that international flights into and out of Japan are as fully booked as domestic flights. Visitors arriving in Japan with open tickets and expecting to make last-minute reservations home during these periods could end up staying longer than they bargained for.

In addition to these three weeks of airport, hotel and railway upheaval, the Japanese have traditionally regarded three short periods of the year as the best times for organizing outings to noted beauty spots. The first of these is the cherry-blossom season, which starts in Kyushu in early March, reaches Tokyo around the beginning of April, and ends in northern Honshu in May. The moon is said to be at its best in early autumn, so September was traditionally a month for organizing moon-viewing parties, a recreation now sadly lapsed. And the often spectacular colouring of the leaves in late autumn makes October and November favourite months for trips to lakes or mountain spas.

Many people would advise against travelling during the rainy season (called *tsuyu* or *baiu*; for most of the country early June to mid-July), but the misty precipitation characteristic of this time of year can enhance some destinations—the gardens of Kyoto temples, for instance—and, in any case, the rainy season usually includes stretches of up to a week when the whole country basks in completely rainless summer weather. Meteorologists insist that there is a second rainy season (*shurin*) during late September and early October, but this period is more obviously characterized by the late typhoons that blow up through the South China Sea and bring torrential downpours to much of southern Japan, especially the Ryukyu islands and Kyushu. It is certainly not a time of misty precipitation; rather of the dispersal of rooftiles and the washing away of grandmothers.

An all-year-round phenomenon is the supposed difficulty raised by the 'language barrier', though this tends to weigh more heavily on the Japanese consciousness than it does on that of the average foreign visitor. It is not many years since the Japan Tourist Bureau did its best to persuade people with foreign faces not to stay at country inns and lodging houses, citing the 'language barrier' as the reason. And the proprietors of the country inns themselves would often fly into mild panics and pretend to be full or closed or under a demolition order when faced with the possibility that a guest might have to ask the way to the bathroom by pointing his finger rather than engaging his host in a ten-minute discussion. Happily, things have changed for the better and, though one can still encounter reluctance to accept foreign visitors at some places, there is nowadays a much wider acceptance of the fact that people who have taken the considerable trouble to reach, say, the interior of Shikoku will in all likelihood not be expecting to find water beds, tenderloin steaks and an innkeeper with a degree in modern languages.

Practically all Japanese people educated in the postwar period have studied English for at least six years at school, and practically none can speak a sensible word of it. This is less their fault than the fault of an educational system which has seized upon the intricacies of English grammar and lexis as a perfect means of testing rote memory and willingness to submit to grinding discipline for the sake of social advancement. Grammar is taught as though it were a series of algebraic equations and vocabulary is introduced with little concern for its potential usefulness in everyday life but with every consideration for its likely occurrence in examination papers. That young people resent learning English and leave school thinking that foreigners and their languages are colossal jokes is hardly surprising.

Needless to say, the visitor who confines his stay to Western-style hotels and does all his booking through major travel agents will find English speakers on the staffs of both, so considerations of language will not much worry him. But the more adventurous visitor, provided he is amply supplied with time and patience, will likely discover that the 'language barrier' is a more formidable obstacle in the imagination than it is in reality.

Quite aside from questions of language, many foreign visitors have returned from their trips to Japan brimming with praise for the helpfulness and honesty of the people they have encountered, and few of their tales are exaggerated. The personal honesty of the Japanese (when they are not filing income tax returns) is, quite rightly, proverbial. Visitors have left their handbags on the back seats of taxis and had them returned within the hour by drivers who have turned off their meters and taken time off work to cruise the streets looking for the owners. Foreign tourists have dropped their wallets in station taxi queues and gone to the station lost property offices hours, or even days, later to find that their wallets have been handed in with the contents intact. The only glaring exceptions to this rule are umbrellas and bicycles, which, no matter how much they cost and no matter how many combination locks protect them, tend to be viewed as fair game for anyone in urgent need of either.

As for helpfulness, it has been the common experience of travellers, particularly in remoter areas, that no sooner have they opened their guidebooks or maps to consult them than someone has approached and asked if he could help. If a visitor has solicited directions, he has frequently found that the person he asked has left whatever he was doing and accompanied the visitor to his destination, sometimes inviting him for coffee on the way. I have walked past houses in remote rural areas and had the owners run out to summon me inside for a cup of tea. I have knocked at a door to ask the way and spent the rest of the afternoon sitting on the veranda drinking beer. Visitors who shun encounters of this kind because they pay too much attention to mutterings about language barriers do themselves a serious disfavour. And besides, if you speak three words of Japanese you will be rapturously applauded for your linguistic mastery. It is only when you are approaching competence that you will be frowned upon as a threat to the national polity.

It seems hardly necessary to emphasize the limitations of a book of this kind. It has often been said that a festival takes place somewhere in Japan every day of the year. There are countless little shrines and temples that no guidebook will ever mention. They may boast no valuable statuary nor any special historical associations, but a combination of circumstance, location, age and atmosphere can turn any one of them into the high point of a visitor's stay. And the unspoiled, little-visited parts of the Japanese countryside still hugely outnumber the famous spots singled out for full-throttle tourist spoliation. The Inland Sea National Park alone contains more than a thousand islands.

Other limitations the book has imposed on itself. It recommends no hotels or restaurants; it does not give advice on how best to waste the nighttime hours; it provides no details of rail, road or air connections to the places it describes. Visitors in need of this sort of information can find themselves inundated with it, if they choose, within minutes of arrival. A lot of it is available free from their hotel information desk or from any large travel agent. See page 238 for most of the reliable sources.

This guide's approach is regional. The Kanto (including Tokyo) and Kinki (including Nara and Kyoto) regions occupy the longest sections because they are the places where most foreign visitors to Japan spend the greatest amount of time, but more than half the book is concerned with other, often remoter, destinations. Each region is introduced by some general remarks aimed at providing the reader with background information on history and geography, as well as with some idea of a district's character and reputation. Following this, the main sights and attractions of each region are described, prefecture by prefecture (the nine regions are divided into a total of 47 prefectures). A prefectural approach has the disadvantage that some notable tourist spots (like the Fuji-Hakone-Izu National Park) spread over two or more prefectures; so that the reader is obliged to look in several different parts of the book for a comprehensive description of what he will see there, though his task is simplified by cross-references. However, this inconvenience is outweighed by the fact that much of the tourist information available within Japan is organized at a prefectural level. Each prefecture has its own tourist offices and these publish many of the brochures, maps and other material available. A prefectural approach facilitates the use of information from local sources to amplify and complement the descriptions and opinions contained in this book.

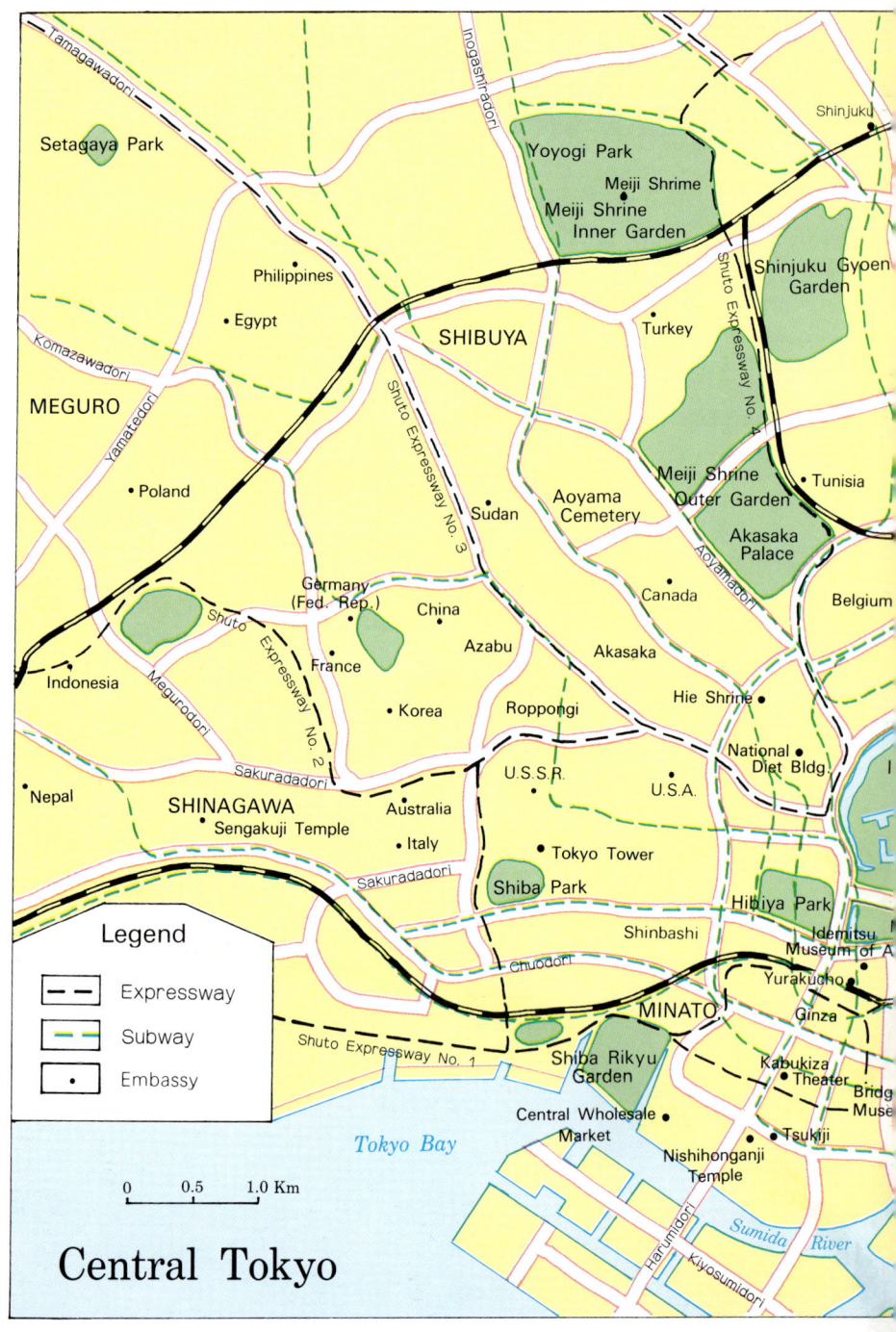

Tokyo and the Kanto Region

Tokyo: History, Size, Crowds, Chaos, Character

When in 1721 the eighth Tokugawa shogun's super-efficient bureaucracy conducted the first of its nationwide censuses, it discovered that the city of Edo (now called Tokyo) had a population approaching 1.3 million. Eighty-two years earlier, the eighth shogun's second cousin had ordered that Japan be closed to practically all foreign contact, so by 1721 information about other countries cannot have been very up-to-date nor very readily available. Possibly, then, not even the super-efficient bureaucracy realized that, on the evidence of its first mammoth head-count, Edo was the most populous city on earth and had probably been so for at least half a century. If it had known that, the bureaucracy would certainly have advertised the fact with great relish, since statistical demonstrations of ways in which Japan outshines all other countries, in whatever field of human activity, have long been a national hobby.

Since 1603, when the Tokugawa shogunate was founded, Edo had been the shogun's administrative centre and the site of the shogun's own castle, but it was not Japan's official capital. The official capital was Kyoto, where the emperor maintained his infinitely sophisticated and totally powerless court. And so it remained until 1868, when the Tokugawa shogunate finally collapsed and the new government, with the present emperor's grandfather nominally at its head, renamed Edo Tokyo (Eastern Capital), thus confirming in name what, for two and a half centuries, the city had been in fact.

Accounts of the origins and rise of the Eastern Capital often imply that, until the first Tokugawa shogun, Ieyasu, decided to situate his government there, the place was a swampy little village; but this is fanciful, and suggests that the authors are somehow confusing Tokyo with Kuala Lumpur. Edo had been a power base of sorts since 1457, when Lord Ota Dokan built a fortress there—which for a time enjoyed a reputation as the strongest fortress in the Kanto region, the pivot of three major highways that were to play a fundamental role in the social and economic development of Japan. These highways were the Tokaido (joining Edo to Kyoto, and extending to Osaka), the Koshukaido (from Edo to Kofu in today's Yamanashi prefecture) and the Oshukaido (which began at Edo and went north into the unpoliced wilds of the Tohoku region). By the end of the 16th century, the fortress had fallen into disrepair but Ieyasu's decision to site his administrative seat there was hardly the example of preternatural longsightedness that his admirers pretend.

It is as well to begin a description of Tokyo aimed at the short-term visitor with at least this much ancient history, since the city today boasts few visible relics of anything older than the Second World War, and these first paragraphs can remain in the visitor's mind as an evocation of things that he will see little sign of.

Certainly, the so-called 'Edo period' (1603–1867) is alive and well on television. Almost every televised example of what the Japanese call *chambara* (swashbuckling action adventures) is set in the colourful, crowded city of Edo during the two and a half busy centuries when the shogun held sway there. The popularity of the Edo period among T.V. viewers probably owes something to the enforced absence of foreigners (the few who turn up are either crucified or beheaded, thus greatly increasing their entertainment value) and it owes something, too, to the inflexible class structure maintained throughout feudal times, a structure wherein everyone knew at a glance both his own place and everybody else's, and was thus rarely at a loss about how to comport himself with the people he encountered—a situation woefully different today, with uncrucified foreigners turning up on all sides and the sons and daughters of company executives wearing torn jeans and 'Prick Up' tee-shirts.

Edo was also the city in which a non-aristocratic Japanese urban culture first came into its own. The city's great entertainments—its fairs, its festivals, its licensed quarters, its Kabuki theatre—flourished in response to the earthy demands of a newly powerful and ebullient merchant class. This—now that the values of the marketplace have eclipsed forever the once dominant mores of the samurai—adds hugely to the ongoing popularity of the Edo period, making it and the city that gave it its name both symbols of an imagined egalitarianism.

But the visitor—whether Japanese or non-Japanese—who comes to Tokyo in search of the old Edo is doomed to disappointment. Few cities on earth change as rapidly and as constantly as Tokyo does; and while the visitor from any other part of Japan is liable to list among his first impressions of Tokyo its vast size, its vast population and the vast amount of chaos generated by the apparent lack of any form of rational town planning, the long-term resident is more likely to characterize the city by the frequency and abruptness of the changes that continually overtake its various districts.

Tokyo is still, by many measures, the largest city in the world. Its size is officially given as 2,145 square kilometres (1,341 square miles), almost twice that of Greater London. This is the figure for the total metropolitan area, including the 23 inner wards and the 26 outer sub-cities. But Tokyo has no green belt, and the urban sprawl extends uninterrupted well beyond the metropolitan boundaries and into the neighbouring prefectures of Kanagawa, Saitama and Chiba, much of whose residential space is occupied by daily commuters to the capital. The traveller between Tokyo and Yokohama, for example, will be quite unable to determine merely by looking out of his train, bus or taxi window when he leaves one and enters the other, and this applies equally to the commuter from Chiba city or one of the 'bed-towns' in

Free entertainment opposite the East Exit of Shinjuku station.

Saitama. The population of Tokyo is usually stated to be in the region of 12 million but, given that the sprawl far exceeds the capital's administrative boundaries, this is a somewhat artificial figure too. If the populations of the indistinguishably adjoining areas are included, the figure more than doubles; which means that something like a quarter of Japan's total population (which now stands at more than 120 million) lives within an area that, for practical purposes, we must call Greater Tokyo.

In terms of population density, Tokyo is nowhere near as badly off today as it was when the shogun's bureaucracy conducted its 1721 census (a fact which may supply a modicum of comfort to the visitor struggling through Shinjuku Station at eight o'clock on a weekday morning). In 1721, Tokyo had a total area of 70 square kilometres (43 square miles) and an overall population density of about 18,500 per square kilometre. Today, if we accept for the sake of argument the official metropolitan figures, the overall density is about 5,500 per square kilometre—positively thin on the ground when you take into account the advent of high-rise buildings. But, of course, populations are never evenly spread, and in 1721 the unevenness perfectly reflected the painful inequities of Japan's feudal class system. More than 66 percent of Edo's land area was owned by the lords and their samurai retainers, and only about 12.5 percent by the far more populous trading class. As a result, in the tradesmen's areas (particularly in parts of what is nowadays Chuo ward) population density reached a horrendous 70,000 per square kilometre. That is about what it reaches in Hongkong today, but in Hongkong people's residences are stacked vertically for 12 or 20 storeys, whereas in old Edo they were all stuck down in the mud. The sheer difficulty of shifting your weight from one foot to the other without mangling the hem of your neighbour's kimono must have been an ever-present worry, and perhaps the high degree of overcrowding among a class of people destined to become the prime shapers of post-feudal Japan contributed greatly to the absence among them of a 'Western' sense of privacy, as well as to the development of elaborate forms of social lubrication (incessant bowing, ultra-polite language, ritualized gift giving, maintenance of a rigid hierarchical order, the accepted difference between what you say and what you really think); forms that helped to stave off the permanent tension that such overcrowding could easily have given rise to. Today the most densely populated ward in Tokyo is Toshima (about 20,000 per square kilometre), which is, not coincidentally, a ward that contains a large number of high-rise housing developments.

As for chaos: it is hard to imagine a more thoroughly mind-numbing introduction to any city in the world than to take the limousine bus from the New Tokyo International Airport at Narita to one of its downtown destinations. The bus travels along some 70 kilometres (43 miles) of concrete expressway which, once the narrow agricultural belt around Narita itself has been passed, is flanked on both sides for as far as the eye can see, and the disturbed brain conceive, by an uninterrupted vista of grey ferroconcrete offices, factories, docks, warehouses and huge characterless housing developments which the Japanese, without any irony, call 'mansions'. At night, the endless sea of neon and fluorescent-lit windows can have a magical attraction, particularly when the skyscrapers of West Shinjuku float into sight. But in daylight, the chief effect is one of horror tinged with whimsy (the whimsy being nowadays enhanced by the fairy-tale spires of Tokyo's Disneyland, which appear briefly on the left-hand side). No two roads seem to run in compatible directions, no two buildings seem to face the same way or to have the same number of storeys or to have been designed with any thought for their surroundings. It is often noted, both by local and foreign observers, that Japanese people tend to promote the ideal of uniformity in their dress, speech, education and behaviour; but uniformity is the very last impression one receives from Tokyo's buildings. The buildings surrounding a well-planned European plaza or flanking a well-laid-out avenue can seem wedded to each other. Tokyo's buildings seem at war with each other. Each is a little island, paying no attention whatever to its neighbours, devouring their sunlight, blocking their approaches, maintaining a ferocious independence in what the architects clearly regarded as hostile territory, or no-man's land at best.

Most Japanese city roads, streets, lanes and avenues have no names, and those of Tokyo are not exceptions. Areas have names, and within these areas blocks are numbered, and within these blocks sub-blocks, and within sub-blocks buildings. But because the roads that surround the blocks strike out and fork in all directions, the blocks are seldom uniform, so the numbers are not necessarily sequential. Some sources derive glee from further horrifying newcomers with the assertion that numbers are assigned to houses not according to their topographical position in a street or block, but according to the (unremembered) date when they were built. This is a nice idea, but fanciful—at least nowadays. Numbers are assigned in as logical a manner as the circumstances permit, which is hardly logical at all. It is somewhat like trying to assign sequential numbers to the leaves of a large tree. They are never regularly arranged and are constantly either falling or sprouting, just as Japanese houses and offices are constantly being ripped down and re-erected. (When Japanese people buy a house they generally tear it down and build a new one immediately, their principal expense and investment being in the land, not in the building). The newcomer can derive some comfort from the fact that life-long residents of Tokyo are obliged— just like himself—to find their way about by means of little maps scribbled on the backs of envelopes. Addresses are normally given only when postal communication is likely. Otherwise your chief recourse is the scribbled map—turn left at the public bath, right at the Chinese restaurant, cross four traffic lights and enquire at the police box.

It is not as though Japanese planners lacked experience in laying out a logically organized city. Kyoto (laid out in 792) had been deliberately modelled on the ancient Chinese capital of Chang'an: its blocks perfectly uniform, its streets intersecting at right angles and aligned with the cardinal points of the compass. Why did planners not follow this familiar example when laying out the shogun's de facto capital of Edo in 1603? One answer is that the land was more hilly. Another is that to have designed Edo along the lines of imperial Kyoto would have been a direct affront to the emperor and an obvious challenge to his, and Kyoto's, fancied pre-eminence. If this is so, it would also account for the fact that no logical replanning was undertaken after the great fire of 1657 (which destroyed half the city's buildings and killed a quarter of its residents) or after any one of the 97 major fires that devastated Edo throughout the 17th, 18th and early 19th centuries (and for which the residents came to feel a curious affection: fires and brawls were called 'the flowers of Edo'). But it does not explain why no extensive replanning took place after the Great Kanto Earthquake of 1923 or the immensely destructive fire-bomb raids of March 1945, since by the time those calamities occurred Tokyo was Japan's capital in name as well as in fact, the shogun had long since disappeared into history and the emperor now made his home there. Some Japanese commentators have tried to suggest that Tokyo is an especially 'Japanese' city precisely because it has never been rigidified in a 'Western' manner. They point to what they see as a similar victory of the Japanese spirit in the carefully preserved 'naturalness' of a Japanese garden versus the straight paths and regimented flower-beds of, say, Versailles. Tokyo is quintessentially Japanese, they suggest, because it has developed 'organically', like cirrhosis of the liver.

Quite apart from fires, earthquakes, bombs, and the fact that many of the buildings in the capital's residential districts are still constructed of timber, and so are as prone to conflagration, typhoon damage and natural degeneration as they ever were, rapid changes are the lifeblood of Tokyo people. From their earliest history the Edokko, the true 'sons of Edo'—particularly the merchants and artisans—were famous for their love of the brash and the new, for fashions and fads, for discarding the outmoded without so much as a sign and for welcoming novelties, the more striking and unlikely the better.

At the very beginning of the 17th century the Edokko were already busily changing the basic topography of their city by reclaiming huge areas of the bay on which it stands—a practice that has continued virtually uninterrupted to the present day. Much of Chuo, Koto and Edogawa wards stands on land reclaimed from the sea, as do the entire Port of Tokyo, the generators of the Tokyo Electric Company, Haneda Airport (until 1978 Tokyo's only international airport, today the terminus for most domestic flights), Tokyo's largest rubbish tip (endearingly named Yumenoshima—'Island of Dreams') and dozens of other major facilities, both commercial and residential. The latest development project is an undersea road tunnel planned to cross the entire width of the bay from Kawasaki in Kanagawa prefecture to Kisarazu in Chiba prefecture.

Inland, Tokyo's propensity for change is enormously aided by the fact that the city has no single centre. Rather, it has a multiplicity of sub-centres, each with its own distinct and still evolving character, each striving to outdo the others in atmosphere and attractions. This too has been a largely unplanned development, since the briefest glance at a map of the city is enough to reveal that the topographical 'centre' of old Edo—and the intended centre of Tokyo—was the Imperial Palace (formerly the shogun's castle), isolated and grandly surrounded by its moats and walls and still flanked by untypically wide roads and rare plaza-like spaces. During the Edo period, the shogun's castle was the hub of government and the chief focus of attention for all the provincial lords who were forced by the shogun to spend alternate years in the capital so as to prevent them being long enough in their own distant fiefs to foment rebellion. (In the years when the lords were allowed to live in their own fiefs, family members were obliged to remain in Edo under what amounted to a system of legalized hostage-taking). But even during these centuries, the capital had more than this one awe-inspiring centre. For the merchants and artisans, the 'centre' of Edo lay about a kilometre and a half, east of the castle, in the most densely populated area of the city. This 'centre' was the Nihonbashi Bridge, and it was recognized as such by the bureaucracy to the extent that distances between the capital and all other points were measured from there (it was over the Nihonbashi Bridge that the major trunk roads entered Edo, but the system of measuring distances from there is curious when you consider how jealously the shogun guarded most other prerogatives; you would expect all distances to have been measured from the dais on which he sat, but perhaps this was also part of a deliberate policy of not offending the emperor).

The main modern sub-centres grew up as a result of private enterprise's taking advantage of the flood of commuter traffic which began shortly after the war. Private railway companies, unable to purchase land for their terminuses in the already congested central areas of the city, were forced to build them an average of just over five kilometres (three miles) away from the castle, in an arc marking the western boundary of what became the Yamanote loop line (see page 226). Because land this distant from the centre was still comparatively cheap, the companies diversified their investments into department stores, theatres and other facilities: the nuclei of today's sub-centres. The Seibu, Keio and Odakyu companies developed Shinjuku, once a simple staging point on journeys west, today the capital's liveliest district, served by a massively complex railway station through which two

million people pass each day—the equivalent of the entire population of Paris. The Tokyu company developed Shibuya, now a major shopping and entertainment area, the site of NHK's (the National Broadcasting Corporation's) headquarters and the pools and stadiums built for the 1964 Olympics. And the Seibu and Tobu companies developed Ikebukuro, not so fashionable as Shibuya nor so frantic as Shinjuku, but the chief shopping and entertainment district of Tokyo's most densely populated ward. The other two major terminuses on the Yamanote loop line—Tokyo and Ueno—both serve mainly lines that have only recently been privatized and predate the postwar boom in sub-centres. Both lie much nearer the palace, in what was Edo proper rather than its outskirts. Tokyo station is close both to the city's major business and banking areas, Otemachi and Marunouchi, and to the traditional, but now sadly eclipsed, shopping and entertainment districts of Ginza and Shinbashi. Ueno is the site of a major park as well as several of Tokyo's principal art museums and concert halls.

Unless they are bent on some special errand, such as the purchase of electrical equipment or the study of industrial robots, most short-term visitors are likely to want to gain three things during their stay in Tokyo: a sense of the city's history, a sense of its importance and function as the nation's capital and as the richest and arguably the most powerful city in Asia, and a sense of its elusive and multi-faceted spirit. The following sections deal in turn with each of these ambitions.

Historical Tokyo

The point has already been made that comparatively little remains in modern Tokyo to recall its colourful feudal-era past. Perishable wooden buildings, natural and man-made disasters have conspired to rob it of visible remains. In addition, an understandable desire to put the disastrous military adventures of the 1930s and '40s firmly out of mind has resulted in a tendency among many Japanese people to ignore—and sometimes actively to dislike—their own history. Where T.V. dramas treat historical subjects, they almost invariably turn them into fairyland fantasies: class distinctions disappear, old Edo bursts at the seams with impossibly dashing Robin Hoods, dictatorship—even military dictatorship—is always benevolent.

The centre of Edo-era military dictatorship was the shogun's castle, now the **Imperial Palace**, constructed on the site of Ota Dokan's 15th-century fortress. The palace itself, having been destroyed during the war, was rebuilt in ferroconcrete in 1968 (the visitor had better accustom himself quickly to the idea of ancient buildings having been rebuilt in recent times, since it is true of most of Japan's castles, and many of her most impressive temples and shrines). The massive stone walls, however, are original and typical of Japanese feudal-era fortifications. The emperor and his consort live today in a fairly modest building not visible from outside the walls. There is, naturally, no public admission to the palace, but the outer garden is sometimes open, and it is occasionally possible to obtain from influential acquaintances invitations to Gagaku and Bugaku (ancient court music and dance) performances staged in a special auditorium within the walls by the Imperial Court Orchestra. Otherwise, entrance is restricted to two days annually—New Year's Day and the Emperor's Birthday (29 April), on both of which the emperor and members of his family wave to the crowds gathered below from behind the bulletproof glass of their balcony.

The visitor who has been to, say, Windsor Castle or the historical residences of other European crowned heads, may be surprised and perhaps disappointed by the sobriety (some might say dreariness) of the external aspect of the Japanese emperor's palace and by the complete absence of any such colourful ritual as the Changing of the Guard. But it will be as well for him to accustom himself quite quickly to this idea too: that understatement, relative smallness of scale and a love of the monochrome and low-key are at the root of much of what the Japanese have traditionally considered worthy of admiration.

Though every feudal lord maintained a residence in Edo, and though these together accounted for more than two-thirds of the city's total land area, none of these residences has survived. Most of the city's modern parks, major hotels and university campuses have been built on the grounds that these residences occupied, so the visitor can at least get some idea of where they once stood. **Tokyo University**, for example, stands on land once owned by the lords of Kaga (modern Ishikawa prefecture), a fitting location since Tokyo University (or Todai as it is usually known) is the most prestigious seat of learning in the country and Kaga was the richest fief.

Edo was a city of rivers and canals, comparable, so some observers reckoned, to Amsterdam or Venice. Just as the visitor can obtain an idea of where the residences of lords once stood by searching out parks, universities and hotels, so he can get a notion of where the rivers and canals once ran by looking at elevated expressways, since many of these have been built on the concreted-over courses of old waterways. One or two stretches of the waterways survive intact, such as that at **Ochanomizu** where the **Kanda River** joins the outer moat of the palace. The name 'Ochanomizu' means, charmingly enough, 'water for making tea', though putting the water here to that particular use today would likely result in a lengthy period of hospitalization (and, conveniently enough, one of Tokyo's many hospitals, Ikashikadai, is situated on the very bank). For a glimpse of how pleasant Edo's waterways must have been in feudal days, the visitor with time to spare can take the orange Chuo Line 20 kilometres (12 miles) out to Mitaka Station, from which a brief taxi ride will bring him to a point where the **Tama** (Jewel) **Canal**, though surrounded by unremitting suburban greyness, is still shaded

(Preceding page) Procession of Shinto dignitaries at the Meiji Shrine, Tokyo, on Culture Day (November 3).

by trees and lined with pleasant rural-like paths. The canal here proved so irresistibly attractive to the novelist Dazai Osamu that in 1948 he drowned himself in it.

Most people in search of the old Edo go first to **Asakusa**. Asakusa is—or rather, was—the centrepiece of what Tokyo people affectionately call the *shitamachi* (the 'low city'). It is definitely to the shitamachi—the old overcrowded tradesmen's area—that a visitor should go in his quest for as much of the spirit of old Edo as survives; though it is no longer quite so definite that he should concentrate his quest in Asakusa. Asakusa has enjoyed several heydays. From 1657 until prostitution was officially outlawed in 1958, it was the site of the **Yoshiwara**, the largest licensed quarter in the country, which in turn spawned all kinds of other, less private forms of entertainment. In the early modern period Asakusa remained the quintessential Edokko district, boasting every imported and novel delight that the fad-mad son of Edo could possibly crave. It was the site of Japan's first 'skyscraper'—the red-brick 'Twelve Storeys', destroyed in the great earthquake of 1923, which had incorporated the country's first elevator. It was the site of Japan's first cinemas, dance halls and cabarets. As late as the mid-1970s Asakusa was still the nightlife capital of the shitamachi, with its stalls, restaurants and *minyo sakaba* (eating and drinking establishments where live folk music and dances are performed). Then, in the 1980s, the blight of change overtook it. The Kokusai Theatre was torn down and replaced by the modern Asakusa View Hotel. *Oiwake* (Crossroads), one of the largest and liveliest of the minyo sakaba was closed, and the entire area began a not-yet-completed transformation from entertainment quarter to business district.

Asakusa's showpiece is **Sensoji** Temple, also called **Asakusa Kannon** Temple (Kannon is the Goddess of Mercy). It is one of the oldest temples in the capital, with records dating from the seventh century, but, like so many other landmarks, it was completely destroyed during the Second World War and rebuilt in ferro-concrete in 1958 (a tumultuous year for both temple and prostitutes). Among the temple's attractions are the rows of small shops (*Nakamise*) within its precincts, that sell traditional items such as dolls, cakes, clogs, kimonos and oiled-paper umbrellas. Visitors fortunate enough to be in Asakusa on 17 and 18 May (or the nearest weekend) will find the **Sanja Matsuri** in full swing. This is one of the capital's largest and most impressive festivals, and during its two days the spirit of old Edo comes as close to resurrection as it ever will. Though radical change is a way of life in Tokyo, the city's three main festivals—this, the **Sanno Matsuri** (15 June of even-numbered years) and the **Kanda Matsuri** (15 May of odd-numbered years)—remain a good deal more authentic, in externals as well as in spirit, than are many of the large provincial celebrations.

Like most of the city's other waterways, the **Nihonbashi River**, spanned by the famous measuring-point bridge (the present bridge dates from 1911), is largely obscured by an elevated expressway, and **Nihonbashi** itself is today best known as the site of the large **Mitsukoshi Department Store**, the forerunner of which was founded here in 1673.

Kanda, whose 17th-century **Myojin Shrine** (rebuilt in 1934) hosts one of the three great festivals already mentioned, is best known for its bookshops. Some of these specialize in second-hand foreign-language books, as well as old maps and prints, and many restrict their stock to specific subject areas such as philosophy and religion. For some reason, Kanda has also become the capital's chief retail centre for ski equipment. (It is worth pointing out that, as was traditionally the case in many Asian cities, whole areas of the shitamachi tend to specialize in the retailing of a single kind of commodity. Thus, **Akihabara**, next-door to Kanda, is the place to go for electrical equipment, **Asakusabashi** for paper ornaments, **Tawaramachi**, next-door to Asakusa, for lacquered Buddhist altars, **Kappabashi**, next-door to Tawaramachi, for kitchen utensils and plastic food).

Tsukiji is the place to go for fresh fish and sushi, owing to the fact that it contains the city's largest wholesale fish market, formally inaugurated there in 1935. Visitors are allowed into the market, but they must go very early in the morning to see anything worth seeing, and they must make up their minds not to be offended by porters cursing them in loud voices if they happen to be standing in the path of a ton of bleeding tuna.

Ueno boasts Japan's oldest Western-style zoo, the **Tokyo National Museum** (the largest museum in Japan), the **Tokyo Metropolitan Art Gallery**, the **National Museum of Western Art**, and the **National Science Museum**, as well as one of Tokyo's leading concert halls, housed in the **Bunka Kaikan** (Culture Centre). It is pleasing to think that working-class Ueno has become such a culturally-minded spot, since the railway terminus is the main arriving point for itinerant labourers from the depressed rural north, and Tokyo sophisticates used to congregate around the station for the humour to be derived from listening to the arriving bumpkins' outlandish accents. Ueno Park is a favourite place for cherry-blossom viewing in late March or early April, a traditional pastime that requires a delicate sensitivity to the transient beauties of nature and an extremely indelicate constitution capable of handling the massive amounts of sake and beer whose rapid consumption the transient blossoms inspire. Nearby is the lotus-shrouded **Shinobazu Pond** with its little island dedicated to the goddess Benten, who in some ways is the presiding deity of the whole city since it was she who led Lord Ota Dokan to found the first Edo Castle.

None of these places has very many visible relics of the feudal age, but the Edo spirit was a bustling, clamorous, out-to-turn-a-quick-trick spirit that can still be found in the narrow shopping streets, markets and nightlife

(Preceding page) A sumo bout between wrestlers in the highest (makunouchi) *division. The* tategyoji *(referee) will point his fan, hidden by Dewanohana's right buttock, to indicate the victor.*

---

districts for which some of the shitamachi areas are noted.

The Edo age lives visibly on in the rituals, costumes, hairstyles and atmosphere associated with the national sport of sumo wrestling, and it is no coincidence that the mecca of sumo, the **Kokugikan**, lies in the shitamachi district of **Ryogoku**. Three 15-day tournaments are held here each year, in January, May and September. (There are six annual tournaments altogether; the others are held at Osaka in March, Nagoya in July and Fukuoka in November.) The former sumo mecca, abandoned in 1984, lies just across the **Sumida River** in **Kuramae**, and a somewhat graceless plan is afoot to turn it into a plant for treating sewage.

For a more subdued shitamachi, the visitor might turn to the **Yanaka** area, famous for its many small, quiet temples. In most cases nowadays one must look for the old Edo atmosphere not in buildings or objects, but in the lifestyle of shitamachi residents. Yanaka is one of the last areas where something of the atmosphere of the old city can still be said to linger, even when its streets are empty.

Away from the *s*hitamachi, in the more fashionable, middle-class areas of Tokyo that lie within the Yamanote loop line, the chief landmarks of historical interest include three large shrines and one not very large temple.

The **Hie Shrine** in **Akasaka** hosts the already-mentioned Sanno Matsuri and, sometimes on summer evenings, performances of classical Noh dramas (which, when given by torchlight, are called *Takigi Noh*). The shrine was founded here at the same time as the first Edo castle was founded, with the object of protecting the castle's inhabitants. It was completely destroyed in the air raids of 1945, and rebuilt in 1959 (not, happily, in ferro-concrete). It is dedicated to Sanno Gongen, the tutelary deity of Mount Hiei outside Kyoto (see page 102), where its parent shrine is situated and from which it takes its name.

The **Meiji Shrine** in **Harajuku** is dedicated to the flesh-and-blood person of the Emperor Meiji, the present emperor's grandfather, who gave his name both to the restoration of 1868, which propelled Japan into the modern era, and to the first period of that era (1868–1911). The shrine was completed in 1920, destroyed in 1945, restored in 1958, and its **Inner Garden** is famous for the irises that bloom there in June. That a human being should be enshrined and receive prayers like those offered to a god is not at all unusual. It happens in the West, too, with saints; but in Japan the deified human may have spent a life completely undedicated to religion in any shape or form, and the reverence accorded his spirit falls somewhere in the shadowy territory between worship and simple secular respect.

Still, this reverence is at the root of the controversy surrounding the third historically interesting shrine, the **Yasukuni Shrine** in **Kudan**, which has survived intact since 1869 and which is dedicated to Japan's war dead. Part of the problem is that the war dead enshrined here include some of those who were executed by the occupation authorities as Class-A war criminals, men like the wartime leader, Tojo Hideki. The second part of the problem is that in recent years, the prime minister and members of his cabinet, ignoring protests from such widely differing sources as Japanese Christians and the government of the People's Republic of China, have taken to visiting the Yasukuni Shrine, just as leaders in other countries visit secular cenotaphs and the tombs of unknown soldiers. Critics purport to see in this a dangerous blurring of the separation of religion from state which is guaranteed under the (American-drafted) postwar constitution. On occasions when the prime minister has declined to visit the shrine he has been criticized for succumbing to foreign pressure, so the whole business has become for him a kind of ceremonial Catch 22. The Yasukuni Shrine is also known for its cherry blossoms—often associated in poems and in the popular imagination with young men who die in battle (cherry blossoms that perish after so brief a life were the theme of the kamikaze pilots' marching song)—and blossom-viewers at Yasukuni tend not to get falling-down drunk under them.

Sengakuji Temple in **Shinagawa** is famous for its connection with the 47 loyal retainers of Lord Asano Naganori, whose graves it contains, and who were responsible for the best-known and most-admired incident in Edo-era history. Their lord was a young man from the provinces who overlooked the necessity of presenting expensive gifts to an older lord, Kira Yoshinaka, who had been assigned to instruct him in the intricacies of court etiquette. Kira insulted Asano, goading him into drawing his sword in anger within the precincts of the shogun's castle, for which unpardonable breach of the peace Asano was sentenced to commit ritual suicide (*hara-kiri*—'belly-slitting'—more properly called *seppuku*). Forty-seven of his most loyal samurai, now masterless (the word for a masterless samurai is *ronin*—the same word applied today to students who fail to gain admission to universities and spend a rootless year in cram schools waiting for the next set of entrance examinations), swore to avenge their lord's death, which they did on a snowy night in 1702. They attacked Kira's residence (400 metres from the present sumo stadium in Ryogoku), killed and decapitated him, bore his head to Sengakuji, their lord's family temple, washed it in the well which still stands in the precincts, and offered it to Asano's departed spirit. Since vendettas were strictly forbidden by law, they were sentenced, despite the widespread adulation their act had earned them, to commit *seppuku* themselves, and each calmly took his own life. The adulation has not much abated. Their exploit is the subject of one of the most perennially popular Kabuki plays, *Chushingura* (The Treasury of Loyal Retainers), and visitors to Sengakuji Temple will still find their graves decked with flowers and wreathed with incense smoke. It is interesting to note that the only other Kabuki play of comparable fame, *Kanjincho* (see page 154), also treats of the unswerving devotion of a loyal subject for his feudal lord, a theme that

Japanese Theatre

The earliest forms of Japanese theatre were simple dances of a pastoral kind, that survive at some festivals, and of a religious and ceremonial kind, that survive in the shrine dances called *Kagura*. As Buddhist and other cultural influences improved the intellectual life of the aristocracy, a more complex ritual and narrative drama developed which, in the 14th century, was refined into the form called *Noh*.

About 240 Noh plays continue to be performed on stages and in a style not much different from that of six centuries ago. Some Western sources refer to them as 'operas', some as 'ballets', but both those terms are misleading. Noh is a slow moving, subtly lyric drama, some of which is danced and much of which is chanted. A small musical ensemble and chorus accompanies the performance, and there are usually no more than three protagonists, with female parts taken by masked male actors. The themes are often from classical Japanese literature and many plays treat of Zen-inspired subjects, such as the transience of human glory. The masks and gorgeously embroidered kimonos make the Noh an almost hypnotizing experience even if the language is beyond the listener (and it is well beyond the average modern Japanese). There are several Noh theatres in Tokyo, the newest being the National Noh Theatre (*Kokuritsu Nohgakudo*).

Kyogen are 'comic interludes' performed between or before the more sombre Noh. Kyogen depend far more for their effect on dialogue than do Noh plays and, though they are shorter and much livelier, their verbal base as well as the absence of masks and exquisite costumes limits their interest for a non-Japanese-speaking visitor.

Kabuki is a melodramatic and often spectacular theatre form that evolved in the 17th century to satisfy the earthier and more extravagant tastes of the newly powerful urban merchants. As in the Noh, female parts are taken by male performers, some of whom achieve a popularity similar to that of film stars. With its revolving stage, its stunning costumes and scenery and its dances and full orchestral accompaniment, it is the most easily approachable form of 'classical' Japanese drama for the casual Western visitor. It is also the most popular form among modern Japanese audiences, though the majority of people never see it except on television. In Tokyo it is performed regularly at the *Kabukiza* and at the National Theatre (*Kokuritsu Gekijo*).

Fans of the *Bunraku* puppet theatre are inclined to rave about the 'magic' moment when they forget the presence of the highly visible puppeteers and begin to believe that the dolls are alive, making it sound like a version of the Indian rope trick. Bunraku is a drama of great skill and concentration on detail, and it has a fine, strong repertoire of plays (the dramatist often called 'the Shakespeare of Japan', Chikamatsu Monzaemon, wrote primarily for puppets). Whether it also has the power to move and thrill must remain a question of personal taste and experience.

(Preceding page) Kabuki actor in bravura pose; a popular subject with nineteenth-century ukiyoe (woodblock print) fanciers.

clearly moves the spirits of Japanese audiences today as it did when lords were lords and subjects were subjects.

Institutional Tokyo

Tokyo Tower (height 333 metres or 1,092 feet), a transmitting station for local television broadcasts, owes much to the example of Monsieur Eiffel's contraption though, being newer (it was built in 1958), it is imbued with less romance. It and the souvenir stalls that cram it attest to the ongoing attraction which idiotic novelties exert on Tokyo people. From the higher of its two observation floors, on a clear day, a breathtakingly comprehensive view of Tokyo and its environs can be obtained, so a trip up the tower is a perfect way for the visitor to disorient himself.

The red-brick west (Marunouchi-side) facade of **Tokyo Station**, built in 1914, survived the war and is today one of the most famous 20th-century architectural landmarks in the city. From time to time it is threatened with demolition, but each time conservationist-minded citizens flock to its defence in sufficient numbers for a reprieve to be granted. The Nichigeki Music Hall in **Yurakucho** was not so fortunate and is the most recent of the capital's well-known landmarks to vanish, having been replaced by a vast prison-like building called **Yurakucho Mullion**, housing newspaper offices, banks, a concert hall, five cinemas and two department stores. As the walls of Kuala Lumpur jail are adorned with colourful murals, so the external wall of this edifice boasts a clock that chimes and opens to reveal cherubs who dance the hours.

The **Tokyo Stock Exchange** in **Kabutocho**, opened in 1878 and now, in terms of market capitalization, the largest stock exchange in the world, is included on a number of guided tours of the city.

The grimly monumental-looking **National Diet Building** (*Kokkaigijido*) in **Kasumigaseki** was completed in 1936 and also, somewhat surprisingly, survived the war. It contains the Upper and Lower Houses of Japan's national legislature (the House of Councillors and the House of Representatives). Admission is not easily obtained.

Equally monumental is Tokyo's **Disneyland** in **Urayasu**, to which admission is only a problem for the impecunious. Since it opened in April 1983 it has become one of the chief sightseeing destinations in East Asia. Some tourists, particularly from neighbouring Asian countries, make it the main object of their visit, and there is an express bus service direct from Narita Airport. It offers attractions and rides closely modelled on those of its parent park in California, as well as the quite unforgettable experience of hearing *Deibii Kuroketto* (Davy Crockett) sung in Japanese. Visitors to Disneyland should be forewarned of the long periods of queueing necessary to gain admission to even the less popular attractions. For each of the more popular, even on a day of pouring rain, you can find yourself waiting without shelter for up to two hours, and to visit the park on a summer weekend, or during school or national holidays, is to court a large degree of frustration. The frustration is not relieved by the fact that Urayasu, where the park is situated, is among the greyest and gloomiest of Tokyo's suburbs (it is actually just across the prefectural border in Chiba) so, if you give up on Disneyland, there is absolutely nothing else to do there for amusement.

Before Disneyland opened, Tokyo's best known amusement park was **Korakuen**, next door to Suidobashi Station, which now looks sadly shabby by comparison. It is still jam-packed on many a summer evening since it houses the new home stadium of Japan's most popular baseball club, the Yomiuri Giants, most of whose fixtures are night games so that they can be televised live during peak viewing hours (at least up to 9.24 p.m., when they are often brusquely cut off as the sponsor changes, regardless of the state of play). The new stadium boasts Japan's first 'airdome', known as the 'Big Egg', completely roofing both field and stands.

The **Nippon Budokan** in Kudan, opposite the Yasukuni Shrine, was built immediately prior to the Tokyo Olympics in 1964 as a mecca for the martial arts (its name means 'Martial Arts Hall') but has achieved greater prominence as a venue for large-scale rock concerts. The first of these was given by the Beatles in June 1966, since when many leading Western rock bands have performed there. On nights when concerts are scheduled, the exits of Kudanshita station are crowded with disreputable-looking ticket touts whose only connection with martial arts is likely to be the ownership of a set of knuckledusters.

NHK's Broadcasting Centre stands a short walk from Shibuya or Harajuku Stations. Like the BBC in Britain, NHK is publicly funded through the collection of licence fees and is thus free from commercial pressures and, in theory at least, from government influence. A sightseeing tour of some of NHK's facilities, including the largest T.V. studio in the world, is on the itinerary of many school trips to the capital. **NHK Hall**, next-door, is the home of the NHK Symphony Orchestra.

Tokyo boasts many special-interest museums in addition to those in Ueno. The **National Museum of Modern Art** is in **Takebashi**, near the headquarters of the *Mainichi Shinbun* newspaper. The **Japan Science Museum** is close to the Nippon Budokan. The **Communications Museum** is a short walk from Tokyo Station's red-brick facade. Some large business corporations who pride themselves on being patrons of the arts also operate museums and galleries. Two of the best known of these are the **Idemitsu Gallery**, also near the Marunouchi side of Tokyo Station, and the **Bridgestone Museum of Art**, not far away on the other side. Major department stores have also become leading contenders in the patron-of-the-

(Preceding page) Distinctive yellow accessories worn and carried by fans of Osaka's Hanshin Tigers baseball club.

arts stakes and most visiting foreign exhibitions are displayed at one or other of these.

But it is not primarily the viewing of foreign art that keeps Tokyo's department stores so crowded. Visits to department stores for the purpose of shopping (window- or actual) are the leading leisure-time activity in the capital, and on weekends or just before the two main annual gift-giving seasons (midsummer and end of the year) the most popular stores—such as Shinjuku's **Isetan**, **Odakyu** and **Keio**, Nihonbashi's **Mitsukoshi** and Shibuya's **Tokyu** and **Seibu**—can become as dauntingly choked with people as rush-hour trains. The degree to which department stores have become leisure-time magnets is certainly a measure of Japan's new-won affluence, but it is also a measure of how completely novel the affluence still seems to many Japanese people. It is almost as though Tokyo's residents regarded affluence itself as one of their forever passing fads: if we don't throng department stores now, they'll have disappeared before we know it. Despite the intense competition among stores, they tend to be laid out in a very similar manner with the emphasis on predictability. Restaurants and galleries are invariably at the top and food halls invariably in the basement. Some have recreation facilities for children on their roofs (and recreation facilities for adults, in summer, in the inviting form of beer gardens). With the rise in value of the yen, the free samples offered by department-store food halls have begun to attract budget-conscious travellers from abroad to the extent that where to obtain a free gourmet lunch is now among the most frequent questions posed to tourist information officers. Free samples still abound, but sales staff are becoming less generous and a good deal more eagle-eyed.

A fashionable alternative to ordinary department-store shopping, particularly popular with the moping young, is the 'fashion building', often architecturally striking, that houses designer boutiques, a café bar or two, a chic restaurant, and other leisure facilities such as theatres and exhibition halls. Among the best known such centres are **Parco** in Shibuya, **La Foret** in Harajuku, the **Axis Building** in Roppongi, and the **Spiral Building** in Aoyama. Falling somewhere between the monolithic familiarity of the older-style department store (in fact it contains a branch of Mitsukoshi) and the newer, more gimmicky eclecticism of the 'fashion building' is the **Sunshine City** complex in Ikebukuro, at 60 storeys the tallest building in Asia, boasting a museum, a hotel, a planetarium and an aquarium. Major trade fairs are also staged there.

Then there are the buildings that house Japan's new religious organizations. The postwar period has seen an extraordinary boom in new religious sects and cults (see page 75), and some of these have become rich enough to encase their spiritual aspirations in remarkable earthly containers. Among the most outwardly striking are the headquarters of the **Reiyukai**

(Companions of the Spirits) near Tokyo Tower, housed in a 1975 building which looks like a Chaldaean ziggurat, and the Arabian-Nights-and-pink-mushroom inspired minarets of the headquarters of the **Rissho Koseikai** (Society to Foster the Establishment of Righteousness) in the surburban ward of **Suginami**, some four kilometres (2.5 miles) west of Shinjuku. Older foreign-looking religious landmarks include the **Tsukiji Honganji** Temple near the wholesale fish market, whose present building was completed in 1935 and purports to have been inspired by ancient Hindu architecture, and the Russian Orthodox **Nikolai Cathedral** in Ochanomizu, which dates from 1884 except for its dome, the original of which was a victim of the 1923 earthquake.

Fluid Tokyo

Most visitors will have heard of (the) **Ginza**, which takes its name from a silver mint that used to stand in the area. Some guides still call it 'Tokyo's fabulous Ginza', thereby helping to sustain a myth that no longer has much basis in reality. Ginza has major department stores, cinemas, the **Kabukiza** theatre, some expensive designer shops and many small picture galleries in its back streets. Some of Tokyo's priciest restaurants and watering holes are there, the latter used mainly for the expense-account pampering of business associates (Japanese corporate entertainment spending now runs to a higher annual total than the government's budget for education). But Ginza has had to endure the ever-threatening ravages of change and, for sheer excitement, it has been eclipsed by brasher, newer pleasure centres such as Shinjuku and Roppongi.

Bordering Ginza on the southwest is **Shinbashi**, once also a favoured pleasure spot, particularly famous for its *geisha* who could sometimes be glimpsed as they rode through the narrow streets in rickshaws (*jinrikisha*—literally, 'person-powered vehicles'). Both rickshaws and geisha are today endangered species, and Shinbashi, too, has been eclipsed. Perhaps the most entertaining nightlife in the Ginza area nowadays—for those without massive expense accounts anyway—is to be found under and around the railway arches in **Yurakucho**, near Ginza's northwest corner. In times of poverty and hardship, such as followed the defeat of 1945, the arches beneath elevated railways provided shelter to people made homeless by bombs and other disasters. Gradually, whole communities grew up under the arches, with food and drink stalls (*yatai*) to cater to them. As prosperity returned, some of the yatai owners, hustled along by the winds of change, transformed their stalls into permanent bars and eating places, still wedged under the thundering tracks. Today, along parts of the Yamanote loop line and a great deal of the Chuo Line, the arches and immediately adjacent streets harbour some of Tokyo's least pretentious and most reasonably priced places to eat

(Preceding page) The skyline of 'Tokyo's Manhattan': West Shinjuku.

and drink. Those at Yurakucho are the best known and most centrally located. Some cater mainly to manual workers, some are ritzier and not quite so inexpensive as they might appear from the outside.

Shinjuku is an area crisply divided by its station. On the west side stand the new skyscrapers of 'Tokyo's Manhattan'—the head offices of major corporations such as Mitsui, Sumitomo and KDD, flashy hotels like the Keio Plaza, Hilton and Century Hyatt, and soon the new city Hall and municipal administration buildings now under construction. On winter nights, when the wind gusts between these huge cold obelisks, West Shinjuku can seem a desolate place, and yet the novelty of having so many tall buildings clustered together in one small area has clearly struck a chord in the Tokyo resident's novelty-loving soul. In a dreadful 1987 disaster film, Tokyo is threatened by a cloud of electrically-charged smog and has to be rescued single-handed by a young municipal engineer. In the film the heart of the city—the first sight to stand revealed when the cloud disperses, the violins soar, and the rays of the sun break through again—is not the Imperial Palace nor the National Diet Building, but West Shinjuku's skyscrapers.

On the east side of the station stands the rabbit-warren of streets lined with bars, coffee shops, restaurants, cinemas, amusement arcades, pinball and mahjong parlours, sex shows and cabarets that give Shinjuku its name for sleaze, bustle and loose living. **Kabukicho**, northeast of the station, has no connection whatever with classical theatre. It is Tokyo's brashest nightlife district with a heavy emphasis on sexual titillation. Since the area is largely controlled by the *yakuza* (organized crime syndicates), its character and reputation have earned it some criticism, particularly from the proprietors of neighbouring toy shops and so on. But, like all other parts of the city—indeed, of the whole country—it is a perfectly safe area to stroll around at any time of the day or night, the only dangers being to one's eardrums and mental and moral equilibrium.

Roppongi is sometimes referred to in trendy tabloids as 'Gaijin Gulch'—*gaijin* (literally 'outside person') being the Japanese word for a foreigner. It is an area of loud, colourful bars, restaurants, coffee shops and discotheques frequented by foreigners and by young Japanese ladies who wish to acquire foreign boyfriends in order to parade them before their acquaintances (though not before their families) as status symbols, akin to multi-system video tape recorders. The Almond Coffee Shop at the corner of Roppongi Crossing is probably the best-known coffee shop in Tokyo, not because it possesses any outstanding attractions (in fact it is supremely dull), but because the corner on which it stands is the second most famous place for arranging to meet people. The most famous meeting place is the statue of Hachiko outside the north exit of Shibuya Station. Hachiko was a dog who died after waiting seven years for her master; a fact which the visitor, if he had not had drummed into him the lesson of Japan's incomparable efficiency, might take for a comment on

(Preceding page) Sunday in Harajuku.

Japanese habits of punctuality, at least outside the business sphere. Next-door to Roppongi is **Azabu**, less lively at night, but the home of many well-heeled foreigners and an area known for its boutiques and café-bars.

Akasaka used to offer Roppongi some competition as a young people's nighttime entertainment area, but its competitiveness has diminished. Change has overtaken it. Its most famous discotheque (Mugen) closed in 1987, and like Asakusa (with which, owing to the similarity of the two names, visitors sometimes confuse it), it is turning into a business district.

The young people's principal daytime entertainment area is nowadays **Harajuku**, where, incongruously enough, the solemn Meiji Shrine stands, as though to remind the place of forgotten virtues. Harajuku is newly famous for its 2,000 or so trendy clothing boutiques, selling items that look as though they were designed for 7-year-olds to chirruping throngs of 17-year-olds with as much money to spend as their grandparents' generation used not to accumulate until they were 70-year-olds. On Sundays in the streets of Harajuku and in nearby **Yoyogi Park**, fantastically-dressed young people dance to rock music supplied by large portable cassette players. These are the *Takenoko Zoku* (the 'Bamboo Shoot Tribe'), who began their career as a daring scion of the counter culture and who now, caught up in Tokyo's infectious passion for bizarre novelty, are a tourist attraction and an institution.

Tokyo's Islands

Equally bizarre, to anyone not familiar with the workings of Japanese city halls, is the discovery that the Tokyo metropolitan area includes a number of tiny remote rural islands which have as little in common with the lifestyle of the capital as today's Kabukicho has with Kabuki. The most easily accessible of these are the **Izu Islands**, off the southeast coast of the Izu Peninsula (see page 135), most of which form a part of the Fuji-Hakone-Izu National Park. The islands are **Oshima** (population 11,000), whose **Mount Mihara** erupted so violently in 1986 that the entire island had to be evacuated, **Toshima** (population 280), **Niijima** (population 3,600, including nearby **Shikinejima**), **Kozujima** (population 2,200), **Miyakejima** (population 4,400), at present a centre of controversy owing to the government's insistence that an airstrip be built there from which U.S. forces can conduct night training flights, a plan that is being pushed forward despite the opposition of 80 percent of the islanders, **Mikurajima** (population 200) and **Hachijojima** (population 10,000). (*Shima* or—*jima* means island). These islands provide attractive opportunities for hiking, camping, fishing, bathing and experiencing eruptions and anti-government demonstrations.

Even more remote are the **Ogasawara Islands** (sometimes referred to by English-language sources as the Bonin Islands), lying more than 900 kilometres (560 miles) south of the capital, to which nevertheless they have belonged since 1968 when, four years earlier than Okinawa, they reverted to Japan from U.S. control. The inhabited islands are **Chichijima** (population 1,300) and **Hahajima** (population 280) and together with some outlying uninhabited islands they form the **Ogasawara National Park**. Further south still are the three specks called **Iojima** (or Iwojima or, on some charts and maps, The Volcanic Islands), which have a total population of 60 and are principally famous for having been the scene of fierce land fighting between Japanese and American troops during the early months of 1945. To reach even the closest of the Ogasawara group from Tokyo takes almost two days by ferry and the service is infrequent, so these islands, though fascinating from the point of view of history and administrative anomaly, are unlikely to figure on most visitors' itineraries.

The Rest of the Kanto Region

The **Kanto** region, of which Tokyo is the heart, also contains the prefectures of **Kanagawa, Saitama, Gunma, Tochigi, Ibaraki** and **Chiba**. 'Kanto' means 'East of the Barrier', the barrier being the Hakone Mountains, the major natural obstacle along the Tokaido Highway which joined this eastern district to the older capitals in the west. The Kanto is a relatively flat area, its plain being the broadest in Japan, rising in Gunma and Tochigi to the southern slopes of the Mikuni Mountains.

The prefectural capital of **Kanagawa** is **Yokohama** (population 2.9 million), today the second largest city in Japan and one of the first ports opened to foreign commerce following the end of Japan's self-imposed feudal isolation. It was opened in 1859, since when the city has been home to a tenaciously-rooted foreign community, whose wealthier members live mainly on the heights known as 'The Bluff', where the original foreign concession was located. As a result—and because it remains the second largest foreign trading port in Japan (after Kobe)—Yokohama, together with Kobe and Nagasaki which also had early foreign communities, is known for its 'cosmopolitan' atmosphere. By this is not meant that it can be compared with the sort of melting pot that, say, San Francisco is, nor in its short history could it ever be. But it has its own **Chinatown**, where the cuisine in the restaurants is as authentic as one is likely to find in Japan. It has a **Foreigner's Cemetery** (Gaijin Bochi) and another cemetery for British and Commonwealth war dead. Several of the Kanto area's leading international schools are also situated in Yokohama, the majority of them established by Christian religious orders.

Jealous efforts have been made by the Yokohama authorities to see that

their city does not lag too far behind its larger fad-loving neighbour in leisure facilities. The **Motomachi** shopping street is famous even in Tokyo, and the **Takashimaya** department store and **Diamond Shopping Centre**, next-door to Yokohama Station, are quite the rivals of similar stores in the capital. Yokohama strikes the visitor arriving from Tokyo as a comparatively clean, up-to-date, pleasantly laid-out city (at least spasmodically), where some priority is still given to matters like the preservation of greenery and the provision of areas where a pedestrian can walk without ending up under a truck. There are some pleasant walks around Yokohama Stadium at **Sakuragicho** and the passenger harbour, near where the **Silk Museum** is to be found. One can live a lifetime in Tokyo and quite forget that it is on the coast, whereas in Yokohama the ocean is always there and still an encouragement to romance.

But for visitors with time to spare for only one of Kanagawa's cities—particularly for visitors interested in history, art, architecture or simply atmosphere—by far the more rewarding destination is the historic city of **Kamakura**.

For almost a century and a half Kamakura was the de facto capital of Japan, and the era of its supremacy (1192–1333) is known as the 'Kamakura Period'. Its supremacy came about because of the fierce rivalry between two powerful military clans, the Heike (or Taira) and the Genji (or Minamoto). From the middle of the 12th century the Heike controlled the court in Kyoto and were the real power in the country. But in 1180 the head of the Genji, Yoritomo, began raising an army in the Kanto region to move against the Heike and, largely because of its perfect defensive position with hills on three sides and sea on the fourth, Kamakura became Yoritomo's headquarters. In 1185 the Heike were finally overthrown. The tale of their defeat and scattered flight is one of the great sources of dramatic and poetic literature in Japan, firmly attesting to the Japanese preference for noble failure over clever triumph. Today, many remote villages in widely different parts of Japan still proudly claim to have been settled by Heike survivors; nowhere are such claims made on behalf of the victorious Genji. In 1192 Yoritomo was proclaimed shogun and the military government that he established in Kamakura, and which was maintained after his death by descendents of his father-in-law, lasted until forces loyal to the emperor attacked Kamakura in 1333, defeated the military regents there, and restored power to Kyoto.

Kamakura (present population 173,000) is a seaside town, and its dusty beach is jam-packed on fine summer weekends with thousands upon thousands of young people, who have mostly come down from Tokyo. But it is principally Kamakura's historical landmarks that will occupy the attention of the short-term visitor. Visitors arriving by train from Tokyo (the journey takes only an hour) can get off one stop before Kamakura, at Kita (North)

Kamakura, in order to visit **Engakuji** Temple, a major centre of Rinzai Zen Buddhism, founded in 1282 and largely restored after the 1923 earthquake. The temple is in a hilly area (the hills around Kamakura contain many pleasant walks and small, out-of-the-way temples) and is well known for its long and picturesque flights of steps, one of which leads up to a belfry in which hangs the largest temple bell in the city, cast in 1301. The Buddhist scholar and explicator, Suzuki Daisetz, whose work is well known abroad and was partly responsible for the popularity—and almost total misunderstanding—that Zen Buddhism achieved among hippies and others in the 1960s lived near this temple until his death in 1966. He is buried across the road in the small temple of **Tokeiji**, formerly a convent famous for having offered sanctuary to women seeking divorce or merely refuge from belligerent husbands, a tradition that continued into the early years of this century.

In Kamakura proper (to which the visitor can easily walk from Kita Kamakura, though the road is loud and dusty) the two chief historical showpieces are the **Tsurugaoka Hachiman Shrine** (founded on this site in 1191, rebuilt in 1828) and the 11.4-metre (37.5-foot) high **Daibutsu** (Great Buddha) cast in bronze in 1252, which stands in the precincts of **Kotokuin** Temple. This is one of two famous Great Buddhas in Japan, the other—larger and five centuries older—being housed at Todaiji Temple in Nara (see page 77). Some prefer the Kamakura Buddha simply because it is open to the sky, although it was originally enclosed in a structure that was destroyed by a tidal wave in 1495. A similar tidal wave on a summer Sunday today would bury the Buddha under a mound of gangly bathers. In the precincts of the Tsurugaoka Hachiman Shrine stand a vermilion drumbridge that visitors may clamber across at the risk of a severely twisted ankle and a famous and ancient gingko tree, from behind which, according to legend, an assassin leaped out in 1219 to lop off the head of Yoritomo's second son, the assassin later being identified as his victim's own nephew. In September each year the shrine hosts an exhibition of mounted archery *(yabusame)* which can be very exciting if you are lucky enough, or tall enough, to be able to see it over the countless heads of jostling spectators.

Kamakura abounds in smaller, quieter temples that amply repay the leisurely stroller's attention. Three of the best-known are **Sugimotoji**, founded in 734, long before Kamakura figured on anyone's map of the nation's power structure, and famous for its statues of Kannon, the Goddess of Mercy; **Hasedera**, also famous for its massive statue of Kannon as well as for the thousand or so tiny statues of Jizo, the Buddhist guardian of children, which have led to the temple being associated specifically with the welfare of infants, born and unborn; and **Hokokuji**, founded in 1334 and famous for its carefully nurtured bamboo grove, viewable upon the paying of an admission charge that includes a bowl of ceremonial tea.

Among the most popular and accessible hot-spring resorts for residents of Tokyo is **Hakone** at the extreme southwestern tip of Kanagawa prefecture; part of the **Fuji-Hakone-Izu National Park**. During the Edo period, Hakone was the site of the shogun's principal barrier gate along the Tokaido highway, and there is a small museum dedicated to this institution. Because it is so accessible, Hakone has been enthusiastically developed by entrepreneurs and consortiums who clearly believe that the ideal weekend in the country is one spent gazing out of the window of a 12-storey hotel at a vista of other 12-storey hotels. Hakone is popular with not terribly adventurous honeymooners, and more popular still among the organizers of even less adventurous company outings. Many of Hakone's hotels earn most of their income not from couples or families, but from large groups, such as associations of traders, who arrive en masse in hired buses and get as helplessly drunk as they can in the shortest possible space of time. This is called experiencing nature.

Saitama prefecture, more than half of which has been invaded by the northern reaches of Greater Tokyo's industrial and residential sprawl, has little in the way of sightseeing attractions to offer the short-term visitor. In the hilly west of the prefecture lies part of the **Chichibu-Tama National Park**, easily reached from Tokyo and famous for its woods and gorges, though the more interesting parts of the park lie still further west in Yamanashi prefecture. Closer to Tokyo, the town of **Kawagoe** (population 259,000) contains some fairly old wattle-and-daub buildings, mostly shops and tradesmen's houses.

Due north of Saitama lies **Gunma** prefecture, where the great Kanto plain peters out into a more typical Japanese landscape of mountains rising steeply to heights of more than 2,000 metres (6,500 feet). Gunma has some notable hot-spring resorts, the most devastatingly overdeveloped being **Minakami**, just south of the border with Niigata, but many are on a smaller scale and offer a more traditional environment in which to relax. Among these are **Kusatsu**, famous as one of the hottest spas in Japan (so hot that ablutions in some of the town's bathhouses are strictly organized and timed by a 'bath-master'), **Shima**, and **Hoshi**, which possesses a wonderful cathedral-like wooden bathhouse that makes up for its lack of outdoor bathing facilities. During the more peaceful years of his life, Admiral Yamamoto Isoroku, the commander of the Imperial Navy who died when his plane was shot down in the Solomon Islands in 1943, used to stay at Hoshi, and his namecard is proudly preserved at the front office of the resort's only ryokan. For visitors with little time to venture into the countryside, Gunma's hot springs, all reachable from Tokyo in three or four hours, provide a relaxing sampler, and

(Preceding page) Yabusame *(mounted archery)* at the Tsurugaoka Hachiman shrine, Kamakura. The archer attempts to split three plywood targets at the gallop.

they also provide a good cross-section of traditional hot-spring styles. At Kusatsu the whole of the little town is given over to the serious enjoyment of bathing and there are many ryokans, bathhouses and bars to choose from, while the single ryokan at Hoshi lies on the edge of quiet wooded hills, 20 minutes by taxi from the nearest bus stop. The energetic visitor can walk over the hills from Hoshi to Shima, a tramp of several hours.

Continuing clockwise round the edge of the Kanto plain, one comes to **Tochigi** prefecture, whose uplands also boast some fine hot springs. The most easily accessible is **Kinugawa** and, because it is so easily accessible (two hours from Asakusa by Tobu-Line express), it has become a slightly shabbier version of Hakone. Better are the resorts that cluster on the plateaus of **Shiobara** and **Nasu**. Another famous military leader, General Nogi Maresuke, the chief architect of Japan's victory in the Russo-Japanese War of 1904–5, used to stay at **Omaru**, a short taxi ride from the main Nasu spa. The single ryokan there preserves the room he stayed in as a museum, and it contains a striking formal photograph of the general and his wife taken shortly before their quiet suicides (the general's in the traditional samurai manner by disembowelment) committed on the occasion of the funeral of Emperor Meiji.

A short distance from the prefectural capital of **Utsunomiya**, at the northern extremity of the Kanto plain, stands the small town of **Mashiko** (population 22,000), the object of a day-trip from Tokyo for many visitors interested in traditional ceramics. Mashiko is the best-known centre for the manufacture of folk pottery in the Kanto region, and has been so since shortly after 1924, when the potter Hamada Shoji, who was designated a 'Living National Treasure' in 1955, established his most famous kiln there. Previously, Japanese connoisseurs had tended to disregard the merits of the traditional coarse-glazed pots of the rural areas (just as connoisseurs of painting had scorned woodblock prints), preferring the finer Chinese-inspired product of kilns like Kutani in Fukui prefecture. But attitudes gradually changed as a result of the success of the *mingei undo* (folk-craft movement) of the 1920s and '30s, which aimed to restore dignity and economic viability to various traditional rural arts, and in which Hamada and the English potter Bernard Leach were highly influential. Mashiko pottery (when not an exhibition piece from the kiln of one of the best-known potters) is comparatively inexpensive, and its heavy but subtle glazes with their abstract designs and natural colours lend themselves well to modern Western-style place settings. Mashiko today is far more of a mecca for souvenir-hunting tourists than a haven for reclusive potters bent on preserving traditional skills, but commercial independence for the artist was as much an aim of the mingei undo as was the injection of new life into lapsing arts, so Hamada would presumably find little to complain about.

But most visitors to Tochigi will head straight for **Nikko** and its famous **Toshogu Shrine**, the mausoleum of Ieyasu, the founder of the Tokugawa shogunate. The mausoleum was completed in 1636 and the immense expenditure of money and effort lavished on it is apparent at a glance—'lavish' being the operative word, since the gaudy, gilded and lacquered structures clearly fly in the teeth of those canons of Japanese aesthetics whose chief concern is with subtlety and understatement. By any standards, the place is an exercise in excess. The mausoleum was built to specifications laid down by Ieyasu himself and is thus one of the world's most spectacular testaments to megalomania. With its flashy colours and hectic cramming in of exotic detail, it seems far more Chinese in appearance and inspiration that does any other shrine or temple in Japan, even those of far earlier date which actually acknowledge the debt they owe to continental methods and tastes. One cannot help but see a rich irony in this when one recalls the extreme xenophobia displayed by the regime that Ieyasu founded, even as the building of the Toshogu Shrine was in progress. Japanese guidebooks and brochures intended for foreigners rarely fail to quote the famous saying about Nikko (possibly coined by the ancestors of the entrepreneurs who developed Hakone), *Nikko o mizushite 'kekko' to iunakare,* which these publications invariably translate as 'Never say "splendid" until you've seen Nikko', but which might equally accurately be rendered, 'See Nikko and say you've had enough!'

On 17 and 18 May (the same dates as Tokyo's Sanja Matsuri) Nikko's 'Procession of a Thousand Armed Men' marches along a one-kilometre route between the picturesque cryptomeria trees that line the approaches to the mausoleum. The participants are dressed in costumes and armour of the early Edo period and annually attract more than 100,000 spectators interested in fancy-dress parades.

A 50-minute bus ride from Nikko lies **Lake Chuzenji**, and the visitor who is planning an overnight stay in the Nikko area might welcome the comparative serenity of the lakeside after the florid self-aggrandizement of the Tokugawas. In summer, serenity is not an easy commodity to discover at Chuzenji, since its location so close to one of Japan's foremost tourist attractions has led to its development as a busy resort in its own right, where boating, water-skiing and lake- and river-fishing are all available to the energetic. The vicinity of the lake is well known for its waterfalls, the most famous being the **Kegon Fall**, about 100 metres (327 feet) high, formerly a favourite spot for romantically-motivated suicides.

Ibaraki (or **Ibaragi**) prefecture has Japan's second largest freshwater lake in **Lake Kasumigaura**, but this is not a developed tourist attraction, mainly owing to the industrial exploitation that the prefecture's flatness and proximity to Tokyo early inflicted on it. It is, by and large, a drab prefecture, formerly known for its mines and for the grim, warlike nature of its people (not for nothing did Yoritomo choose to raise his army in the Kanto region), and today Ibaraki is the home of a coastal industrial belt with massive port facilities and the largest oil refinery in the world, as well as Japan's Atomic Energy Research Institute and atomic power stations at **Tokai** village (the bombings of Hiroshima and Nagasaki have left many Japanese people with what they call a 'nuclear allergy', and this allergy finds expression both in popular opposition to atomic energy in any form and in the government's carefully maintained pretence that U.S. Naval vessels with nuclear capability do not bring their armaments into Japan). The prefectural capital is **Mito** (population 216,000), which posesses one of the 'Three Most Beautiful Landscape Gardens in Japan' called **Kairakuen**, completed in 1843. For the other two celebrated gardens see Kanazawa (page 151) and Okayama (page 164). At **Tsukuba** stands the recently built 'Academic New Town' or 'Science City', in 1985 the site of a six-month-long scientific and technological exposition, and now a leading research and development centre, featuring the world's largest particle accelerator. Visitors interested in accelerating particles should head there without delay.

Chiba prefecture has gained recognition among international travellers due to the siting of Tokyo's New International Airport at **Narita**. Visitors with longish waits in transit at Narita might consider a trip by bus or taxi into Narita city (population 68,000), and particularly to **Shinshoji** Temple, a large complex founded in the tenth century, which belongs to the Shingon sect of Buddhism, famous for its rigorous asceticism. Among the outward manifestations of this are fasting, pouring icy water over one's naked body in the middle of winter, and walking 100 times round the main hall of Shinshoji rubbing beads and reciting sutras, a practice visitors can see at all times of the year. The street leading up to Shinshoji is lined with shops selling traditional items such as handicrafts, sweets and rice crackers, and is a cheaper source of last-minute souvenirs than are the shops in the airport.

The **Boso Peninsula** is flattish and has little to offer the sightseer other than the famous **Kujukurihama** (Ninety-Nine-League Beach) which is actually 57 kilometres (35 miles) long and lies along the peninsula's east coast. The lighthouse at **Cape Inubo** in the city of **Choshi** provided the last sight of the homeland to early emigrants bound by ship across the Pacific to the United States or South America, and has thus achieved a small degree of romance.

Other destinations suitable for one- or two-day trips from Tokyo include Mount Fuji and its five lakes and the Izu Peninsula. These are dealt with on pages 135–138.

Nara, Kyoto and the Kinki Region
The Ancient Capitals, their History, their Primacy

The **Kinki** (Around the Capital) region consists of the 'urban prefectures' of **Kyoto** and **Osaka**, and the ordinary prefectures of **Nara, Shiga, Mie, Wakayama** and **Hyogo**. The distinction between 'prefecture' (*ken*) and 'urban prefecture' (*fu*), of which Kyoto and Osaka are Japan's only examples, may conceivably have some meaning for the bureaucrats who dreamed it up, but it is of no earthly use to anyone else, and in the case of Kyoto is downright misleading, since the outlying parts of this 'urban prefecture' are as rural as anywhere else in the region. Perhaps the distinction was awarded Kyoto simply as a means of setting it apart from most of the rest of the country, but history and art have achieved that goal without the need for any bureaucratic fiddling. Another potential source of confusion where nomenclature is concerned is that the whole area is more commonly referred to as **Kansai** (West of the Barrier), just as Kanto is East of the Barrier (see page 51). *Kinki* is a term more often found in official designations than in ordinary speech, but it serves as a useful reminder of the central role that the region played in Japan's development as a nation.

No single word has more powerful associations for the Japanese people than the word *Yamato,* written with two ideograms that mean, literally, 'Great Harmony' or 'Great Us'. It is a poetic, spirit-stirring name for Japan and the Japanese race (as Albion is for England and the English), implying especially a purity unsullied by external influences. *Yamato* was the name of the great battleship that set out for Okinawa four months before the end of the Second World War in a last-ditch effort to turn the tide, and which carried only enough fuel for the outward journey—an example of heroic, unpragmatic self-sacrifice that the Japanese deem typical of their spirit at its most wholesome. *Yamato* was also the name of the first political power base—or court, or state—in Japan, said to have been established in the Nara basin by the legendary Emperor Jimmu in 660 BC. Historians treat this date as a complete fiction, and regard the Yamato state as having existed much later—between the third and seventh centuries AD—but it still represented the first attempt to unify the country under a single rule and was 'pure' in that its culture predated the tremendous continental influences—in particular those deriving from the introduction of Buddhism—which were to play such a crucial role in shaping Japanese society in later centuries.

The capital of the Yamato state was moved from place to place with the passing of each ruler, and little trace of the sites of these earliest power bases remains, though most, if not all, were located in what is today Nara prefecture. But in 710, by which time the Buddhist religion had become the most important influence on the life, art and intellectual aspirations of Japan, the court and bureaucratic machinery had grown so cumbersome that the need for a more stable base was felt, and a permanent capital was established at Nara city. Nara (then called **Heijokyo**—Capital of the Peaceful Fortress) remained the capital until 784 and, in the three-quarters of a century during which it held that position, the unification of the country continued, with imperial forces pushing north into the wild regions occupied by tribes such as the Ainu, who were racially quite different from the founders of the Yamato state. In 784 the particularly energetic Emperor Kammu, said to have grown wary of the power and political ambitions of Nara's belligerent Buddhist priesthood, ordered a new capital built at Nagaoka, out from under the intimidating shadow of the great temples, and eight years later, his passion for pristine horizons still seemingly undimmed, he began laying out yet another new capital a few kilometres to the northeast. The court was trundled to this newest site in 794 and the city that sprang up around it was known at first as **Heiankyo** (Capital of Tranquillity), and then as **Kyoto** (simply, Capital City). Kyoto remained the imperial capital of Japan for more than a thousand years.

There is a fashion among some foreign residents of Japan who play host to visitors from abroad to steer them away from the old capitals of the Kansai on the grounds that 'everyone goes there'. More knowledgeable than 'everyone', these residents prefer to direct their guests toward thatch-roofed lodging houses in remote rural areas or microphone-equipped bars where salaried workers sing pop songs to each other, so that their guests can experience the 'real' Japan. There is no doubt that microphone-equipped bars can harbour an abundance of delights. There is no doubt, either, that unless the visitor is tremendously lucky or presciently choosy in his timing, he will have to share the chief sights of the old capitals with large crowds of other sightseers. But nor can there be any doubt in a sane mind that the cities of Nara and Kyoto together are the cradle, nursery and full-blown flower of Japanese culture. To avoid them or omit them for want of time is an act of stupendous folly.

Among the 'everyone' who crowd the chief sights of Nara and Kyoto are the hordes of Japanese schoolchildren who are taken there on educational visits. Naturally enough, those two historical cities are the chief focus of many of the school trips which are included in the standard syllabus for junior and senior high school pupils—a fact that can prove an unlooked-for irritation to the foreign visitor since a good proportion of the pupils will find the sight of him quite as remarkable as any of the historical monuments they have been taken to see, and will comment to this effect in loud and giggly voices. One solution is to try to time your visit so that it coincides with one of the longer school holidays—the months of July and August, and the weeks on either side of the New Year. A drawback to this plan is that Nara and Kyoto (Kyoto especially) lie in a basin, and are thus subject to more extreme temperature highs and lows than are hilly or coastal regions. In midsummer

(Preceding page) Photographed together for the umpteen thousandth time: holy Mount Fuji and the holy bullet train.

Kyoto is uncomfortably hot and in January it is tingly cold. In July Kyoto is crowded for another reason (the Gion Matsuri—see page 84), and on New Year's Eve and the three days following, some of the major shrines and temples become so congested that it is hard enough to squeeze through their gates, let alone enjoy their sights. But the visitor prepared to put up with the frostiness of late December or mid-January to mid-February will usually find himself rewarded with at least a whiff of that tranquillity for which the city was originally named.

Though Nara and Kyoto (only half an hour apart by express) are often linked as a single historical 'package', the two cities are very different in character and the visitor should approach them in very different frames of mind. It is part of the object of what follows to suggest some of the differences between the two, particularly those differences that dictate the peculiar kind of beauty that each contains.

Nara

Nara's beauty is monumental, and resides in such qualities as size, strength and symmetry. It is a spacious, public beauty; a beauty amid which to congregate and applaud. Though Nara (present population 298,000) is the older of the two great capitals, and though many of its treasures owe their origins and forms to the influences of continental Asia (these having found their way to Nara, via T'ang China and Korea, along the Silk Road), it is still a city with which a Western visitor can feel an immediate kinship. Mostly, this is because the chief sights of the city centre—the temples of Todaiji and Kofukuji and the Kasuga Shrine—lie on the edges of open parkland, through which the visitor can stroll and in which he can enjoy the sort of panoramic vista that is crucial to most Western ideas of what constitutes an attractive place.

With Buddhism came, for the first time, a fully-developed means of writing down language (the Japanese script is wholly borrowed or adapted from the Chinese—see page 234) and, as with the religious institutions of the West during the dark and early middle ages, the Buddhist temples of the Nara period were the principal repositories of learning and culture. It is thus fitting that the chief surviving monuments of Nara's greatness are not palaces or mansions, but the massive brooding religious edifices that were the apex of its intellectual, as well as of its outward, glory.

The visitor arriving from Kyoto by the rapid and comfortable Kintetsu Line express emerges from Kintetsu Nara station to find himself within 200 metres of Kofukuji Temple, which has occupied this site since the year of Nara's founding and whose five-storey pagoda is one of the city's most immediately recognizable landmarks. But his patience will be repaid if the visitor postpones his visit to Kofukuji for the moment and instead takes a bus or taxi some four kilometres (2.5 miles) west to **Yakushiji**, a temple almost as old, and which provides a more illuminating introduction to Nara's temple architecture.

Yakushiji (named after the Buddha of Healing) was founded on this site in 718 and, like so many of Japan's historical monuments, has been largely destroyed and rebuilt several times. This is immediately obvious from the spanking new condition of two of the temple's freshly restored buildings, the Kondo (Golden Hall), completed in 1976, and the West Pagoda, completed in 1981. The old Yamato state had maintained relations with China, but there had been no large-scale attempt to imitate continental civilization. This changed with the introduction of Buddhism in the mid-sixth century, and from the time of Japan's first great lawgiver, Prince Shotoku, Chinese manners, learning, customs, writing, architecture and most other arts were imported with as much fervour as have been the habits and inventions of the West in modern times. The two restored structures in Yakushiji are quite unlike anything else standing in Nara today and, like Nikko on a brasher and more baroque scale, they seem to contradict those canons of Japanese taste wherein the subdued and the monochrome are accorded pride of place. Many Japanese visitors to Yakushiji, though quick to admire the craftmanship and dedication to tradition that have raised these new structures, are equally quick to express a preference for the stark, age-darkened buildings like the East Pagoda (said to date from the temple's founding), which, they like to infer, are somehow more 'Japanese'. The bright primary colours of the new structures strike them as distinctly Chinese in flavour—which, of course, they are, being perfectly faithful to the temple's seventh-century Chinese-inspired design. So it is worth keeping in mind, when making the rounds of Nara's temples, that they were all once as brightly decorated as these two parts of Yakushiji are. Having made a start with freshly painted buildings, the visitor will perhaps have a sharper eye for the traces of red that can still be found, say, on the rafters of the Great Buddha Hall in Todaiji, and this sharper eye may help in turn to sharpen his imagination so that he sees the great temples not only as they stand brooding and dark today, but as they once stood.

Behind the East Pagoda is another very old building which has miraculously survived more than eight centuries: the Toindo (East Temple Hall), erected in 1285, in which stands the bronze statue of Sho-Kannon (the original manifestation of the Goddess of Mercy), cast at the end of the seventh century, probably in Korea, and presented as a gift to the Japanese emperor by the King of Paekche. Other fine statues, including that of Yakushi Nyorai, the Buddha of Healing who gives the temple its name, are kept in the Kondo.

A second reason for choosing Yakushiji as the springboard for a tour of Nara is that an old Nara-period road begins just outside its north gate, and the visitor with time and a taste for leisurely strolls can follow this road a little

(Preceding page) Festival lanterns on one of the floats paraded during Kyoto's Gion Matsuri.

over three kilometres (1. 8 miles) to the formerly great temple of Saidaiji, passing as he strolls two of the ancient capital's most important historical monuments.

The first of these, which he reaches within minutes of leaving Yakushiji, is **Toshodaiji**, perhaps the most exquisite of all Nara's temples. Here, more than anywhere else, one blesses the centuries that have worn away the reds and greens and blues and golds, and left the almost-black of the wood and the crisp white of the plaster and wide gravel paths to reveal without the distraction of colour the temple's perfect architectural harmonies. 'Toshodaiji' means 'Temple of the One who was Invited and Brought from China' and was founded in 759 by the Chinese priest Chien Chen (Jian Zhen), whom the Japanese call Ganjin. In 742 Chien Chen was invited by envoys of the Japanese emperor to visit Japan in order to instruct the priests there. Chien Chen was forbidden to leave China by imperial decree and his various attempts, one of which ended in shipwreck, occupied 11 years and cost him his sight. The hardships Chien Chen underwent in his efforts to reach Nara are a measure not only of his determination and stoicism, but of the hazards of eighth-century sea travel, even at a time when Japan was particularly anxious to preserve and strengthen the umbilical cord that precariously joined it to the continent. It has been estimated that, in Chien Chen's time, fully half the ships that set out to cross the sea between China and Japan either turned back or were lost.

The first sight that greets the visitor as he enters Toshodaiji through the Great South Gate is one of the most striking he will see in all Nara: the Kondo, or main hall, which has survived intact from the date of the temple's founding and must rank as one of the most beautifully proportioned buildings in the world. Much of its strength derives from the eight great pillars that support its roof along the south facade, lending a peculiar sense of weight and rootedness to the entire compound, and making one wonder whether the architectural heritage of classical Greece was not among the many influences that found their way along the Silk Road. Among the statues housed in the Kondo is a seated dry-lacquer figure of the sombre Buddha of the Law (Vairocana), said to have been made by two of the Chinese artist-priests who accompanied Chien Chen to Nara. The flanking statues are all by Chinese sculptors.

Most of the other originally Nara-period structures in the compound—the lecture hall, the drum tower—have a simplicity and grace and a way of complementing each other to create a completely satisfying aesthetic whole that is not matched in any other Nara temple, with the possible exception of Horyuji. At the very back of the compound, away from the main buildings and beyond a small lotus-pond, stands the unassuming grave of blind Chien Chen the founder, who never saw the material loveliness of the temple he established and so never knew how great a legacy his adopted country had received from him.

The old road now crosses the Kintetsu railway line and turns north again to lead the stroller past the southeast corner of the key-hole shaped island and lake that mark the tomb of Emperor Suinin, one of the semi-legendary Yamato-era or pre-Yamato rulers, said to have lived for 139 years and to have reigned as emperor for a full century (29 BC–AD 70), dates and figures that all attest to the early and energetic development of the fairy story. But the tomb is genuine enough, and so is the fact that it houses the remains of a notable ancient ruler (alone perhaps, since the custom of retainers immolating themselves on the deaths of their lords is said to have ended in Suinin's reign). Six more of these mysterious key-hole shaped burying grounds lie a little over a kilometre northeast of here, beyond the site of the now vanished imperial palace, and there are many more near Osaka and throughout the old Yamato basin. A small controversy has developed around these tombs owing to the reluctance of the authorities to consent to their being excavated. The authorities state, quite credibly, that the tombs should be left alone in order not to disturb the august spirits of those for whom they were built. But critics have suggested that this reluctance is due more to a fear of what might be found if the tombs were systematically examined. Such excavations as have taken place (mostly at later tomb sites in Kyushu) have revealed paintings very similar to tomb frescoes that exist in Korea and, so critics charge, the Japanese establishment (particularly that part of it that spends so much of its time 'proving' the uniqueness and racial purity of Japanese people) would likely suffer embarrassment if too many early links with the 'inferior' culture of Korea were uncovered.

But this controversy need not detain the stroller, indifferent as he is bound to be to spurious claims of cultural and racial uniqueness, and if he continues north for about another kilometre, the old road will bring him finally to the gate of **Saidaiji**, 'The Great Temple in the West', founded here in 765 and formerly of a scale to compare with Todaiji, 'The Great Temple in the East', which it was built to complement. It is now much reduced in size and grandeur and none of its present buildings is earlier than 18th-century.

The three-kilometre (1.8-mile) stroll described above, with visits to Yakushiji and Toshodaiji, could well occupy the best part of a day. Visitors with less time to spare might squeeze it into a morning and then, from Saidaiji station, take the Kintetsu Line two stops to the Nara terminus and continue their tour of the chief sights of Nara with visits to Kofukuji, Todaiji and the Kasuga Shrine.

Kofukuji was moved to this site in 710 (some of the city's temples were originally founded elsewhere and re-established in Nara after it had become the capital), and its chief buildings, including the famous five-storey pagoda, were rebuilt, after repeated destruction by fire, in the early 15th century. Kofukuji means 'Happiness-Producing Temple', an appropriate name in that

The Great Buddha Hall of Todaiji temple, Nara; the largest wooden building on earth.

its pagoda and main hall were built to house a powerful regiment of benevolent Buddhas, including the Buddha of Compassion (Amida), the Buddha of Healing (Yakushi), the Historical Buddha (Sakyamuni) and the Buddha of the Future (Miroku Bosatsu). But the temple's most arresting sculpture is the slender and exquisitely human three-faced and six-armed Ashura, which dates from the early eighth century and is kept today with most of Kofukuji's other treasures in the temple's ferroconcrete museum. One can't help wondering how much happiness their removal from 15th-century wood to 1950s' ferroconcrete produced in the Buddhas.

A stroll east from Kofukuji through Nara Park takes the visitor past excavations that have uncovered the foundations of a solid Nara-period road, to the **Nara National Museum**. By this time the visitor cannot help but have noticed the famous **Nara deer**, who graze at large through the park and the precincts of the temples and shrines that surround it, and who may already have attempted to relieve him of half the items he is carrying (those who congregate in the approaches to Todaiji's Great Buddha Hall are most adept at this, having continual daily practice from the tourists who feed them rice crackers bought at the nearby souvenir stalls). The connection between deer and Buddhism is a long one, and owes much to the supposedly gentle nature of these animals—fitting symbols for a faith that, unlike Islam and Christianity, has usually refrained from aggressive proselytizing or from seeking converts by force. The Historical Buddha's first sermon was preached in a deer park at Varanasi in India, the first place he entered after obtaining his enlightenment. As the visitor continues east and reaches the beginning of the long and picturesque flight of stone steps that leads up to the **Kasuga Shrine**, he will notice that bas-relief sculptured deer form a repeated motif on the stone lanterns that line these steps. The shrine is dedicated to Shinto gods, not to any manifestation of the Buddha (see page 75), but the deer's presence here is a clear testament to the accommodating line taken by both faiths since Buddhism arrived in Japan. In fact, the Kasuga Shrine was originally linked to Kofukuji by virtue of the fact that both were ancestral places of worship for the Fujiwara family, the real power behind the throne from the mid-ninth to the mid-eleventh centuries, and among the Shinto shrine's official functions was protection of the Buddhist temple. The deer came to be regarded as incarnations of the many local deities and of the Fujiwara ancestors themselves. Each year in mid-October a ceremonial horn-cropping takes place in a compound erected to the right of the long flight of steps.

The Kasuga Shrine (whose name is written with ideograms that mean 'Spring Day') is in fact a complex consisting of four small shrines, each of which is dedicated to a different deity—two of these being legendary ancestors of the flesh-and-blood Fujiwaras. That gods should father human descendants is, of course, not uncommon; it happens throughout Greek mythology, and the best-known Japanese example is that of the imperial family who, until the present emperor renounced his divinity following the defeat of 1945, claimed direct descent from the Sun Goddess, Amaterasu Omikami. For centuries the Kasuga Shrine buildings were demolished and rebuilt every 20 years, a practice of ritual renewal that continues today at the Grand Shrine of Ise (see page 103). The chief structures of the main Kasuga Shrine were last rebuilt in the mid-17th century and those of the next-door **Kasuga-Wakamiya Shrine** in the mid-19th. Many of the shrine buildings have rows of metal lanterns hanging from their eaves. These are lit twice a year, together with the stone lanterns that flank the steps, on 3 February (traditionally a date on which the dark spirits of winter are ceremonially banished) and on 15 August, when the lantern-lighting takes on an added significance owing to this date's marking the (mainly Buddhist) Festival of the Dead (see page 121).

In its situation among steep wooded hills, deriving most of its attraction not from grandly monumental architecture but from the pleasantness of its sylvan setting, the Kasuga Shrine presents a sharp contrast to most of the Nara-period temples with their clean, flat compounds and crisp, Chinese geometry. As such, it helps to delineate a crucial difference between the Nara-period Buddhist temple and the Shinto shrine, and between the faiths that inspired them. Pre-Zen Buddhist temples preserve a teaching, or a moral system, or ideas such as 'salvation' and 'law'; but Shinto shrines are the signposts to a non-didactic spirit-in-nature, a spirit that lodges not so much in the man-made structures as in the trees and hills and rocks and waterfalls to which the structures were built to pay homage. This is not always true. It is not true, for example, of the Meiji and Yasukuni Shrines in Tokyo which were erected specifically to honour the souls of newly-dead men. Nor is it true of such bureaucratically-inspired examples of shrine-building as the 'Heian Shrine' in Kyoto. And there are many Buddhist temples of a later date than the Nara period which draw their chief outward beauty from a sense of being wedded to their surroundings. But if the visitor will keep in mind the difference between an ordered 'teaching' and an unconfinable 'spirit-in-nature', it will help him to appreciate better both the different functions and characters of the temples and shrines he visits, as well as the fact that the two were never mutually contradictory or exclusive.

For a sight of one more exquisite example of Nara-period sculpture, very different in character from the meditating Buddhas, the visitor can walk south along a short woodland path that leads from the precincts of the Kasuga Shrine, across a modern road, to the temple of **Shinyakushiji** (New Yakushiji), which stands down a winding back street that ends in rice paddies. This temple, like Saidaiji, is greatly reduced from its former splendour, but in a dark, stable-like hall it houses an image of the Buddha of Healing, from which it takes its name, surrounded by clay statues of the

Religion in Japan

It is sometimes said that the modern Japanese are the most secular-minded nation in the world. Nevertheless, a recent nationwide survey revealed that 95,860,000 Japanese people regard themselves as adherents of the Shinto faith; 87,750,000 are Buddhists; and 2,020,000 profess to be Christians. In a country whose total population is just over 121 million, it is clear that a large number of those surveyed are hedging their bets.

Shinto (literally 'the Way of the Gods') derives from the animistic cults that pre-dated Buddhism in Japan. Where these survive in their most original forms (the rural northeast and Okinawa), one still finds older country people consulting female shamans. Shinto's vast pantheon inhabits mountains, rivers and waterfalls, and some of the gods, but by no means all, concern themselves with human welfare. The myths of the founding of the nation and the divine descent of the imperial family were early incorporated into the faith, and from them specifically derives the nationalistic aspect of Shinto which shaped much of the social climate in the 1930s and '40s. An observance such as *hatsumode* (the first prayer of the new year) is far more an affirmation of Japaneseness than an expression of any form of supernatural belief.

Buddhism was introduced into Japan from Korea and China in the sixth century and was officially adopted as the state religion during the Nara period (710–94). Buddhism and Shinto were never in serious conflict and complemented rather than opposed each other, with Shinto deities coming to be regarded as the protectors of Buddhist temples. An attempt to separate the two faiths was made at the beginning of the Meiji period when Buddhism was disestablished and Shinto (or the nationalistic face of it) came to monopolize state support. Since the war, with freedom of religion guaranteed under the postwar constitution, they have partly resumed their complementary roles: Shinto ceremonies often accompany early infancy and marriage, while Buddhism looks after the dead.

Perhaps to counter the oppressive weight of unalloyed materialism, the postwar period has seen a remarkable proliferation of 'new religions', many of which could better be described as new Buddhist or Shinto sects. The best-known and most powerful is the *Sokagakkai* (founded in 1930), a lay splinter group of Nichiren Buddhism, which now claims a Japanese membership of 10 million and another million worldwide. The group has a 'political wing' in the form of the *Komeito* (Clean Government Party), with an established presence in the Diet. Until 1979 the president of Sokagakkai was the humourless, silk-suited, limousine-chauffered Ikeda Daisaku, regarded by his followers as an embodiment of the Buddha.

For comments on the relationship between Shinto and Buddhism, and for an outline of the development of Buddhism in Japan, see the sections on Nara and Kyoto. For a brief account of the introduction and persecution of Christianity, see the section on Kyushu.

February Setsubun ritual at Takayama, Gifu prefecture. Beans will be scattered, accompanied by the cry "Oni wa soto! Fuku wa uchi!" *(Devils out! Good luck in!)*

Twelve Guardian Generals who defend the Buddha's law. Many of these are justly celebrated, but the outstanding sculpture is that of the fierce, teeth-baring **Basara**, whose right hand holds a sword and the fingers of whose left hand are curiously and tensely poised. Buddhist mythology has its figures of terror just as it has its embodiments of sublime peace, and, unlike those in the Christian myths, the figures of terror are often on the side of right.

The visitor can now head north again, past **Sagi-ike** (The Heron Pond) and back through the park to **Todaiji** Temple, easily the most visited temple in Nara on account of its containing the 16.2-metre-high (54-foot), bronze **Daibutsu** (Great Buddha), larger than the similar statue in Kamakura, and housed in a structure (the **Daibutsuden**, or Great Buddha Hall) which is the largest wooden building on earth. The striking proportions of this building are best appreciated if you approach it, as most visitors do, through the **Nandaimon** (Great South Gate), itself a huge structure that dates from 1199.

Todaiji was founded in 745 and its chief object of worship, the bronze Buddha, was completed in 749, having been cast under the supervision of a Korean metalworker named Kimimaro. The great fires that have twice reduced the Buddha Hall to ashes—once in 1180, once in 1567—were both deliberate acts of war in the millennium-long struggle for supremacy between power-hungry warlords; a struggle in which the priestly orders were often embroiled, even when they did not willingly embroil themselves. The great bronze Buddha had already had his head knocked off by an earthquake in 855. During the fire of 1180 he lost it again together with his right arm, and during that of 1567 he lost it a disorienting third time. He was restored to his present state in 1692, and the hall was rebuilt on a somewhat smaller scale than it had originally possessed in 1709, and again extensively renovated in 1914. That the Great Buddha seems to lack the ageless serenity of many of the finest Nara temple sculptures can, of course, be blamed on the vicissitudes of war and earthquakes, on decapitation and emergency surgery. But, disasters apart, if sculptures like Kofukuji's Ashura and the Buddha of the Future in Chuguji have anything to communicate beyond an infinite capacity for love, it is that size alone, even size as momentarily overpowering as this, is a barren quality without the deeper mystery carved into those figures' faces; a mystery of which the great bronze Buddha has little visible trace.

On the heights to the east of the Daibutsuden, beyond the belfry, are the **Nigatsudo** (Hall of the Second Moon) and **Sangatsudo** (Hall of the Third Moon—'moon', in these cases, meaning the months of the old lunar calendar). The present Nigatsudo dates from 1669 and from its platform the viewer can see the distant five-storey pagoda of Kofukuji rising above the rooftiles and trees of the Todaiji complex. The Nigatsudo is the site of an important annual two-week-long ritual called **O-mizutori** (Water-Drawing), which takes its name from the climactic event enacted each year on 12 March—the drawing up of water from the well below the building. This is preceded by a nighttime procession of priests, each carrying a large brightly blazing pine torch, who, when they reach the platform of the Nigatsudo, swing and shake their torches to produce a massive shower of sparks and embers that wraps the entire building in flame. This ceremony, dating back to the mid-eighth century, is the most hallowed in the old capital and is, in origin, a combination of purification ritual (the flames purging the temple of winter spirits) and absolution from sin, symbolized by the gift of sacred water. Many of Nara's annual observances involve the use of fire; another famous ritual being the spectacular grass-burning on **Mount Wakakusa** (Mount Young-Grass), above the Kasuga Shrine, which takes place each year on 15 January (Coming-of-Age Day).

Northwest of the Daibutsuden stands the log-cabin-like **Shosoin** repository, in which are—or were—stored some of the outstanding treasures of the Nara period, many of them, like the masks and five-stringed lute, providing crystal clear evidence of the extent to which the Silk Road brought foreign cultural influences and artifacts to early Japan from as far away as the Middle East and, perhaps, the Mediterranean. These treasures are not usually on public display, owing, so the authorities maintain, to their fragility. But they are exhibited annually for a brief time during the safely unhumid weather of autumn.

In Nara Prefecture

One of the most important temples associated with the old capital stands not in the city of Nara itself, but some 14 kilometres (8.5 miles) southwest of it. This is the temple complex of **Horyuji**, the oldest existing temple in Japan, founded by Prince Shotoku in 607, a bare 20 years after the official espousal of Buddhism, destroyed by fire in 670 and rebuilt at about the time that Nara became the capital. As an example of T'ang Chinese religious architecture Horyuji is unrivalled in the world, and its treasure house and neighbouring nunnery contain two of the most superb sculptures the visitor will ever see.

The larger west compound is the one the visitor enters first, with its main hall (Kondo) and five-storey pagoda (reassembled after the Second World War using the original eighth-century timbers) arranged to right and left of the gateway after the Korean fashion (many of the craftsmen employed in the temple's construction were Korean), rather than one behind the other as was usual in China. Both these buildings contain treasures—the Kondo has several bronze statues of Buddhas, including Sakyamuni (The Historical Buddha) and Yakushi, cast at, or shortly after, the time of Horyuji's founding, notable for their unmysterious, naively complacent expressions. The pagoda contains clay bas-reliefs of scenes from the Buddha's life, death and ascension to paradise.

But for Horyuji's most riveting sculptured treasure the visitor must go to the 20th-century treasure house, where he will see among many other things, if he is lucky (since it is not always displayed), the tall, impossibly slender form of **Kudara Kannon** with its sublime, still somehow homely features. The origins of this statue are a mystery. It has been claimed for a seventh-century Japanese sculptor of Korean descent, but also for the artists of southern China and the Korean kingdom of Paekche (the Japanese name for which was 'Kudara'). A modern mystery is why the curators of this treasure house have stuck the statue behind reflecting glass, a plan that makes the full appreciation of its lovely face a practical impossibility. Another celebrated image of Kannon (the Goddess of Mercy) is housed in the **Yumedono** (Hall of Dreams), the beautiful octagonal pavilion at the centre of the east compound. This statue has been ascribed to no less an artist than Prince Shotoku himself, and has been worshipped since shortly after his death as the repository of his soul. The statue is rarely on public view.

A few dozen metres from the Hall of Dreams is the nunnery of **Chuguji**, originally the home of Prince Shotoku's mother. In its modern treasure hall stands arguably the finest piece of sculpture in Japan, the wooden, incense-blackened **Miroku Bosatsu** (Buddha of the Future), whose distinctly feminine aspect has also caused the figure to be identified with the Goddess of Mercy. The only comparably beautiful statue of Miroku Bosatsu is the one in Koryuji Temple in Kyoto (see page 84) which has not the softness of the Chuguji figure, but is more purely androgynous. The Chuguji figure is also attributed by legend to Prince Shotoku, though the complete irrelevance of its provenance cannot but strike the awed visitor who looks long enough at its softly shining face. It doesn't matter who carved it. It is sufficient that such a perfect thing exists.

Perhaps the most satisfying thing about the finest Nara sculptures—this, the Ashura, the Kudara Kannon—is the degree to which they communicate to the viewer a seeming longing to inspire in him the same perfect calm that inspires them. Their chief aim is not to be merely beautiful, but actively to pass on the quality that sustains their beauty. Compare this accessibility with the defiant loftiness of, say, Michelangelo's David, who stares away over his magnificently untouchable shoulder as though the viewer were completely beneath his contempt. There is no contempt, no cold magnificence, in the faces of these Nara figures. Rather, they seem like encouraging relatives (the *homeliness* of the Kudara Kannon; she is just like somebody's auntie!) who derive a palpable pleasure from the viewer's confidence in their concern.

If the reflecting glass of Horyuji's treasure house proved an irritant, how much more so will the tape-recorded commentary switched faithfully on every 10 or 12 minutes by the lady custodian of Chuguji's Miroku Bosatsu. This worthy person has responded in the past to requests that the tape

Rebuilt pagoda at Kiyomizudera temple, Kyoto; colours the years will wear away.

recorder be turned off, but always with a puzzled frown, and the visitor who threatens her with physical violence does so at the risk of his soul. Besides, the visitor had better accustom himself to tape-recorded commentaries before he sets out to view the chief sights of Kyoto, otherwise he could end up leaving old unsullied Yamato in a straitjacket.

Within easy strolling distance of Horyuji stand the two small unfrequented temples of **Horinji** and **Hokkiji**, both founded in the seventh century. Hokkiji is remarkable for its lovely three-storey pagoda which survives in its original state.

The mountainous **Yoshino** area, in the south of Nara prefecture, an area famous for its cryptomeria and cherry blossoms, is part of the **Yoshino-Kumano National Park** (see also page 107).

Kyoto

When in the West we speak of 'a beautiful city', we often have in our minds a place which, viewed from some point of vantage, presents a pleasing overall prospect. Kyoto is not like that at all. If your first sight of Kyoto is from the platform where the bullet train deposits you, its superficial ugliness can move you to despair. Kyoto's beauty is not like Nara's—monumental, expansive, public. Kyoto's beauty is elusive and has to be sought out with patience and forethought.

Partly this is because Kyoto has continued to grow and flourish as a living city, while Nara has tended to settle reclusively into the sombre business of being a museum. Modern city growth has on all sides threatened the peace and loveliness of old Kyoto—threatened, but not extinguished. Nara's claim on the visitor's attention has often to do with size—the great bronze Buddha, the extent of the compounds of Todaiji and Horyuji, the largest wooden building on earth. But the best of what Kyoto has to offer is often small in scale and of a delicacy that the encroachment of raucous modernity seems always to underline, and sometimes enhance—the rock garden at the Daisenin, the Shisendo hermitage, the Jakkoin nunnery, a single gate, a single patch of crumbling wall, the window of a doll shop that contains for its display one single, painstakingly chosen doll.

You cannot enjoy Kyoto from a point of vantage (even from such traditional points of vantage as Mount Hiei or the platform of Kiyomizu Temple), let alone from the top of the banal lighthouse-shaped tower of the Kyoto Tower Hotel. You have to go down among the narrow back streets where the old and the new clash so echoingly and begin ferreting out the private corners of that beauty which is the heritage of Kyoto's privacy-minded people.

In three or four days, the diligent, sensitive visitor might come close to understanding and appreciating what, for want of a more properly descriptive term, we shall have to call the 'heart' of Nara. But to come within striking distance of the 'heart' of Kyoto would take as many years, and even then the discovered 'heart' would be an unashamedly private invention, as different from the next man's image of 'the real' Kyoto as you are different from him. I hope that the visitor will not mind my being completely subjective in the advice I have to give.

The advice is in two parts. In the first part I shall briefly describe most of the famous sights of Kyoto which any bus tour will take the visitor to see, and on which I urge him, with little more than personal prejudice for a reason, not to spend more than half his total time. In the second part I shall try to point him in the direction of other sights (some equally famous, some largely ignored) where I have found and been able to enjoy some vestige of what I regard as the 'real' Kyoto beauty. I cannot guarantee that the visitor will find that beauty there in equal measure for, as well as being a private matter, the charm of this old city is almost wholly dependent on such unpredictable factors as the weather, the season, the time of day, and whether or not the visitor is in love. Part of the beauty of the great monuments of Nara lies in the impression of strength they convey. But the private, elusive beauty of Kyoto is far less vigorous a thing, and it is easily spoiled. Talk too loud, look too hard, think too much, and it is gone.

Kyoto: The Skin

Kyoto (present propulation 1.5 million) contains about 20 percent of all Japan's listed national treasures—an embarrassment of riches—so the chief problem for a visitor with limited time is one of choice. Perhaps his best means of approaching the famous sights in this first section is to allow convenience of location to make the choice for him. It doesn't really matter in what order he sees these things, only that he get round as many as interest him and still leave himself time to follow at least some of the suggestions in the next section. The temples and shrines are introduced here roughly in the order of their founding.

Heian is the name given to the period, almost four centuries long, between the establishment of the capital at Heiankyo (Kyoto) in 794 and the removal of real power to Kamakura in 1185 (see page 53). It was, for the privileged classes, an age of elegance and sophistication, derived from the manners and interests of the still-preeminent imperial court. The clearest legacy of the period is Kyoto's grid-like street plan, modelled on that of the T'ang Chinese capital of Chang'an. Directions to Kyoto's taxi drivers often consist in naming the intersections of major thoroughfares (as in New York), and the main east-west avenues are still numbered one to nine.

The style of architecture on which it is based requires that the **Heian Shrine** be mentioned early, though it is not a Heian shrine at all but a late

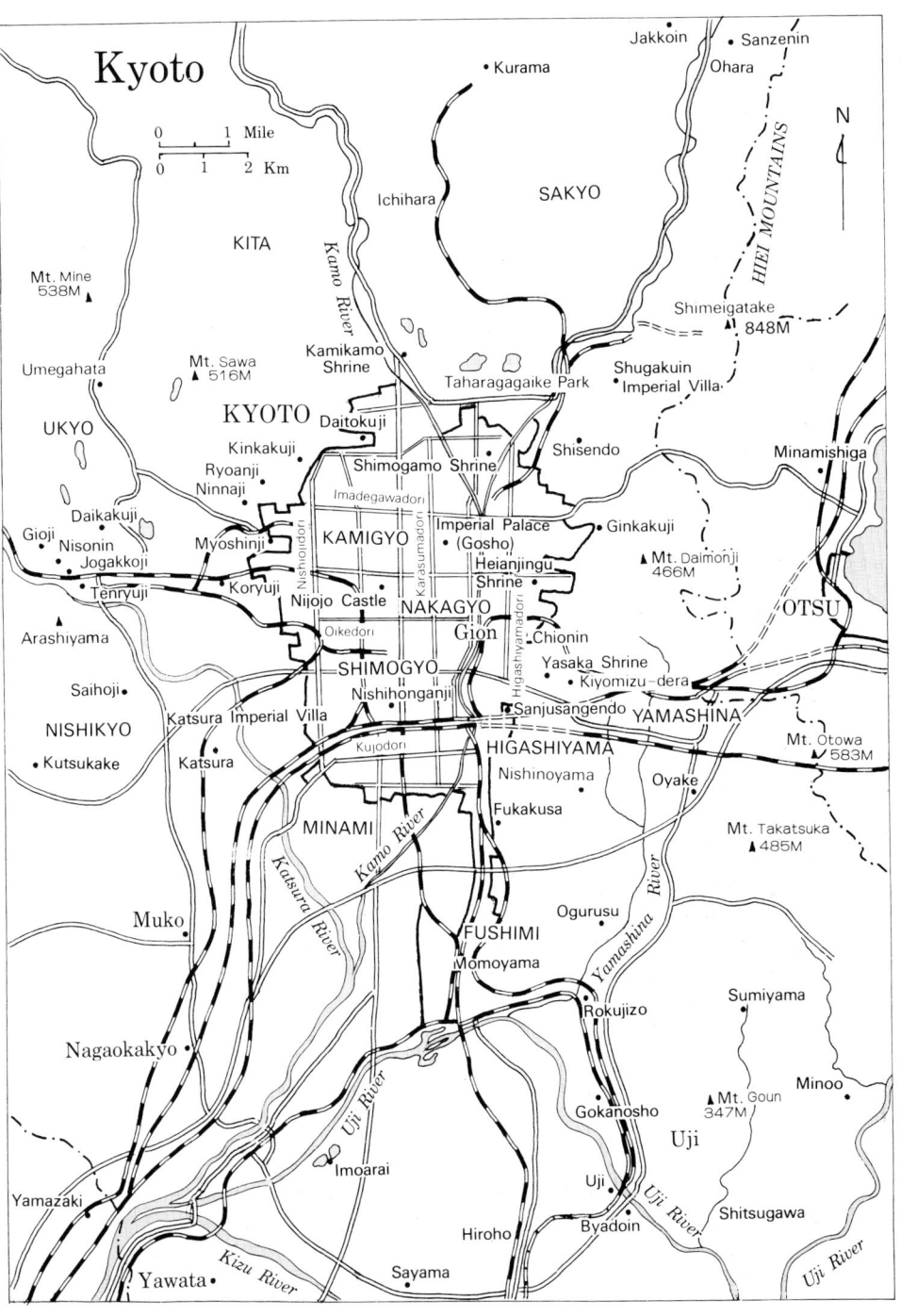

19th-century replica of the earliest imperial palace in Kyoto, built to a scale of about half the size of the original on former parkland in 1895 to commemorate the 1,100th anniversary of the city's founding. It possesses, in consequence, the spiritual depth of a stage set for an extravagant production of Gilbert and Sullivan's *The Mikado,* an operetta already a decade old when the 'Heian Shrine' first opened its gates.

The **Yasaka Shrine**, on the other hand, is genuinely Heian in origin, though its present buildings were constructed in the mid-17th century. Its location in **Gion** (it is sometimes called the 'Gion Shrine'), which is the old theatre and entertainment quarter of the city, well-known for its geisha, has given this particular religious edifice a not unattractive atmosphere of worldly bustle, especially on New Year's eve, when a bonfire is lit in the shrine compound, and people can be seen strolling through the precincts twirling in their hands the smouldering strings with which, traditionally, they would have kindled the first hearth fire of the new year. The shrine's most famous annual observance occurs in July and is Kyoto's best-known festival (see Gion Matsuri page 98).

Of the principal temples within the city proper, **Koryuji** is the oldest, having been established during the time of Prince Shotoku, in 622, long before Kyoto became the capital. Its main hall still dates from 1165, but the visitor's attention will be chiefly claimed by the exquisite late-sixth or early-seventh-century statue of **Miroku Bosatsu** (The Buddha of the Future), the first piece of sculpture ever designated a National Treasure, which is housed today in the temple's modern museum. Opinions differ as to which of the two similarly posed statues is the finer, this or the one in Chuguji (see page 79). Chuguji's may strike the viewer as the more accessibly human, while this in Koryuji seems to hover tantalizingly between the human and the purely spiritual. The story is told of a student who, during the days (not so long ago) when the statue was less rigorously protected than it is now, was so captivated by its beauty that he leaned across to caress it and accidently broke off one of the delicate fingers of its right hand. Horrified at the enormity of what he had done, and prevented by sheer terror from confessing, he carried the finger around in his pocket for several days while the country went into an uproar and the police conducted a frantic search. Eventually he plucked up the courage to hand the finger over to the authorities, who restored the statue and placed it behind the carefully guarded plate glass where it meditates today on how to effect the salvation of mankind. The student's salvation was quick to arrive, and he became something of a folk hero, more admired for his love of the ethereally beautiful than frowned on for his folly.

Visitors interested in folly will find the **Toei Eiga Mura** (Film Village), a stone's throw from Koryuji, entirely to their taste. Here they can see how one of the major Japanese film companies goes grandly and energetically about the task of reducing the country's history to a series of swashbuckling

confrontations between baddies who speak out of the corners of their mouths and goodies who speak with their quivering chins tucked back into their Adam's apples.

Of temples founded after Kyoto became the capital, **Kiyomizudera** (Pure Water Temple, taking its name from a spring on the steep hillside where it stands) is among the most famous and ancient, having been established here in 798. Most of the present structures date from the 17th century. The temple's chief architectural feature—and main tourist attraction—is the stilted platform on which the main hall stands, commanding a view over part of the city. Below the platform, paths disappear into the wooded hillside, affording a short, but pleasant stroll. Kiyomizudera is approached along a street lined with shops that sell, among other souvenirs, examples of the pottery to which the temple has given its name. The district has been famous for its ceramics since it was settled by Korean potters brought back to Japan following the campaigns in Korea during the 1590s.

Ninnaji Temple was founded in 888, but most of its buildings have been reconstructed (several during the last hundred years) in the style of the late 16th century, so it is not typical of the period of its founding, although it preserves an atmosphere of calm elegance better than do its more famous neighbours, Ryoanji and Kinkakuji. This temple is a recognized centre for the gentle arts of tea ceremony and flower arrangement and, throughout feudal times, the head priest was a member of the imperial family.

During the Kamakura period (see page 53), when political power shifted for the first time to the Kanto region, Kyoto, though still a seething hotbed of plot and counterplot, was thrown back to a large extent on cultural and philosophical pursuits, such as the assimilation of several new schools of Buddhism, all Japanese in origin. These included the 'Pure Land' sect founded by Honen, the 'True Pure Land' sect founded by Shinran, and the 'Nichiren' sect, named after its highly egotistical founder, Nichiren, regarded, on his own recognizance, as an incarnation of the Buddha. Each of these new Japanese sects was, in one way or another, an attempt to popularize and simplify the hitherto esoteric doctrines of the adopted continental faith. But the most important artistic development within Japanese Buddhism during this period came once again from the continent. This was the introduction from China of Zen (Ch'an) Buddhism toward the end of the 12th century.

For the most striking example of original Kamakura-period architecture in Kyoto one turns to **Sanjusangendo**, a long wooden structure built in 1266, and belonging to **Myohoin** Temple, which was actually founded in Heian times. Inside, the entire 118-metre (390-foot) length of the hall forms a vast exhibition platform for 1,001 statues of the Goddess of Mercy which are among the most breathtaking sights in the city—not because of their beauty, but because of their sheer massed numbers. In the gallery behind the main exhibition, through which the visitor passes before reaching the exit, stand some genuinely moving sculptured figures, in particular that of the praying woman, **Mawara-nyo** and of the lean, bearded hermit, **Basu**. Since 1606 the building's long veranda has been the site of a famous annual archery contest, still held on 15 January (Coming of Age Day, a national holiday). The name Sanjusangendo means 'Hall of Thirty-Three Spaces' and refers to the number of gaps between its supporting pillars.

Another, even larger, Kamakura-period temple is the **Chion-in**, the earliest of whose present buildings dates from the 17th century. The temple's massive bell was cast at about the same time, and is a major attraction for visitors to Kyoto on New Year's eve when, throughout the country, temple bells ring out the 108 sins of the old year. The Chion-in bell is so huge that the priest appointed to strike it (an exhausting business, so the priests relieve each other very frequently) must throw the whole weight of his body at the bell, being hoisted off the ground by the momentum of the heavy wooden striker in a somewhat unpriestly display of trapezery.

The collapse of the military government in Kamakura and the return of political power to Kyoto marked the beginning of the Muromachi period (1333–1568), an era so plagued by civil wars and armed rivalry between supporters of the court, of the powerful Ashikaga family (for much of the era de facto rulers of the nation), and of numerous provincial lords, that the latter half is also known as the Sengoku period or 'Period of the Country at War'. Nevertheless, the chief architectural monuments of these centuries are particularly noted for their elegance and refinement.

Rokuonji Temple, far better known as **Kinkakuji** (The Temple of the Golden Pavilion), was the retreat of the third Ashikaga shogun, Yoshimitsu, who entered the priesthood on his retirement in 1394 and subsequently both built the famous pavilion and laid out the temple's large garden. The pavilion was intended as an expression of the earthly wealth and power of the retired shogun's family rather than as a monument to religious zeal—just as was, more than two centuries later, Ieyasu's Toshogu Shrine at Nikko (see page 59) so a comparison between the two buildings provides an illuminating lesson in the decline of aesthetic taste from Ashikagas to Tokugawas. The original pavilion was completely destroyed by arson in 1950, and this astonishing act of vandalism forms the climax of Mishima Yukio's 1956 novel, *Kinkakuji,* in which the author suggests that the culprit, a Buddhist acolyte, destroyed the pavilion partly out of an inability to tolerate the existence of so perfect an object of beauty in an imperfect, ugly world. The present pavilion, completed in 1955, is a replica of the original.

Ginkakuji (The Temple of the Silver Pavilion) was built almost a century after the construction of its golden forebear, in 1488. It was built by Yoshimitsu's grandson, the eighth Ashikaga shogun, Yoshimasa, not as a place to retire to but as a distraction from the cares of office. Yoshimasa

(Preceding page) Intolerable in a wretched world: the Golden Pavilion, Kyoto, restored after arson.

made his pavilion a centre for the refined hobbies to which he was addicted—tea ceremony, painting and flower arrangement—and to his consequent neglect of the affairs of government can be attributed the beginning of his family's fall from power. The Mount-Fuji-shaped sand hill, which is the most striking object in the pavilion's famous garden, has often been praised as an example of Zen artistry and has always struck this observer as supremely silly.

But for the most famous example of Zen artistry in Kyoto one must go to **Ryoanji** Temple, founded in 1473, whose garden of 15 rocks and raked sand has come, perhaps more than any other single work, to symbolize the simplicity and metaphysical profundity to which Zen art aspires, or, more often, professes. Do these rocks 'represent' islands in an ocean? Or mountain peaks above a sea of cloud? Or tigers carrying their cubs across a river? Or are they just boulders scattered randomly about a patch of flat sand which has been raked in a finicky way? The visitor will wish he knew. He may also wish he knew how the monks manage to rake the sand into those circles without leaving footprints. And, if he stays longer than five minutes, he will also wish he knew why a temple whose introductory pamphlet invites visitors to sit down and meditate quietly on the profundities of its garden plays an endless tape-loop of explanatory babble designed to prevent them doing any such thing.

The three decades between the end of the Muromachi period and the beginning of the Edo period (see page 21) form the brief Azuchi-Momoyama period (1568-1600), during which the long era of civil war was gradually forced to a close, and the warring provinces brought to heel, by the unifying policies of two ruthless and powerful warlords, Oda Nobunaga and Toyotomi Hideyoshi. Between them they created the conditions on which Ieyasu could found the strong centralized government of the Tokugawas. Painting and other arts continued to flourish, but the period has not added much to the Kyoto visitor's itinerary. The **Nishi** (West) **Honganji** Temple dates from 1591, and the **Higashi** (East) **Honganji** Temple from 1602. Both are large temples of the 'True Pure Land Sect' founded by Shinran, and are popular with visitors, not so much on account of their intrinsic architectural merits (though Nishi Honganji is highly regarded), but on account of their proximity to Kyoto station.

The chief architectural legacy of the Edo period is secular, not religious. The most accessible example of it is **Nijo Castle**, begun in 1569 by Nobunaga, but much expanded in 1601–03 by Ieyasu, who used it as his Kyoto residence, the first real permanent evidence of the heights of power he had attained. Visitors to Tokyo who were disappointed by the Imperial Palace's lack of glamour may find their disappointment assuaged somewhat by the spacious gardens and interior grandeur of Nijo Castle (Nijo means simply 'Second Avenue', the name of the thoroughfare where it is located), though the exterior is hardly less sombre. An explanatory tape-loop boasts endlessly of the castle's size—33 rooms, 800 tatami mats, 3,300 square metres (3,950 square yards)—and many of its ceilings and panels are decorated with a richness which foreshadows the baroque extravagance that was eventually to dictate the form of the Nikko mausoleum. An interesting architectural innovation is the 'nightingale' floor, constructed so as to emit a low squeaking sound when anyone walks across it. It was designed to afford the shogun's bodyguards warning of the approach of possible intruders and one marvels that it did not drive the permanent staff of the shogun's household completely barmy.

The **Katsura Imperial Villa** (built in 1624) and the **Shugakuin Imperial Villa** (built in 1659) attest to the fine things that emperors could create and inspire when they didn't have to bother themselves with governing. Katsura is famous for the restrained beauty of its architecture and possesses a lovely garden, while Shugakuin, situated on the lowest slopes of Mount Hiei, has an attractive rusticity that must have made it a perfect setting for the tea ceremonies regularly conducted there. These villas are only open to visitors who have made prior application to the Imperial Household Agency, and then only when they consent to be shown round by a talkative official guide. Applications can be made through offices of the Japan Travel Bureau and should be filed at least a week in advance.

Kyoto's most spacious landmark is the **Gosho** (Imperial Palace), originally built here in 1790, destroyed in 1854, rebuilt in 1855. Its outer gardens are always open for the visitor to stroll through, but entrance to the palace itself is subject to the same restrictions as is entrance to the imperial villas (except that applications may be accepted at 24 hours' notice instead of a week's). The palace is the starting point of the procession which forms the basis of the Aoi Matsuri (see page 98) in May.

Kyoto: The Bones

And now, having made the rounds of these monuments, many of them outstandingly beautiful, the visitor may feel compelled to ask in what way they are not the elusively 'real' Kyoto. What is it that they lack? Here, the author falls back, as he warned he would, on personal predilection. They lack little or nothing in terms of material splendour. No temple I am about to mention has a statue that remotely matches in loveliness Koryuji's Miroku Bosatsu. None has a building so striking, and so strikingly filled, as Sanjusangendo. None has the aura of wealth and power that hangs over the Golden and Silver Pavilions or Nijo Castle. None has a view so famous and so wide as that from Kyomizudera. It follows that, in this author's view at least, the hard-to-define but distinctive Kyoto beauty resides in something other than statuary, striking buildings, wealth and worldly power and

20-year-olds celebrate their coming of age with a shrine visit on Adult's Day (January 15). The kimonos may never be worn again. The arrows are bought for luck.

wide–ranging prospects. For statuary and striking buildings, one should really go to Nara; for the display of worldly riches to Nikko; for vast eye-pleasing prospects to the mountains. Kyoto's beauty resides, I think, in a particular kind of atmosphere; in the sensation of uncomplicated peace for which the city was first named.

I have not stressed up to now the *kind* of Buddhism practised in the temples this guide has described because a book of this nature, and of these limitations, is obviously no place for a discourse on the many Buddhist sects and the complexities of their widely differing ideas and practices. Yet, it is impossible to point the visitor toward the particular atmosphere of tranquillity that distinguishes the temples I am now going to recommend he visit without at least attempting to say something about the way in which Zen Buddhism differs from other forms.

Up to the beginning of the Kamakura period Buddhism had developed in a more or less straight line from the esoteric (*mikkyo*) forms introduced from China and Korea. The main Japanese sects, *Shingon* (Koryuji, Ninnaji) and *Tendai* (Kiyomizudera, Sanjusangendo) based their worship mainly on complex rituals and on the teachings found in the ancient mandalas and sutras, teachings to which secret or semi-secret formulas were sometimes believed to hold the key. The founding of the purely Japanese schools of Buddhism during the Kamakura period can be seen as a populist reaction against the entrenched mysticism of this earliest kind of Buddhism. The new sects maintained that a knowledge of esoteric formulas was unnecessary, and that the unlettered had as much chance of achieving everlasting peace in the Buddha's 'Western Paradise' as did the most learned and deeply initiated among the clergy, merely through the profession of faith. This profession might take the form of simple prayers or the repetition of the Buddha's name, comparable to the Pater Nosters and Ave Marias of Catholicism. The notion of 'salvation' fostered by these sects is also akin to the Christian notion of Heaven, and the Buddha and his incarnations came to be regarded as 'saviours', shouldering the responsibility for dragging mankind out of sin and propelling him into paradise on the strength of 'I believe'.

Zen, introduced from China, proposed a completely different view of man's place and destiny. No supernatural intervention was going to 'save' man; indeed 'salvation', in the sense of admission to a happy afterlife, was not man's chief object. His object was present enlightenment (*satori*), which was obtainable only through discipline of body and mind, a discipline for which he was himself wholly responsible. Through enlightenment man would come to understand the nature of existence and his relationship with all else that lived or was inanimate. He would lose his ego — that most damaging commodity which kept him from a knowledge and enjoyment of true peace— and see that in his insignificance still dwelt the essential Buddha-nature. Man himself is Buddha. Hence Zen's overriding concern with the here-and-now,

with the transient present, not some dreamed-of future glory. Enlightenment does not lurk behind pearly gates. Like Kyoto's elusive beauty, it must be actively sought for—in a rice field, on a mountain top, in a freezing cold temple corridor. 'The truth is everywhere. The truth is where we are', wrote Dogen, the founder of the Soto sect of Zen. 'One step separates earth from heaven.'

Though Chinese in origin, the Zen teachings achieved their finest and most lasting fruits in Japan. Among these fruits is the distinctive atmosphere of peace and simplicity that pervades Kyoto's Rinzai Zen temples, and is, I believe, directly related to Zen's reverence for the here-and-now, and not for subservience to, or ultimate union with, a godhead that moves in mysterious ways. The two main Japanese Zen sects, Rinzai and Soto, differ in the kinds of discipline they encourage, but are united in their determination to remove the barriers of mind that keep man from his potential enlightenment. The oneness of the human and the natural (a quality seen by many as a prerequisite for 'Japaneseness' in the arts) is the mainstay of the unassuming beauty that characterizes these temples and that clearly differentiates them from, say, the great religious buildings of Nara. You could remove all the natural objects—rocks and trees and moss—from the vicinity of almost any of the great law-preserving temples in Nara, or from Sanjusangendo or Kiyomizudera for that matter, and the places would still be awesome and grand. But if you removed those links with nature from the compounds of Daitokuji or Myoshinji or Saihoji, you would strike at their very essence.

If the visitor has been to see all of the sights mentioned in the previous section, he has already visited three Rinzai Zen Temples: Kinkakuji, Ginkakuji and Ryoanji. **Daitokuji** (founded in 1324) and **Myoshinji** (founded in 1337) are the largest Rinzai Zen centres in Kyoto, but they differ from those of the first section in two important ways. First, they are not single temples as Ryoanji is, but large clusters of smaller temples, each jealously guarding the sense of privacy which this author at least finds essential to the 'real' Kyoto beauty. Second, they have not opened themselves up to tourism to the extent that those in the first section have. This may sound elitist, but it is possible to argue that the sheer fuss made of, say, Ryoanji's rock-and-sand garden has lessened, rather than heightened, its impact on the viewer. You approach it half expecting a shock of revelation, whereas it would likely impress you far more deeply if you could come on it unawares. In Daitokuji and Myoshinji you can stroll down quiet paths, linger at gates leading to empty temple gardens, and come completely unawares on many small corners of private loveliness. Most of the temples within the complexes are not open to the public. Those that are open include, in Daitokuji, the **Daisenin**, also famous for its rock-and-sand garden, the **Hoshunin, Sangenin, Ryogenin, Zuihoin, Kotoin** and **Obaiin**, and, in Myoshinji, the **Taizoin** (the suffixes -*ji* and -*in* both mean 'temple', -*in* usually denoting a smallness of scale).

Saihoji, another Rinzai Zen temple, founded in 1339, is sometimes called **Kokedera** (Moss Temple) on account of its spacious garden lushly carpeted with various species of moss. Until 1977 admission to this temple was unrestricted, with the result that large crowds of trampling sightseers began seriously to endanger the very sight for which the temple was famous. Admission is now only granted to visitors with prior permission. There is a waiting list and the number of visitors per day is strictly limited. If you are lucky enough to obtain permission, you will be doubly lucky if it has rained shortly before—or even during—your visit since, after a rain, the moss is at its most luminescent.

It would, of course, be wrong to suggest that early 14th-century Rinzai Zen Temples have a complete monopoly on peace and solitude. Kyoto has other quiet corners where these qualities may be found and enjoyed. If the visitor has devoted most of a day—as he surely should—to Daitokuji, Myoshinji and (with luck) Saihoji, he might end it by relaxing for an hour at the **Shisendo** hermitage, an unassuming little retreat built in 1631 by the poet Ishikawa Jozan, and the possessor of a carefully tended garden on the edge of wild woodland.

A second day could profitably be spent in the **Arashiyama** area of western Kyoto, beginning at the Heian-period temple of **Daikakuji**, formerly a villa belonging to the Emperor Saga who retired there in 823. Emperor Saga was a poet by inclination and hobby, and he so preferred this outlying rural suburb (called Saga) to the capital's bustling centre that he took it for his posthumous name. Daikakuji reminds one a little of Ninnaji, with its maze of covered walkways and corridors but, unlike the raked bare spaces at Ninnaji, the spaces between the walkways at Daikakuji are crowded with overgrown plant-life, reminders of its location in the rural wilds. The temple overlooks a small lake.

Strolling toward the Rinzai Zen complex of **Tenryuji**, founded in 1340, the visitor can turn right just before he reaches it to begin a walk that will take him along narrow rural lanes to several small, comparatively secluded temples. First, he comes to the tiny cottage where the 17th–century poet Kyorai lived, and where he will find the poet's grave. Further on stands the steep hilly Muromachi-period temple of **Jojakkoji**, further still the Kamakura-period **Nisonin** and, finally, at the end of the visitor's stroll, the tiny but lovely Heian-period thatch-roofed temple of **Gioji**, named after the Lady Gio who was loved in her youth by the great Heike leader, Taira no Kiyomori, and who in later life became a nun and spent her last days in this tranquil spot at the foot of Mount Atago.

At least part of a third day can be spent in the northeastern suburb of **Ohara**, where the two chief attractions are both Heian-period temples. The larger is the **Sanzenin**. The smaller, and more poignantly connected, is the

(Preceding page) The garden of the Jakkoin nunnery, Ohara, Kyoto. Bone-penetrating peace.

little nunnery called **Jakkoin**, famous as the retreat of Kenreimon-in, the daughter of Kiyomori and mother of the eight-year-old Emperor Antoku, who plunged into the sea with her son when defeat for the Heike became certain at the climax of the decisive sea battle of Dannoura in 1185. Antoku was drowned, but Kenreimon-in was rescued by her enemies and ended her days here, a nun. It is hard to imagine a more perfectly peaceful place to spend the last years of one's life, away from the clamour of court and war. Like Gioji, the Jakkoin possesses everything implied by the 'real' Kyoto beauty—privacy, tranquillity, and the unmistakable note of sadness which comes with the realization that such places are so lovely because they are so few.

The visitor can easily combine a trip to Ohara with an excursion to Mount Hiei and the Enryakuji Temple complex (see page 102).

Festive Kyoto

I have said nothing at all about Kyoto's thriving modernity, because I have assumed that it will not be what the visitor is primarily looking for. But Kyoto is a bustling, fashion-conscious city with its own subway, major department stores and well-known shopping street (**Kawaramachi**). For night life, the small streets behind the Kawaramachi-Shijo (Fourth Avenue) intersection offer the most interesting possibilities. The **Minamiza**, Kyoto's Kabuki theatre, is located near Shijo station. Running north to south between Shijo and Sanjo (Third Avenue) is the narrow street called **Pontocho**, famous in the past—and lingeringly today—for its ultra-sophisticated geisha clubs and restaurants. These line the alley, unassuming almost to the point of invisibility, behind their opaque slatted windows, guarded by exquisitely refined, unforgiving, unbudgeable matrons who, unless the visitor has been invited by a very rich and very trusted client, will not allow him to cross the the threshold for love—or, even, for money.

The principal festivals in Kyoto are, on 15 May the **Aoi** (Hollyhock) **Matsuri**; in July the **Gion Matsuri**; and on 22 October the **Jidai Matsuri** (Festival of the Ages). The first and last of these are mainly spectator-oriented costume parades. The Aoi Matsuri (dating from the sixth century and thought by some to be the oldest festival in the world) begins at the Gosho and proceeds to the two Kamo Shrines (**Shimogamo Jinja** and **Kamigamo Jinja**) where an imperial messenger presents a sacred horse. The participants wear costumes modelled on those of the Heian period, and the event commemorates the successful attempt by Emperor Kinmei in 553 to placate the local gods who had grown impatient at the impiety of the people (or, more likely, their espousal of Buddhism) and were flooding the area with violent storms. The Gion Matsuri dates from the ninth century and commemorates the end of the great plague of 869. Large floats topped with halberds (symbolizing protection) process through the city, culminating in a parade on 17 July. The Jidai Matsuri had its origin in the same tide of 19th-century bureaucratic enthusiasm that gave birth to the Heian Shrine. Participants wear costumes modelled on those of the various ages of Kyoto's history, from Heian to Meiji, and march to the Gosho from the Heian Shrine. On the same night (22 October) the little village of **Kurama**, some 12 kilometres (7 miles) north of Kyoto and easily reached on the Keifuku Line, celebrates a spectacular fire festival, the *Kurama no Hi Matsuri,* in which participants carry huge pine torches through the little streets of the village and drag them, as they disintegrate dangerously, up the steps of the village shrine. The torches, like the Gion halberds, are symbols of the gods' protective favours, though at the festival's climax they are so boisterously handled that one wonders how the village survives its own protection.

In Kyoto Prefecture

In the city of **Uji** (population 153,000), about 12 kilometres (7.5 miles) south of Kyoto, stands the **Byodoin** Temple, originally a private villa of the Fujiwara family, which became a temple in 1052. The main hall is known as the 'Hall of the Phoenix' both because of the shape of the whole structure, like a bird with outspread wings, and because of the bronze ornaments that top it. It is regarded as the finest example of Heian temple architecture to remain standing in its original state.

Otherwise, the principal sightseeing attraction in Kyoto, outside the prefectural capital, is located on the Japan Sea coast. This is the sand bar, a little over 3 kilometres (1.8 miles) in length, which stretches across the **Bay of Miyazu** and is called **Amanohashidate** (The Floating Bridge of Heaven). The Japanese love to arrange things—their natural wonders included—in categories that reflect a strict hierarchical order, and Amanohashidate has gone down in the ledgers as one of the 'Three Most Beautiful Scenic Views' in the country. (For the other two, see Matsushima on page 120 and Miyajima on page 160.) One can walk the length of the sand bar, pleasantly wooded with pine trees, or take a sightseeing cruise around it. But, traditionally, the finest view of it is obtained from the heights of **Kasamatsu Park** on the northern side of the bay, where visitors stand on one of three small stone benches with their backs to the sand bar, bend down and look at it through their open legs. This curious method of looking at a landscape is said to create in the viewer the impression that the bridge is truly floating in space. It is also likely to create in the foreign visitor not forewarned of the custom the impression that he has wandered unawares into the grounds of the prefectural mental asylum.

The Rest of the Kinki Region

Osaka (population 2.7 million) was the site of the 1970 World Exposition, an event that, together with the 1964 Tokyo Olympics, catapulted Japan onto the modern international stage and squarely into the modern preoccupation with being 'truly international' that has plagued the country ever since. At the time of Expo '70, Osaka was the second largest city in Japan, and it is now the third, having been topped by Yokohama. It is an almost exclusively, and exhaustingly, commercial city, its hotels and public buildings geared for conferences and trade fairs; and it is hard to know what the uncommercial visitor might do there, apart from spend his entire time crawling between the thousands of bars that crowd the city's southern quarter. He could go to see the reconstructed ferroconcrete seven-storey **Osaka Castle**, the original of which was subjected to a famous siege by Ieyasu in 1615, and thus treat himself, perhaps for the first and only time in his life, to the sight of a feudal fortress with elevators. Or he could visit **Shitennoji** Temple, which boasts of being the oldest in Japan, in order to admire the 1950s craftsmanship displayed in its reconstructed buildings. He could shop in the huge intimidating-looking department stores around **Umeda** Station or in the garish underground arcades. If it is 24 or 25 July, he could go to the **Tenmangu Shrine** to find the **Tenjin Matsuri** in full swing—one of Japan's largest merchants' festivals, and a rival in liveliness to Tokyo's Sanja Matsuri. If it is one of several periods during the year when Bunraku puppet plays are performed at the **Asahiza**, he could take the opportunity to witness this unique form of theatre—the elevation of *waza* (skill) and *kata* (form) above all considerations of content and meaning. Or, at the misnamed **Shin-Kabukiza** (New Kabuki theatre), he could sample Osaka's other major contribution to theatrical art, *manzai*—quick-fire verbal comedy routines usually performed in screeching voices by teams of two comedians dressed in loud check jackets. Then, his throat dry from vicarious screeching, he could stroll through **Dotonbori**, the city's major nightlife area, and wash some of the dust and carbon monoxide, at least temporarily, out of his throat.

Osaka's chief contribution to Japanese life has been the unapologetic, cut-throat mercantile instinct. To the T.V. generation the city has also contributed an aggressively blunt style of speech and behaviour, which some profess to find endearing. Osakans specialize in calling a spade a spade. Tokyo bureaucrats are more likely to call a spade an item of Earth-Realigning Equipment. The citizens of Kyoto would likely call one an Honourable Moon-in-the-Water-Stirring Altering-of-the-Ineffable-Landscape Device. No two neighbouring cities could offer a greater contrast in the mechanics of voice production than do Kyoto and Osaka—the cultivated, gently sibilant, birdlike tones of Kyoto, where the men all sound disturbingly like women, and the throaty chin-thrusting rasps of Osaka, where a lot of the women sound disturbingly like men and the men sound like bulldozers.

The rivalry between Osaka–Kobe, the commercial and industrial heartland of the Kansai, and Tokyo–Yokohama, the equivalent in the Kanto, is deeply entrenched, and has been intensified by Osaka's yielding second-city status to Yokohama. A large new airport is being constructed on a man-made island in Osaka Bay, and this could help nudge the pendulum back west. In the meantime, unless the visitor is studying the economic implications of tonsillitis, he is probably better off elsewhere.

About a fifth of the total area of **Shiga** prefecture is occupied by Japan's largest lake, **Lake Biwa**, named, because of a faint similarity in shape, after the ancient lute-like instrument called the *biwa* (see page 132). Like anything statistically outstanding (largest, longest, oldest and so on), Lake Biwa has attracted the scrutiny of ledger-compiling bureaucrats. Those of the 15th century were responsible for designating eight points around the lake's shoreline the 'Eight Beautiful Views of Omi' (Omi is an old name for the locality), while those of the 20th century, with a bravado typical of the period of postwar optimism, named the entire area a 'Quasi-National Park' (*Kokutei-koen*, as opposed to *Kokuritsu-koen*, 'National Park'). For meaningful differences between National Parks and Quasi-National Parks, consult your nearest town hall official. Those interested in putting the aesthetic sensibilities of the bureaucratic mind to the test will want to know that the 'Eight Beautiful Views of Omi' were: Mount Hira, Katata, Karasaki, Miidera Temple, Awazu, Seta, Ishiyama and Yabase. The southern end of the lake is very tourist-oriented, with boat trips and other activities centering on **Otsu** (population 215,000), the prefectural capital. The west shore is less developed, but served by both trains and sightseeing buses. **Hikone**, on the east shore, has a well-preserved early 17th-century castle.

On the border between Shiga and Kyoto prefectures lies **Mount Hiei**, easily accessible from Kyoto via cable car and the Eizan Line of the Keifuku Railway. On the heights of the mountain, just on the Shiga side, stands the **Enryakuji** Temple complex, which predates Kyoto by six years, having been founded here in 788. It is a sprawling set of impressive buildings joined by pleasant hilltop walks. The monks of Enryakuji were notoriously bellicose, making frequent armed forays into Kyoto until as late as the 16th century, at which time the entire temple complex was destroyed by the powerful warlord Oda Nobunaga. Most of the present buildings are thus of comparatively recent date.

The names of certain of the cities and rural areas of **Mie** prefecture have become household words because of the particular industries that have grown up in them. **Yokkaichi**'s petrochemical complexes will not long detain the visitor, but **Matsusaka**'s beer-fed cattle produce some of the finest and most expensive meat in the country, so Matsusaka beef has become synonymous with gourmet eating and extravagant household spending. Further south, among the intricate fjords of **Ago Bay**, the visitor will find himself at the centre of Japan's cultured pearl industry, pioneered by Kokichi Mikimoto at the turn of the last century. Some 1,000 tons of cultured pearls are now produced here annually. Long before Mikimoto, the warmish, shallow sea around the **Shima Peninsula** provided an ideal theatre of operations for Japan's famous white-clad *ama* (woman divers), who can still sometimes be seen operating from boats in which their husbands lounge chain-smoking. Their principal prey is agar-agar, *wakame* (a species of seaweed) and, occasionally, abalone and lobster, depending on the season. It was these ideal conditions that Mikimoto exploited and, today, the chief monuments to his success stand some 20 kilometres (12.5 miles) north of the bay in the small city of **Toba** (population 29,000), where there is a Mikimoto Museum and, on **Pearl Island** in the city's harbour, a model pearl farm open to visitors, who have included Queen Elizabeth II of Great Britain. The coast west of Ago Bay is pleasantly unspoiled.

But not all the cultured pearls, beef steaks and women divers in the world should keep the visitor from what must be his chief destination in Mie prefecture—**Ise Jingu**, The Grand Shrine of Ise, the most revered Shinto shrine in Japan and an object of pilgrimage for people from all over the country, regardless of wealth or class, for some 1,300 years. Even during the later feudal period (when the shogun's efficient police made unrestricted travel an impossibility for the aristocracy, let alone for the rigidly controlled lower classes), a farmer or an artisan might still hope to visit Ise once before he died—the only decent break from labour he would ever know; the journey of a lifetime.

To see Ise after seeing the Toshogu Shrine at Nikko is like clawing one's way out of a bath of lukewarm treacle and plunging naked into a pool of clear, cold water. Ise Jingu stands in a forest of cedar trees, and has two chief centres, or compounds, the Inner (**Naiku**) and Outer (**Geku**) Shrines, about six kilometres (3.7 miles) apart. The first is dedicated to the Sun Goddess, Amaterasu Omikami, the second to the God of Plenty. The most reliable estimates of when the shrines were founded date the Inner to the fourth century and the Outer toward the end of the fifth. The Inner Shrine is the more revered since it houses the sacred Mirror (a part of the imperial regalia consisting of Mirror, Sword and Jewel) which, according to legend, was brought down to earth by the Sun Goddess's grandson. Many shrines throughout Japan house mirrors, and this is their great archetype. The visitor will not see it. In fact, he will be hard put to crane his neck to glimpse the building that houses it. Whether he is Japanese or foreign, aristocrat or artisan, he will not (unless he is a member of, or emissary from, the imperial family) be permitted closer than the outermost of the four wooden fences that surround and protect each of the two main compounds. The mystery is all.

(Preceding page) Transplanting rice seedlings from their beds to the paddies in May: a crucial and delicate operation.

Without the mystery the gods crumple, the legends turn to ash in the mouth, Japan descends to the unspeakable level of a merely human-founded nation, like any other.

And yet perhaps the mystery is not quite all, for there is a pleasing uncluttered external purity about the structures themselves, even the vision-impeding fences. 'Mystery' in connection with religious buildings conjures up, maybe, in the minds of most Westerners, an image of deep crypts or dark gargoyled corners. But Ise is all light and air and plain, unpainted cypress wood, doweled and jointed in the oldest style known, without the use of nails.

For the foreign visitor, the deepest mystery surrounding Ise may well lie in the remarkable fact that, every 20 years, both the Inner and Outer Shrines are completely demolished and rebuilt in exactly the same manner and proportions on the adjacent sites that until then have stood empty save for one small structure that houses the base of the 'heart pillar', said to date from the shrines' founding, and which is incorporated into each rebuilding in order to emphasize the continuity of spirit. The practice of demolishing and rebuilding shrines every 20 years was mentioned earlier in connection with the Kasuga Shrine in Nara (see page 73), where it has been discontinued. It survives famously at Ise, and it would be hard to think of a more perfect symbol for the alliance of continuity and novelty that has characterized the progress of Japanese tradition through the centuries. At each rebuilding (the last was completed in 1973), the old shrine structures offer models for the new, the new are fresh reworkings of the old, and the whole costly, time-consuming practice testifies not only to the survival of extraordinary practical skills but of the impulse that first led to the enshrinement of the Sun Goddess's mirror. More than in a merely old building one feels, if one is Japanese, the rekindling of the ancient pride in being a race set apart, a pride that the disasters of war and defeat have done little to diminish. Besides which, the repeated rebuildings offer this lesson to the foreign visitor, equally pertinent when viewing other famous monuments in Japan: that 'age' may be less a matter of years marching by than of the atmosphere and associations that the marching years carry with them.

On the coast just outside the city of Ise, at **Futamigaura**, stand the often photographed **Meoto Iwa** (Wedded Rocks). These are two naturally occuring offshore rocks that have been joined together by a straw rope and signposted as holy by the construction of a small *torii* gate. Their holiness derives partly from the idea that they represent the god Izanagi and the goddess Izanami, the mythical creators of the Japanese islands, but more especially from the animistic impulse which imbues all nature with a sentient and sacred spirit.

The **Kii Peninsula** is made up of the three prefectures of Nara, Mie and

Wakayama, in the southern half of which, straddling the border with Mie, is the area called **Kumano**, part of the Yoshino-Kumano National Park. This area has long been regarded as the abode of a multitude of gods, and its three major shrines, known collectively as the **Kumano Shrines**, are located at **Nachi, Hongu** and **Shingu**. These shrines differ in purpose and in atmosphere from Ise Jingu, for they do not so much enshrine an idea (the special origin and descent of the Japanese race) as point up the sacredness of the land that surrounds them. It is not in the shrine structures that the gods necessarily dwell, but in the hills and waterfalls of the countryside where they stand. Waterfalls are traditionally associated both with Shinto (as favourite habitations of the gods) and with Buddhism (as the haunts of hermits and ascetics who discipline their minds and bodies by standing stock still underneath them while the torrent thumps down on their heads). Nachi has one of the highest waterfalls in Japan (130 metres or 426 feet), as well as many picturesque smaller ones.

The visitor to Wakayama prefecture will find it quite hard to avoid places of religious significance, since there are so many. **Mount Koya**, most easily accessible from Osaka, has a celebrated monastery founded in 816 by the great Shingon priest Kukai, better known by his posthumous name of Kobo Daishi. Kukai was easily the busiest founder of Buddhist temples in Japan's history and many of the temples he founded are still the objects of very active pilgrimages (in particular the 88 temples of Shikoku—see page 175). The monastery on Mount Koya is vast and sprawling, not unlike the Enryakuji complex on Mount Hiei (see page 102), and among the most important focuses of interest is Kukai's own burial place.

Near the little city of **Gobo** (population 30,000) stands the small temple of **Dojoji**, founded in 701 and famous as the site of a lovers' reunion so gruesomely striking that it has been turned into one of the most popular plays in both the Noh and Kabuki repertoires. On his way to visit the Kumano Shrines, a young Buddhist monk stayed at a house where the owner's daughter fell madly in love with him. Desperate to free himself from her clutches, the monk promised her that he would visit the house again on his return from Kumano, but in fact returned by another route, whereupon the young woman set out in pursuit of him. Soon, the woman's frustrated passion changed her into a fire-breathing serpent and, in terror of his life, the monk begged the priests of Dojoji to hide him under their bronze bell. But the woman-serpent divined his hiding place and curled herself round the bell, making it glow red hot, so that, by the time she had vanished and the priests eventually raised the bell, nothing remained of her lover but his charred bones. In the Noh play, it is the serpent herself who emerges from under the bell when it is raised, while the Kabuki dance-play *Musume-Dojoji* ends with her poised triumphantly on the bell's top, a grim symbol of the unquenchable fire of female determination.

(Preceding page) Matsuyama castle, Shikoku: one of the few not rebuilt in modern times.

Near the tip of the Kii peninsula is the small town of **Taiji**, once the main centre of Japan's whaling industry, now driven on hard times by the international outcry against whaling and by the pressure on Japan to accept an internationally agreed moratorium—developments which have left some of the inhabitants of Taiji openly bitter.

The prefectural capital of **Hyogo** is **Kobe** (population 1.4 million), which ranks with Yokohama as one of Japan's two main 'cosmopolitan' port cities. In point of fact, Kobe accounts for the larger volume of foreign cargo (160 million tons per year), but it was opened to international commerce several years later than Yokohama, in 1867, so arguments about which is the 'senior' of the two ports rebound against each other. Kobe is certainly the pleasanter city for the casual visitor to stroll in, sandwiched as it is between the sea and green hills, the summit of one of which (**Mount Rokko**) can be reached by cable car. Like Yokohama, Kobe is known for its foreign community and for the restaurants this community has established. In Yokohama the best foreign restaurants are Chinese; in Kobe they are Indian, although Kobe beef is famous among steak lovers (the beef of Matsusaka—see page 102—is more often used in *sukiyaki*). In 1981 a six-month international exposition called 'Portopia' was held on a man-made island in Kobe Bay. The island is now a residential and recreation centre. On the other side of Mount Rokko lies the overdeveloped hot-spring resort of **Arima**, popular with residents of Osaka and Kobe, two cities that share with Tokyo and Yokohama the dubious distinction of being so sprawlingly built up that it is impossible to tell from the window of a train or bus where one begins and the other ends.

Some 50 kilometres (31 miles) west of Kobe lies the city of **Himeji** (population 446,000), whose famous castle, built in 1581 by Hideyoshi and enlarged in the early 17th century, is widely regarded as the most elegant feudal fortress in Japan. It is also one of the very few not to have been destroyed and rebuilt in modern times, though it was extensively repaired in the 1950s and '60s, which is why it looks so pristine.

Between Kobe and Himeji is the city of **Akashi** (population 255,000), from where the **Akashi Kaikyo Ohashi** (Great Bridge Across the Akashi Strait) will soon transport the visitor to the island of Awajishima without his needing to take the ferry. When it is completed, the bridge will be the longest suspension bridge in the world, unless, in the meantime, some Korean construction company erects a longer one elsewhere, as happened at Penang to the chagrin of the Japanese, who had previously possessed in the Kanmon Bridge (see page 163) the longest suspension bridge in the Orient. Eventually, Japanese bureaucrats will probably draw up a hierarchical list of the 'Three Most Beautiful Suspension Bridges' and their 'Eight Most Scenic Struts'. The other end of Awajishima will soon be joined to Shikoku by a Great

Bridge Across the Naruto Strait, all of this bridge-building having been spawned by former Prime Minister Tanaka's grandiose scheme to 'remodel the Japanese archipelago'.

Awajishima itself (population 170,000) is a flattish, mainly agricultural island (except for the highway built to convey motorists rushing between bridges) and is well known for a rural form of Bunraku puppet theatre. How long its comparatively unspoiled state (and its puppet theatre) will survive the remodelling of the archipelago remains to be seen.

Hyogo is one of only three prefectures to span the entire width of Honshu and, although most of its population and chief centres of tourism are crowded along its southern coast, it offers a particularly wide variety of landscape: from the industrialized belt that hems the Inland Sea, through steep mountains and small out-of-the-way village communities in the interior, to its rugged and beautiful northern coastline, the entire length of which is a part of the **Sanin Kaigan National Park** (see also page 168).

The Tohoku Region
Homely Wilds

When, in Japanese gangster films, people flee from the vengeance of their bosses or from rival gangs, they invariably head north into the tangled safety of the Tohoku region. When Yoshitsune fled from his brother Yoritomo's attempts to have him assassinated in 1187, it was north into the Tohoku wilds that he fled. When salarymen sit in karaoke bars singing ballads about mournful, windy places to breathless Osaka bar girls, it is often of Tohoku that they sing. And when the newly urbanized Japanese find themselves pining for the old rural ways, for a simpler, uncluttered, more truly 'Japanese' style of life, it is often Tohoku that springs to their minds. In recent years the Tohoku region has become the paradigm of what the Japanese call *furusato,* a word that means literally 'old home country', and is used nowadays not only of a person's actual birthplace and the place where he feels his heart to lie, but of a Never-Never-Land of thatched cottages with kettles singing cheerfully on sunken hearths, where their sons are charcoal burners, their daughters pale-skinned and lovely as the snow, and every neighbour has a heart of gold and an impenetrably thick accent. If Yamato is the spirit-stirring womb of nationhood, Tohoku is humanity's cradle.

Throughout much of Japanese history, this great, mountainous, northeastern chunk of Honshu was an unpoliced wilderness. Originally, it was the home of the Ainu and other non-Yamato tribes, who, by the close of the ninth century, had either been wiped out or driven from Honshu into the island now called Hokkaido; the victims of a series of genocidal campaigns mounted by the forces of the Yamato, Nara and Kyoto courts. (The word *shogun* is an abbreviation of a longer title, *seiitaishogun*—Great Barbarian-Subduing General—that was first earned in 794, at the height of these campaigns.) But Tohoku's wildness survived the genocide inflicted on its earliest inhabitants. Up to the 19th century the region was not known as Tohoku (East-North), but as *Michinoku* (Beyond the End of the Road). The most famous account of a journey in Japanese literature is the poetic record by the haiku master, Matsuo Basho, of his travels through Tohoku in 1689–91. His book is called *Oku no Hosomichi,* a title that has been translated into English as 'The Narrow Road to the Deep North', but which might more accurately be rendered 'The Narrow Roads at the Back of Beyond'. Even in modern times, a sense of the wilderness persists, and in very modern times has actually intensified. With industrialization, large parts of this still mainly agricultural region have suffered a gradual decline in population as families have left the land that they have farmed, perhaps for centuries, in order to make supposedly more convenient lives for themselves in city offices and factories. Iwate prefecture, for example, has the lowest population density (93 people per square kilometre) of any part of Japan except Hokkaido. Today, the six large prefectures that make up the Tohoku region account in total for only about eight percent of Japan's population, and are among those regularly recording the lowest per capita incomes.

But, for the short-term visitor, Tohoku can be a rich and rewarding experience. It is a region where customs have generally died hard, where local arts and crafts have survived with comparative tenacity or been revived in recent decades, where good, unspoiled hot springs abound, and where the landscape of lakes, rice-plains and mountains has a stirring, rugged grandeur. In winter, the snowfall is fierce and long, especially on the high plateaus and on the Japan Sea side of the mountains. Many smaller roads are closed for the duration of the snows and, when they reopen in April or early May, they must be bulldozed out afresh between towering banks of unthawed ice. Summer is a good time to visit Tohoku, for summer is short there and the inhabitants make the most of it by mounting some of Japan's most spectacular August festivals (see page 121). If the visitor has opted to stay in Western-style hotels during his trips to Tokyo and the Kinki region, he might seize the opportunity Tohoku affords to sample the more traditional hospitality to be found at ryokans and minshukus. Tohoku consists of the six prefectures of **Fukushima, Yamagata, Miyagi, Iwate, Akita** and **Aomori**. Two broad rules of thumb when travelling in the region are: the further north you get the emptier becomes the countryside, the less urbane the people; and the Japan Sea side of the region (the side directly facing Siberia) has a much harsher climate, giving rise to a more arduous lifestyle for the inhabitants, than does the Pacific side. The Pacific side is the more easily accessible via the Tohoku Shinkansen bullet train that joins Tokyo (Ueno) with Sendai and Morioka, and will eventually reach all the way to Aomori and from there, if the newly independent railway companies can scratch together the money, beyond, through the Seikan Tunnel, to Hokkaido. The Pacific side is also the more industrialized and urbanized, the largest and most prosperous city in the Tohoku region being Sendai, the prefectural capital of Miyagi.

Just north of the border between Tochigi and **Fukushima** prefectures, stands the former castle town of **Shirakawa** (population 43,000), near where the shogun's main inland barrier gate between the Kanto and Tohoku regions stood. These gates were a principal means whereby travel could be controlled, taxes levied and road blocks effected. The main purpose of the castle at Shirakawa, one of those belonging to the lords of the region, the Matsudairas, was thus to guard the major artery of transport leading north from Edo.

But the Matsudairas' chief seat of power was **Aizu-Wakamatsu** (present population 115,000). 'Aizu' is the old name for the western part of Fukushima and Aizu-Wakamatsu is the main centre of tourism in the prefecture and a natural starting point for visits to Lake Inawashiro and

Mount Bandai. It is a city of mainly traditional industries, in particular sake-brewing and lacquerware. The castle is known as **Tsurugajo** (Castle of the Crane); the donjon was reconstructed in 1965. The Matsudairas were loyal supporters of the Tokugawa shoguns and some of the bitterest fighting in the campaigns that finally toppled the shogunate, leading to the restoration of power to the Emperor Meiji in 1868, took place in this area. As a result, Aizu-Wakamatsu is somewhat boastful of its samurai heritage, and a large samurai house (*buke-yashiki*) has been renovated in the city and provides a fascinating glimpse of domestic life among the privileged classes in the feudal age. In the nearby museum there is a gruesome display of waxwork models of the women of the clan, all dressed in white, committing gory suicide rather than fall into the hands of the imperial forces.

But the most poignant monument to Aizu's vanished samurai heritage stands on **Iimori Hill** in the western suburbs, approached either via long flights of stone steps or an absurd 'slope conveyor', a large effort-reducing escalator which testifies resoundingly to the decline of samurai vigour. On Iimori Hill stand the graves of 19 young military cadets who committed ritual suicide here after escaping from a rout on the western shore of Lake Inawashiro. They were all between 16 and 17 years old and were members of the 341-strong *Byakkotai* (White Tiger Company), a loyalist unit deployed against the revolutionary army on the rainy afternoon of 22 August 1868. 288 of the company survived the skirmish, 33 died in battle; but none of those have captured the Japanese imagination like the 19 who, seeing smoke pouring out of the Castle of the Crane and believing the battle irrecoverably lost, took their own lives in a last gesture of defiance and despair. Ironically, they were mistaken in their perception of the state of battle. The castle had not fallen, and in fact did not fall until early November. But the rashness and uselessness of their deaths have only increased the aura of glory that surrounds them.

Just outside the city to the southeast lies the hot-spring resort of **Higashiyama**, urban rather than rural, but not yet overdeveloped, so it preserves a degree of old-world charm. Further east is **Lake Inawashiro**, the fourth largest lake in Japan, on the shore of which stands a small museum dedicated to the memory of one of Japan's very few international humanists, Dr Noguchi Hideo. Dr Noguchi spent much of his life in Africa attempting to isolate the virus that causes yellow fever. He succeeded in 1928, but died of the disease two months later in Accra, where, at the University of Ghana, there is a Noguchi Memorial Institute. Dr Noguchi's example of selfless sacrifice is a favourite among publishers of inspirational children's biographies.

To the north of the lake towers **Mount Bandai** (1,819 metres, 5,968 feet), the centre of the southern sector of the **Bandai-Asahi National Park**. Mount Bandai erupted spectacularly in 1888, creating an eerie landscape of pools and lakes on its north slope. The heights offer spectacular views of the surrounding countryside and there are several popular ski resorts in the area. Mount Bandai is one of the many mountains scattered throughout Japan that are thought in some way to resemble Mount Fuji, and it is thus sometimes called 'Aizu Fuji', though the resemblance clearly lies in the eye of the beholder. Other popular ski grounds are to be found on the slopes of **Mount Azuma** (2,024 metres, 6,640 feet) which lies west of the prefectural capital, Fukushima City.

Near the Pacific coast, in the city of **Haramachi** (population 46,000), is held each 23-25 July Fukushima's best-known festival, the **Soma Nomaoi** (Wild Horse Chase of Soma). Like other parts of the northeast, Fukushima prefecture was originally a famous centre for horse breeding, and this fame is recalled each year in the mounted procession, horse races, herding, and spectacular pitched battle fought by riders in feudal costume for the possession of banners lofted into the air by means of fireworks.

The most notable destinations for visitors to **Yamagata** prefecture are mountains, in particular the Three Holy Mountains of Dewa (**Dewa Sanzan**), 'Dewa' being an old name for Yamagata and Akita combined. The three mountains are **Gassan** (1,980 metres, 6,496 feet), **Yudono** (1,504 metres, 4,934 feet), which is really an outcrop of Gassan, and **Haguro** (419 metres, 1,376 feet), a foothill north of the main range. Gassan especially is bathed in an aura of chilly mystery, which partly derives from the inclement, misty weather that shrouds its slopes and the snow that survives in patches throughout the year, and partly from the mystic and shamanistic practices of the Shugendo sect of esoteric Buddhism, to which the mountains are sacred. These practices included the occasional mummification of priests (or, to be more accurate, the smoking of corpses until the flesh was tough enough to withstand decay) and mummified and skeletal remains are still to be found on the mountains, sitting in their robes of office and accepting the suppliance of pilgrims hardy and unblenching enough to make the climb. The alliance of early Buddhism with the older forms of shamanism and animistic spiritualism is seen very clearly at certain rural religious sites in Tohoku, particularly here and at Osorezan (see page 131). The summit of Gassan is beyond the scope of an ordinary visitor's itinerary, but Haguro is easily climbed via the two-kilometre (1.25-mile) causeway of stone steps that leads to the Haguro Shrine at the summit, which was founded in the seventh century. In the woods near the foot of the causeway stands a fine 14th-century pagoda. Originally all three of the holy mountains were inhabited by *yamabushi* (mountain-dwelling ascetics), who cultivated mystic powers (mainly that of exorcism, but they could also leap high in the air and walk barefoot over burning coals) and embraced a life of astonishing hardship. Once again, it is worth stressing that the shrines and temple buildings the visitor will see here are more like

A provincial tub-maker. The government encourages traditional handicrafts by designating the finest practitioners 'Living National Treasures'.

signposts to the numinous spirit of the mountains themselves than they are the actual 'houses' of gods.

South of Gassan and, like it, a part of the northern sector of the Bandai-Asahi National Park, stands the peak of **Asahi-dake** (1,870 metres, 6,135 feet), the centre of an unspoiled area of alpine woodland.

Another notable mountain religious site in Yamagata (one whose name means simply 'Mountain Temple') is the **Yamadera** complex, not far from the prefectural capital, Yamagata city. As at Haguro, a visit involves a vigorous climb up a narrow causeway, spasmodically paved with chunks of stone. The Buddhism practised at Yamadera is more orthodox than that associated with Gassan and Haguro, since the complex's parent temple is Enryakuji on Mount Hiei (see page 98). But, again, the distribution of buildings over the sides and summit of a spacious hill is partly intended to underscore the numinous nature of the entire area. The temple was founded in 860, 22 years after its Kyoto parent. The main hall on the summit was rebuilt in 1963.

Also near **Yamagata** city (population 237,000) is the small city of **Tendo** (population 53,000), famous among players of *shogi* (Japanese chess) as the principal centre for the manufacture of the wooden pieces used in the game. While the intricate and sometimes highly original design of Western chess pieces has made them popular collectors' items even among non-players, the same fate is hardly likely to overtake the pieces used in *shogi*. The pieces all have the same basic flat five-edged form, are all the same colour (natural wood—this because, unlike in Western chess, an opponent's piece removed from the board can be reused by its captor, so no distinction of colour is possible) and are distinguished from one another only by size and by the (to a novice illegible) ideograms engraved or painted on them. Still, sets of these pieces can vary enormously in price, depending on the quality of the wood and on the skill of the calligrapher. Fans of *shogi* are prone to boast that it is the only traditional board game to have defied computer programming. Computers have become proficient at Western chess and have made considerable progress with *go*, but the almost innumerable permutations that arise out of the reuse of captured *shogi* pieces have so far confined the game to merely human players.

Yamagata city itself is the site of the prefecture's largest and best-known festival, the **Hanagasa Matsuri** (see box on page 121).

In the north of the prefecture, on the coast just below **Mount Chokai** (2,230 metres, 7,316 feet) stands the industrial city of **Sakata** (population 103,000), originally well-known as a centre for rice-distribution and the manufacture of sake. Further up the **Mogami River**, on which Sakata stands, are some fine rapids which visitors can shoot safely in thin craft guided by boatmen who employ the traditional combination of tiller and long punt.

On the border between Yamagata and **Miyagi** prefectures stands **Mount Zao** (1,841 metres, 6,040 feet), a popular playground for skiers. And, toward the coast, at the southern end of the largest plain in Tohoku stands the prefectural capital, **Sendai** (population 665,000), formerly the chief seat of the powerful Date clan, whose most famous son, Masamune, built a castle here in 1602. The castle was known as **Aobajo** (Castle of Green Leaves). It was mostly destroyed during the fighting at the time of the Meiji Restoration, and the surviving structures were completely demolished in the large-scale fire bombing that Sendai suffered during World War II. In fact, much of the city required extensive rebuilding after the war, and its newness, together with its size and commercial stature, helps account for its sense of prosperity and absence of the backwoods feeling that clings to many of Tohoku's cities (it is, for example, the only city in the Tohoku region to posses a subway system). Commercial prosperity is particularly noticeable during Sendai's main annual festival, the **Tanabata Matsuri** on 7 August (see page 121).

Sendai is known for its handicrafts and among the most expensive items available in the city's furniture and woodcraft shops are the heavy wooden chests called *tansu,* old specimens of which have become sought-after collectors' pieces. Far cheaper and more easily portable souvenirs are the folk dolls called *kokeshi,* traditionally made from two spartan pieces of wood, a globe for the head and a cylinder for the body, painted in designs that differ from region to region and from one dollmaker to the next. These dolls are sold throughout Tohoku and a major centre for their production is the city of **Shiroishi** (population 41,000), not far from Mount Zao, which hosts an annual kokeshi fair in early May. Japanese tourists, like foreign visitors, tend to regard kokeshi merely as quaint, curious ornaments to grace a hallstand or a television table, and if you ask a Japanese friend to explain the meaning of the word *kokeshi,* he will probably not be able to do so, nor, despite owning several examples and having bought others as gifts for relatives and friends, will he have given the matter any thought. In fact the original meaning is rendered obscure by the fact that, today, the word is always written in the phonetic *hiragana* syllabary, without the use of potentially revealing ideograms (see page 234). But it is likely that the name derives from *ko,* meaning 'child' and *kesu,* meaning 'to cut off', and that the harmless-looking dolls were originally carved as fetish substitutes for children murdered at birth, a practice that continued in impoverished rural areas into our own century. The popularity of kokeshi among Japanese tourists today is thus an eloquent testimony to the survival of a folk tradition as well as to the modern generation's ignorance of its implications.

The chief tourist attraction in Miyagi prefecture is the bay dotted with some 260 small pine-clad islands at **Matsushima,** 22 kilometres (13.5 miles) northeast of Sendai. Like Amanohashidate (see page 99) and Miyajima (see page 160), Matsushima is one of Japan's 'Three Most Beautiful Scenic

Tohoku's Four Great Summer Festivals

O-Bon is an annual nationwide observance, celebrated privately by placing food and drink on the graves of dead family members, and publicly by dancing to entertain their returned spirits. Summer is a comparatively slack time for rice farmers and O-Bon is traditionally celebrated in the seventh lunar month (giving rise to the spurious but much touted theory that Japanese people tell ghost stories in summer to induce refreshing chills). Since the adoption of the Western calendar, O-Bon has been celebrated in August, the middle of that month usually corresponding quite closely to the old lunar date. It is still the custom among many families for relatives who have moved away to return to the ancestral house for O-Bon, making it not only a festival of the dead and a pre-harvest holiday, but a celebration of *furusato,* one's birthplace and spiritual home.

Among the most spectacular of the August festivals connected with O-Bon are the 'Four Great Festivals of Tohoku': the Sendai *Tanabata,* the Yamagata *Hanagasa,* the Aomori *Nebuta* and the Akita *Kanto.* All take place during the first week of August and are staggered so that travel agents can whisk spectators round all four in as many days.

Tanabata is Chinese in origin and commemorates the yearly meeting of the two stars Altair and Vega, originally a shepherd and a weaver who fell in love and were banished to opposite ends of the Milky Way because their passion got in the way of their industry. Tanabata (formerly celebrated on the seventh night of the seventh lunar month) is observed nationwide on 7 July by decorating bamboo branches with slips of paper bearing wishes. In Sendai Tanabata culminates on 8 August, closer to the old lunar date, and features colourful lanterns and streamers hung in the city's main streets.

The Hanagasa of Yamagata city (usually 6–7 August) is a dance festival in which participants wear sedge hats (*kasa*) decorated with artificial flowers (*hana*). The dancers (up to 10,000 of them) process through the streets of the city as happens also in Tokushima (see page 175), distinguishing them from most Bon dancers whose movements are confined to concentric circles.

The Aomori Nebuta (usually 4–7 August) is a parade of huge sculpted and painted lanterns (*nebuta*) shaped like warriors, wrestlers, horses and other figures. It has been suggested that the prototypes of these lanterns were invented by a crafty Yamato general to frighten the barbaric tribes he was fighting. Lanterns of one kind or another figure large in O-Bon, where traditionally they light the way for the ghosts, arriving and departing.

Lanterns are also the chief feature of the Akita Kanto (usually 5–7 August), but here they are of normal size and hang in bunches of up to 46 from wooden poles with crossbeams (*kanto*) which are raised and balanced on the hips, hands, shoulders, foreheads and other parts of the men who handle them. As the *nebuta* display the talents of the manufacturer, so these display the skills of the bearer.

Views', and the beachfront and nearby historical sites have suffered a consequent degree of spoliation. **Zuiganji** temple, founded in 828, has an explanatory tape loop that competes with the bullhorns of the guides who shepherd tourists round its compound. There are loudspeakers at the beach, in the corridors of the 39 hotels, and on all of the boats that ferry visitors around the bay or ply between the pier at Matsushima and the port of **Shiogama** (still a worthwhile trip because of the views of the sometimes curiously shaped islands that it affords). Many of the loudspeakers and tape loops offer the incessant gabbling commentaries without which Japanese tourists seem unable to enjoy their natural environment, and the remainder repeat at full volume the famous folk song that celebrates both bay and temple:

> *Zuiganji temple at Matsushima—*
> *There is no temple like it!*
> *How fine! How true!*
> *And what a great catch of fish!*

Conceivably, something has been lost in translation. The poet Basho viewed Matsushima in an equally celebratory mood. 'Much praise has already been lavished upon the wonders of the islands of Matsushima', he wrote. 'Yet if further praise is possible I would like to say that here is the most beautiful spot in the whole country of Japan'. He was similarly enthusiastic about the lovely old shrine at Shiogama, rebuilt in 1607, eighty-odd years before his visit: 'I was deeply impressed by the fact that the divine power of the gods had penetrated even to the extreme north of our country, and I bowed in humble reverence before the altar'. And in 1948, three years after the catastrophic fire bombing of nearby Sendai, the English poet Edmund Blunden, in an equally reverential mood, left this poetic memento of his visit to Zuiganji temple:

> *Here abide Tranquillity,*
> *Courtesy, Humility;*
> *The traveller pauses in deep rest,*
> *To go his way blessing and blest.*

And does so still in his hundreds of thousands, the echoes of the bullhorns tingling in his ears.

North of Matsushima lies the **Oshika Peninsula**, whose small ports were formerly busy centres of the whaling industry, now fallen on less prosperous times; and a short boat ride from the tip of the peninsula lies the picturesque little island of **Kinkazan** (Hill of Golden Flowers), so named, says Basho, because of the fecundity of the old gold mine that once stood there. In a manner more reminiscent of Chinese than of Japanese superstition, its former wealth together with the occurrence of the ideogram for 'gold' in its name have led to the island's acquiring a reputation for bestowing

financial security on anyone who visits it for three consecutive years—
something the neighbouring whalers presumably omitted to do. Kinkazan is
also well known for the deer and wild monkeys that inhabit it.

Iwate, the largest of the six Tohoku prefectures, has as its capital **Morioka**
(population 229,000), famous for its ironware, called *Nanbu tetsubin*
('Nanbu' being both the family name of the lords who built Morioka Castle
and the old name for Iwate and eastern Aomori). Heavy knobbed kettles are
the most practical form into which the iron is worked, but small lantern-
shaped windbells are more popular with weight-conscious travellers.
Morioka stands in the imposing shadow of **Mount Iwate** (2,041 metres,
6,696 feet) which is also called, predictably, 'Iwate-Fuji'. (The '-Fuji'
designation is reserved for mountains that stand, like their archetypal
namesake, in splendid isolation.) Morioka Castle was built in 1597 and its
massive outer walls still stand, the steps that lead up and around them
deliberately constructed in an irregular fashion to prevent their being
mounted at speed—a cunning feature of Japanese castle architecture.

Iwate, like Fukushima, was an area noted for its horse-breeders, the most
famous of them rearing their stock on the high pastures of **Sotoyama**, in the
hills northeast of the capital, then driving them over the higher passes to fill
orders from all parts of the region. The traditional farmhouses of Iwate,
called *magariya,* very few of which remain standing, were built in such a
way that the horse's stable and farmer's living room stood next to each other
under a single roof. The horses bred in Sotoyama were solid farm stock and
their robust tradition is commemorated each year on 15 June in the **Chagu-
Chagu Umakko Matsuri** (*umakko* means 'young horse' or 'horse and
child', *chagu-chagu* imitates the jangling sound of ornamental bridles). The
festival's main event is a 15-kilometre (9.5- mile) procession of some 80
horses, gaily decked out and ridden by young children in feudal costume.
They process through the streets of Morioka, beginning and ending at two
shrines whose chief business is the blessing and protection of the region's
horses.

Iwate is cleft into two mountainous halves by the valley that runs through
it south to north, and in this valley stand not only Morioka but most of the
prefecture's other cities and towns. Of particular interest to the visitor is one
of the very smallest of these towns, **Hiraizumi**, situated at the southern end
of the valley not far from the border with Miyagi. In the 12th century
Hiraizumi was the most important independent centre of culture and power in
the Tohoku region, and remained so until Yoritomo succeeded in arrogating
practically all power to himself with the institution of the military
government at Kamakura (see page 53). It was to Hiraizumi that his brother,
Yoshitsune, fled (see page 154), in Hiraizumi that he was offered sanctuary,
and in or near Hiraizumi that Yoshitsune was eventually hunted down and

forced to commit suicide (though there are Arthurian-style survival legends, one of which has him escaping to Mongolia where he resurfaced as Ghenghis Khan). Hiraizumi is the site of what is regarded as the most important and magnificently endowed temple in the Tohoku region, **Chusonji**, founded here in 1105 by the powerful Fujiwara family (see page 73), whose original home Hiraizumi was. Particularly impressive is the small **Konjikido** hall, the outer walls of which were originally plated with gold. A short walk from Chusonji is the temple of **Motsuji**. Founded in the 12th century, it was rebuilt in modern times, and each 20 January is the site of a nighttime performance of ancient dances, precursors of the Noh theatre, which date from Heian times. The dances are called *Ennen no Mai*. A similarly ancient performing art, more rural in theme and aspect, is the set of Kagura and other dances preserved in the villages near **Mount Hayachine** (1,914 metres, 6,279 feet), east of Morioka.

South of Hayachine, in the rugged, sparsely populated hills to the east of the central valley, stands the small city of **Tono** (population 31,000), which enjoyed a brief spell of fame in 1910 with the publication of Yanagita Kunio's *Tono Monogatari* (Tono Stories). Yanagita was the founder of Japanese folklore studies and his Tono book was the first concerted attempt to produce an oral history of a Japanese rural area. Most of the book is devoted to legends and superstitions, but the villages and hills around Tono still preserve to a remarkable degree the progress-resisting style of rural life for which karaoke singers pretend to pine.

The coast of Iwate is justly famous for its rugged splendour, and almost the entire length of it has been turned into the **Rikuchu Kaigan National Park**, offering boat cruises, clifftop hikes and a wide choice of simple traditional accommodation.

On the high mountainous border between Iwate and **Akita** prefectures lies the **Hachimantai Plateau**, one of the central attractions of the **Towada-Hachimantai National Park**. The continuing volcanic activity here gives rise to a great many natural hot springs that issue through the brittle crust at temperatures barely below boiling point. Though several of the larger springs have been developed into resorts, these resorts retain a genuinely rural atmosphere, partly owing to their being frequented by groups of elderly local people who stay for weeks to enjoy the benefits of the springs' curative powers, and partly because some at least preserve the now often frowned-upon custom of mixed bathing. The best-known resorts are **Tamagawa, Yuze, Kuroyu, Goshogake** and **Magoroku**, all on the Akita side of the prefectural boundary. In winter, the slopes of the Hachimantai Plateau are crowded with skiers. The hot spring and ski resorts can be reached most conveniently by bus from Morioka, or from the small Akita cities of **Kazuno** and **Odate**.

Tengu (forest demon) mask surrounded by wooden rice scoops inscribed for luck. The tengu can confer virility and physical strength.

At the southern end of the Hachimantai Plateau lies **Lake Tazawa**, at 425 metres (1,400 feet) the deepest lake in Japan. It is almost perfectly circular and has one or two beaches for swimming and pleasure boating, and a fair selection of hotels, ryokan and minshuku.

Just south of the lake is the small, pleasant town of **Kakunodate** (population 17,000), a former seat of the lords of the region, the Satake family. Nothing remains of the castle, but some small samurai houses are preserved in one long street that runs between the station and the river. Much less grand than the *buke-yashiki* at Aizu-Wakamatsu, these houses have about them the plaintive feeling that inevitably arises out of a combination of seclusion and decay.

Like Iwate, Akita is a mainly rural prefecture where, in the low-lying areas, large-scale rice production is the dominant feature of the landscape. Akita was formerly a part of the province of Dewa, Iwate of Nanbu, and the men of Dewa and Nanbu have rarely, if ever, been able to agree on the relative merits of their agricultural produce. Sake is a major industry in both prefectures and competition between local brands (of which there are very many) is particularly keen. The term *jizake* (local sake) is used to distinguish the product of smaller local breweries from the blended sakes manufactured in bulk and distributed nationwide. True sake connoisseurs spend a great deal of time hunting out obscure *jizake* (much as lovers of 'real ale' hunt out obscure beers in rural England) and then usually order the second grade (*nikyu*) brew, claiming that the first-grade (*ikkyu*) and special-grade *(tokyu)* brews have been refined beyond the point where the true taste can be enjoyed. The difference in grade depends mainly on how much of the rice kernel has been used in the brewing. The more polished the kernel the less remains, the less that remains the higher the grade, the higher the grade the less fierce—in theory—the hangover. This somewhat specialized information is included here in the hope that the acquiring of a taste for *jizake* and hot springs will compensate the visitor to Akita for its comparative dearth of other forms of recreation.

The prefectural capital, **Akita** city (population 285,000), is one of the dullest cities in the region, except inside its sake shops and during its annual **Kanto Matsuri** on 5–7 August (see box on page 121).

Jutting out into the Japan Sea north of Akita city is the rugged **Oga Peninsula**, a tour of which provides a good introduction to the grimness and isolation that are inextricably associated with the whole of the Japan Sea coast. In winter, the hardships of life here are especially apparent, with the fishmongers of the peninsula having almost nothing on sale but the tiny sandfish called *hata-hata,* which, together with *kiritanpo* (baked mashed rice) are Akita staples, not out of choice but out of gloomy necessity. In the villages of the Oga Peninsula a New Year's eve ritual called **Namahage** is enacted, one of the last genuine Japanese folk festivals to survive in an

uncommercial form (so uncommercial that the casual visitor will almost certainly not be permitted to see it). Partly this is because it takes place inside private houses, and partly because the villagers still take it seriously as a major means of strengthening community spirit. The *Namahage* are masked demons, impersonated by young men of the villages, who invade all the houses in turn (except those where a death has occurred during the year), shouting, stamping, drinking massive quantities of the sake they are offered (with no sign of worrying about what grade it is) and threatening to the point of terror the children and young wives of the families, which is the main purpose of their visit. The theory is that terrifying young children and women newly married into the village is a good way of reminding them of their comparatively low place in the social pecking order so that they do not get ideas above their station, and of their obligation to work hard for the good of the community and not be lazy and self-absorbed. From the screams, tears and barely restrained violence that accompany the demons' visits, one has to conclude that it is an immensely successful technique. It is also immensely enjoyable (if you are a demon) and a spur to adulthood for the male children who realize dimly through their screams and tears that one day they will be rollicking demons themselves. Visitors' rituals such as this were once common throughout rural Japan and have all but disappeared.

On the border between Akita and **Aomori** prefectures lies **Lake Towada**, the most popular tourist attraction in northern Tohoku, particularly in autumn when the leaves on the surrounding hillsides turn so attractively gold and red that you can't get near them for the crush. The crush tends to converge on the lakeside resort of **Yasumiya**, where there is a small beach and many restaurants, souvenir shops and places to stay; but there are quieter and more inviting places to stay at other points on the lake's shore. A good plan is to approach the lake on foot along the course of the **Oirase River**, a picturesque stream consisting of rapids and small waterfalls, along which a woodland path has been carefully laid down for strollers. The river joins the lake at **Nennokuchi** which has a bus terminal.

Due north of the lake stands **Mount Hakkoda** (1,585 metres, 5,200 feet), which provides good skiing facilities in winter, good camping in summer, and good hot springs all year round. And due east of the lake, in the village of **Shingo**, stands an even more remarkable sight: the grave of Jesus Christ. This claim may occasion a raised eyebrow among less credulous readers, but the humble grave is there for all to see, Jesus having allowed his brother to be crucified in his place (and, in case an uncrucified Jesus would not prove attractive enough to sightseers, his brother's grave is here too, Joseph of Arimathaea having presumably inherited not only the ability to walk on water, but to bear bodies across vast oceans). It is not hard to see how, one bright 17th-century morning, a bearded foreign missionary fleeing

the Tokugawa persecutions (see page 194), took the time-honoured recourse of flight into Tohoku, turned up in the village of Shingo and found the villagers so accommodating that he stayed on to attempt their conversion. His Japanese was minimal and was made even less useful a tool of faith by the villagers' gift of a fearsomely incomprehensible tongue. In the end, the villagers somehow managed to persuade themselves that the missionary himself was the Man he preached, and when he died they buried him under a cross which, crucifixion being the commonest form of execution in feudal Japan for all the lower classes, they regarded as a symbol of his own persecution. This is admittedly conjecture. But whatever the truth of the matter, the Shingo villagers scored a major triumph. The Japanese pay a fortune in licensing fees to Disneyland, but they got Jesus free.

Of the three largest cities in the prefecture, **Aomori**, the prefectural capital (population 288,000), is perhaps the least interesting, except during the first week of August when it stages the spectacular **Nebuta Matsuri** (see box on page 121). Until the ferry service was discontinued in April 1988, Aomori city was the chief rail and ferry terminus for passengers going to Hokkaido, who could transfer from train to boat without setting foot outside the station (or, if they had been in sufficient contact with the villagers of Shingo, try walking across the Tsugaru Strait).

Hachinohe (population 238,000), on the Pacific coast, is a sprawling industrial and fishing centre, which also stages an interesting festival, the **Emburi**, in February, consisting of dances at the local shrine and in the streets of the city performed by men wearing large hats trimmed with decorative horses' manes (another festive reminder of the strong tradition of horse-breeding throughout northeast Honshu).

The real urban heart of the prefecture, however, is the old castle town of **Hirosaki** (population 175,000), an attractive city, famous for its late-blooming cherries, for its apple blossom, and for the state of preservation of its small, elegant castle, built in 1610. Hirosaki also stages a **Neputa Matsuri** in the first week of August, at once less spectacular, less tourist-oriented and more imbued with the solemn, warlike spirit of the north country than its larger counterpart in the prefectural capital. The Hirosaki festival features the appearance on the streets of the *Tsugaru Joppari Daiko* (Drum to Rouse the Passions of Tsugaru, 'Tsugaru' being the old name for the western half of the prefecture), said to be the largest drum in Japan. Hirosaki is also the production centre for a colourful and not inexpensive form of lacquerware.

West of Hirosaki stands the imposing **Mount Iwaki** (1,625 metres, 5,331 feet), which is yet another 'something-or-other-Fuji' (in this case, of course, 'Tsugaru-Fuji') and can be climbed via a track which begins at the **Iwaki Shrine**, whose present buildings date from the 17th century. The orchards at the foot of the mountain and in other parts of the prefecture grow the carefully-tended, huge and expensive red apples for which Aomori is also famous.

The northern half of the prefecture is divided between two peninsulas, Tsugaru in the west and Shimokita in the east. **Tsugaru** is the better-known, owing in part to the renaissance of its virile folk music tradition, an event which reached its peak in the 1970s and has now somewhat diminished. The folk music of Tsugaru is characterized by virtuoso performances on a long-stocked, heavy *shamisen* (see page 132), normally a humble accompanying instrument but in Tsugaru a wonderful device for the display of individual and idiosyncratic skills. The people of Tsugaru are widely thought to possess the most impenetrable of Japan's many regional dialects, and this is partly ascribed to their habit of hardly moving their mouths when they speak (the winters, it is said, are too cold to permit their mouths to open fully). The winters are also exceptionally long, so that the people of Tsugaru, because of their need to cram a whole year's work into six snowless months, have a reputation for quick action and inexhaustible energy, both of which are reflected in their music. The novelist Dazai Osamu, who drowned himself in the Tama Canal (see page 32), was a native of Tsugaru, and the house where he was born in the small town of **Kanagi** is now a ryokan. Dazai's reputation was made in Tokyo, and he is regarded by his Tsugaru countrymen much as D.H. Lawrence is among Nottinghamshire miners and Arnold Bennett among the people of the Potteries: as a man who simultaneously turned his back on his roots and exploited them for his own gratification.

The other peninsula, **Shimokita**, is shaped like an axe, and near the centre of the axe-blade is one of the most impressive and disquieting religious sites in Japan. This is **Osorezan** (The Terrible Mountain), whose temple, **Entsuji**, stands on the shore of a blue, lifeless crater lake and was founded in 845. The entire precincts of the temple are a desert of volcanic lava, grey dust and strong-smelling sulphur springs. Throughout the precincts stand small statues of **Jizo**, the Buddhist guardian of children, since this wasteland is commonly regarded as being an earthly manifestation of *Sainokawara*, the grim Limbo of the Buddhist underworld, where Jizo wages a constant battle against demons who seek to drag the souls of dead children down to Hell. Worshippers often leave straw sandals here to protect Jizo's sacred feet from the sharp, hot lava, and pile up pebbles into mounds, each pebble a prayer for the peace of a tormented soul. Within the temple compound are three dilapidated old hot-spring bathhouses open to anyone who can stand the smell and heat. And on 20–24 July each year the temple hosts the **Itakoichi** (Medium Market) during which blind or half-blind female spirit mediums from as far away as Mount Iwaki congregate in tents and offer to contact the dead relatives of festival pilgrims. The Historical Buddha is known to have inveighed against the 'low arts' of fortune telling and mediumship, but his sentiments have gone unregarded here, where, for all its Buddhist trappings, an older faith strains up through the lunar surface like the mustard-yellow and blood-red springs. Few religious centres in the world are as devoid of embellishment as Osorezan and few leave a profounder mark on the visitor's memory.

Japanese Music

The earliest extant form of Japanese music is *Gagaku,* performed by a 16–20-piece orchestra containing instruments of mainly Chinese or Southeast Asian origin, and dating, in Japan, from the eighth century. Simplified pieces, performed by much smaller ensembles, sometimes accompany ceremonies at Shinto shrines. The basic repertoire derives from T'ang China.

The *biwa,* a four-stringed lute, introduced into Japan from China at about the same time, is used in Gagaku and also to accompany long recitative-like narrative ballads, such as deal with the exploits of the Heike clan. These are not much heard nowadays.

The most familiar of the classical instruments today are the *koto,* a 13-stringed horizontal harp or zither, which is probably the most melodious-sounding Japanese instrument to the Western ear; the *shamisen,* an extremely versatile three-stringed lute or banjo, used in all forms of accompaniment, from Kabuki and Bunraku through geisha ballads to folk songs; the *shakuhachi,* a vertical bamboo flute of varying length with five finger holes, for which there is a large solo repertoire and which is also played in ensembles and accompanies folk songs; and the *fue,* or horizontal flute, which accompanies Noh performances and is sometimes heard elsewhere, though the usual non-theatrical ensemble is limited to koto, shamisen and shakuhachi. Professional recitals of Japanese classical music are rather rare, most major concert halls being used full-time for the performance of Western music.

Several types of drum exist, including the *tsuzumi,* a finger drum supported on the shoulder, and the *taiko,* which can be any kind of stick drum, such as that used in Noh accompaniments, but the most familiar forms of which are the larger drums that accompany the folk dances at summer festivals.

Folk music is alive and well in most parts of Japan, especially Okinawa and Tohoku, which have the largest repertoires of songs. Whereas many Western folk songs are about unrequited love or the exploits of courageous men, most Japanese songs celebrate places, underlining the wistful feeling for *furusato* that runs through so many avenues of Japanese life. Professional folk-song performances, especially on television, are so slick and prettified that one quite forgets to listen to the lyrics, many of which are actually about hardship and oppression. Folk songs are best heard when performed spontaneously in bars or at the long lively sessions that mark the successful conclusion of festivals.

Modern Japanese ballads (*enka*) are popular with karaoke singers and combine a folk-like feeling for place with the slushy romanticism of the soap opera. Japanese pop music is almost completely derivative, not from its Western counterparts but from itself, to the extent that many foreign visitors, even those with musical training, are hard pressed to distinguish one song from another and harder pressed to see why they should bother.

The Chubu Region
The Belly and the Back

As geographical divisions go, the **Chubu** (Middle) region is an unhandy one, comprising all the bulk of Honshu between Kanto and Kansai, and stretching across the greatest width of the island, from the Pacific to the Japan Sea coast. At its centre towers the most formidable range of mountains in Japan which, since an English mining engineer so christened them in 1881, are known as 'The Japan Alps'. The inhabitants of this mountainous inland area (particularly that part of it called **Shinshu**, nowadays Nagano prefecture) are noted for their traditional outlook, often tending in the older generation toward hidebound conservatism, particularly where such delicate matters as the marriage of their daughters are concerned. It is a region which, because of the comparative inaccessibility of much of its terrain, has resisted progress to the same extent that in the past its steep slopes resisted paddy farming. The best-known traditional industry of the region was the silk industry that centred on Lake Suwa, and was notorious for its heartless exploitation of the loom girls recruited from local villages.

South of the mountains, along the narrow coastal strip of the Pacific belly, ran the main historical artery of transport between Edo and Osaka, the Tokaido highway, and consequently it is this southern part of the region that was best prepared for rapid modern development and that has suffered most from the blights as well as from the double-edged blessings of large-scale industrialization. The visitor who takes the Shinkansen bullet train from Tokyo to Kyoto and beyond will find himself travelling, for the most part, through a landscape where few horizons are not marred by smoking factory chimneys or slate-grey conurbations.

North of the mountains, by way of contrast, the entire stretch of the Japan Sea coast and its neighbouring inland areas are often referred to collectively as *Ura Nihon* (The Back of Japan), a name that NHK resists using in its radio and television broadcasts for fear the residents of the area will be offended to the point of refusing to pay their licence fees. This was a neglected area throughout most of Japan's history, partly because it was so far removed from the main channels of inter-urban communication, but more especially because of the immensely heavy snowfalls that are its chief climatic feature. Snow storms arrive in Japan from the northwest, a year-end gift from Siberia. The Japan Alps (many of whose peaks rise to between 2,000 and 3,000 metres, 6,500 and 10,000 feet, or higher) prevent most of these storms from reaching the Pacific coastal areas so that, although it can be bitingly cold in winter, Tokyo generally has little snow. But in the hills and on the plains of *Ura Nihon*, the snow falls so thick and lies so long that, in the remoter hamlets, people spend much of the winter burrowing about like moles and constructing tunnels through the snow to their neighbours' doors. In the larger towns it is common to find the pavements of shopping streets strongly roofed against snow, and the prefectures of Niigata and Toyama especially are known as *Yukiguni*, 'Snow Country'. That is also the title of Nobel-prize winning author Kawabata Yasunari's 1937 novel, set in one of the hot-spring resorts that provide the few real glimmers of comfort along the otherwise gloomy Back of Japan.

The Pacific Belly

Because of the vastly different social and climatic features of the two halves of the region, it seems sensible to deal with them separately. The southern and central part of Chubu contains the prefectures of **Shizuoka, Yamanashi, Nagano, Gifu** and **Aichi**. Those with a coastline are conveniently linked to Tokyo by the Tokaido Shinkansen bullet train while landlocked Gifu is easily accessible from Nagoya, and Nagano can be reached by express either from Shinjuku (for Matsumoto) or from Ueno (for Nagano city, the prefectural capital).

Shizuoka is close enough to Tokyo to offer several destinations suitable for one- or two-day trips from the capital, most notably Mount Fuji (which straddles the border with Yamanashi prefecture) and the Izu Peninsula, both of which are parts of the **Fuji-Hakone-Izu National Park** (see page 55).

Its relatively mild climate has made the **Izu Peninsula** a popular leisure-time destination for residents of Tokyo. The east coast of the peninsula has consequently suffered a good deal of development, particularly in and around the hot-spring resort of **Atami** (which waggish Japanese have rechristened 'tatami' on account of its undecorous reputation and the horizontal nature of many of the pursuits to be enjoyed there). But the west coast is largely unspoiled and, in addition to the majestic views of Mount Fuji it offers across Suruga Bay, is pleasantly wooded and has some unpretentious resorts of its own, like **Toi. Shuzenji** in the north-central hills of Izu is the peninsula's best-known inland hot-spring resort, and it, in turn, is flanked by a number of smaller and more rural spas. Shuzenji affords a good introduction to hot-spring bathing for the novice; the little sloping town is interesting to stroll around and the river that runs through its centre has a small open-air communal bathing facility which is not much used. The Asaba Ryokan at Shuzenji is famous for the Noh stage in its garden, where torchlight performances are sometimes given. **Mount Amagi** (1,407 metres, 4,616 feet) in the east of Izu has romantic associations deriving from Kawabata Yasunari's haunting 1926 novella *Izu no Odoriko* (The Izu Dancer). The associations of the small city of **Shimoda** (population 31,000), at the tip of

the peninsula, are historical, the first foreign consulate in Japan having been established there in 1856 by the American diplomat Townsend Harris. For a while the shogun sought to restrict foreign representation and trade to this comparative backwater, and it was largely Harris' persistence that resulted in the broadening of diplomatic and commercial relations and the opening of Yokohama and other ports to foreign trade.

Japanese people are wont to bemoan the Westerner's alleged habit of regarding **Mount Fuji** and geisha girls as the twin symbols of their nation while wilfully ignoring the cultural assets of which the Japanese themselves are most proud, such as silicon chips. Where the Western fixation with geisha is concerned, Japanese people are often right to express a degree of scorn; the newly-landed G.I.s who stood in the streets of Tokyo and Yokohama in late 1945 shouting, 'We want geisha girls!' clearly exhibited a lamentable ignorance of an old and honourable institution. But for the ongoing Western obsession with the other half of the combination the Japanese have mainly themselves to blame. Every NHK telecast during the 1964 Olympics opened with a shot of Mount Fuji accompanied by the meticulously recorded bong of a deeply resonant temple bell. Calendars and the covers of official guidebooks intended for foreigners' use almost invariably feature a coloured photograph of Mount Fuji, usually with a bullet train speeding by so that modern amenities will not go wholly unremarked. Mount Fuji is an awe-inspiring sight, so imposing that it was a major landmark for American bomber pilots on their way to reduce the capital to ash. Partly because of its splendid isolation, partly because of its almost perfectly conical shape, partly because of the divinity accorded it through the centuries, partly because (despite the formidable barrier raised by the Japan Alps) it is, at 3,776 metres (12,389 feet), the tallest mountain in Japan, and partly because though now a dormant volcano (its last eruption was in 1707) the possibility exists that it could flame again into dangerous life, Fuji does exert a very special influence on the imagination of Japanese and visitor alike.

As with certain beautiful women, it is best to maintain as distant a relationship as possible with Mount Fuji. Not to see it is a sad deprivation, but to see it too close is to court the waning of a dream. There is a climbing season (1 July to 31 August) during which tens of thousands of people make the ascent, most taking a bus either from **Kawaguchiko** in Yamanashi (to the 'Fifth Station' on the mountainside) or from **Gotenba** (to the 'New Fifth Station') and then continuing to the summit on foot. Along the track that winds up the higher slopes there are refreshment stalls (supplies dragged up by tractor) and huts to rest or sleep in. Many climbers plan to reach the summit in the early hours of the morning and watch the sun rise, though this last ambition is often frustrated by the cloud cover that Fuji attracts. Though nowadays the higher slopes are not so littered with beer cans and lunch boxes as they were 15 years ago, they are still a long way from appearing divine.

Japanese people say that not to climb Mount Fuji once in your life is foolish and to climb it more than once is foolish. They say this of other mountains too (notably Asama, see page 139), but where Fuji is concerned, I think an unanswerable case can be put forward by the first category of fool. You do not approach the Sacred Mirror at Ise because by doing so you would render it less sacred, and the same can be said of too close an acquaintance with this awesome, dream-ridden mountain.

On the **Yamanashi** side of Fuji lie its five lakes, Lakes **Yamanaka, Kawaguchi, Saiko, Shoji** and **Motosu**, which, interspersed as they are with dense, in part primeval, woodland and with spas such as those at **Shimobe** and **Oshino**, provide an alternative rural retreat to the Izu Peninsula. The chief town and springboard for a tour of the area is **Fujiyoshida** (population 54,000), while to the north lies the prefectural capital, **Kofu** (population 199,000), the old castle seat of the warlike Takeda Shingen, for years a sharp thorn in Nobunaga's and then in Ieyasu's side, and the 'Shadow Warrior' of Kurosawa Akira's 1980 film *Kagemusha*.

Easily accessible from Kofu is the spectacular **Shosenkyo Gorge**, with its falls and sharp 50-metre (160-foot) cliffs, a part of the Chichibu-Tama National Park (see also page 55); while in the southwest of the prefecture stands **Mount Minobu** (1,148 metres, 3,766 feet), yet another mountain of religious significance, this time to the more than 10 million adherents of the Nichiren sect of Buddhism, Nichiren having founded the temple complex of **Kuonji** during his residence here from 1274 until shortly before his death in 1282. Nichiren was an irascible, humourless character who found intolerable the idea that anyone should dare question the tenets he preached, and it was at Mount Minobu that he wrote the documents upon which the transmission of his doctrines are founded and which state, clearly and completely typically, that all who disregard their contents are slanderers of the Buddha's law. Nichiren's self-centered and abrasive proselytizing sets him apart from other great Buddhist teachers who, for the most part, have been men of peace and tolerance, the virtues upon which, in the dim past, Buddhism was founded.

In the decades since the war, Yamanashi prefecture (particularly the region around Kofu) has become noted for its viticulture, and the only really drinkable Japanese wines are produced here. None has yet achieved greatness, or can even honestly be called memorable, although a wine of the 'Mercian' label (manufactured by the Sanraku Ocean company) did win a medal at an international wine competition in Hungary in 1964, which is why Mercian wine labels are conspicuously adorned not only with sentences in French (*mis en bouteille au chateau*) but with medals. In general, Japanese white wines are either too acid or too syrupy (though Yamanashi wines are not as syrupy as those produced in the north of Honshu and in Hokkaido, which often taste like apple juice) while some of the reds can fur your tongue like the inside of a kettle. In any case, a lot of 'Japanese' wine turns out to be a mixture of local product and nondescript imported *vin de table*, a fact which surfaced amid some scandal in 1985, and which does not bode especially well for the future competitiveness of the Japanese wine industry.

Straddling the prefectural boundary between Yamanashi and **Nagano** are some of the region's most impressive peaks, here a part of the **Minami Arupusu** (Southern Alps) **National Park.** Favourites with climbers are Mounts **Akaishi-dake** (3,120 metres, 10,236 feet), **Shiomi-dake** (3,047 metres, 10,000 feet), **Shirane** (3,192 metres, 10,472 feet), **Senjo-ga-take** (3,033 metres, 9,950 feet), **Koma-ga-take** (2,966 metres, 9,731 feet) and **Yatsu-ga-take** (2,899 metres, 9,511 feet)—*take* or *dake* meaning 'peak'. Some of these, like the last named, have huts and lodging houses well below the summits which are accessible to ordinary hikers without the need of special equipment, but for the most part this is fully-fledged mountaineering country and the peaks should be approached with the wary respect that frequent rapid changes in weather patterns and regular annual fatalities require.

From Tokyo (Ueno), the most easily accessible part of Nagano prefecture is the high plateau that lies to the south of the active volcano, **Mount Asama** (2,542 metres, 8,340 feet), one of those mountains that fools climb twice or not at all, although in recent years even the wise have frequently been prevented from climbing by rumbles and spouts. The plateau was crossed by the old **Nakasendo** highway, like the Tokaido one of the great feudal Japanese roads and a link, though a less direct one (69 post stations as compared with 53 on the Tokaido), between Edo and Kyoto. The train journey from Ueno as far as **Yokokawa** at the foot of the steep **Usui Pass** is uneventful, but an extra locomotive must be added at Yokokawa to manage the gradient, and the short delay required to couple it provides the visitor with an opportunity to skip smartly out onto the platform along with practically every other passenger on the train to buy Yokokawa Station's famous packed lunch, a form of *kamameshi* (boiled rice topped with assorted odds and ends) which comes complete in its own take-away earthenware bowl and is said to be a particular favourite of the empress, who perhaps sees a need for spare kitchenware. All major railway stations in Japan sell packed lunches and their contents and quality vary from region to region, but Yokokawa is one of the last to offer its lunch in an attractive and reusable container.

The visitor emerges from the tunnels of the Usui Pass to find himself in the resort town of **Karuizawa** (resident population 14,000), 'discovered' by Archdeacon A.C. Shaw and other enterprising foreign missionaries in 1888 and used by them much as highland retreats were used by Raj society in India during the long hot summers. Nowadays, Karuizawa is popular among the energetic Japanese young who come from Tokyo in the warm weather to play

A two-tiered bento (boxed lunch) containing the coloured extra-glutinous rice prepared for festive occasions.

tennis and in winter to skate. The little town itself has a famous 'Ginza' shopping street, department stores and fashionable coffee shops (one of which, according to a persistent rumour, charges 10,000 yen for a cup of coffee)—all to prevent the energetic young on their day's excursion into the countryside from feeling too lost. For miles around the land has been divided up by equally energetic real estate agents into small lots which are purchased by university professors and similar countryfolk who erect weekend villas on them. Along the lanes stand bunches of neat white signposts indicating these professorial retreats.

More interesting are the old post and castle towns of the region, such as **Komoro** (population 42,000) and **Ueda** (population 112,000), which, for all their size (Ueda is the third largest city in the prefecture), preserve a sleepy old-world atmosphere, and are usefully close to such hot springs as **Bessho**. Round the skirts of Asama, at the base of its northern slope, lies the intriguing lunar landscape of **Onioshidashi** (literally, 'Shoved Out by Demons'), which was created by the massive eruption of 1783. This and the small museum there are easily reached from Karuizawa by bus.

North and west of the prefectural capital, **Nagano** city (population 324,000), which is famous for its **Zenkoji** Temple, founded in 642 and rebuilt in 1707, are other peaks, not quite so towering as those of the Southern Alps, straddling the prefectural borders with Gunma and Niigata, most of them a part of the **Jo-Shinetsu Kogen National Park.** They include Mounts **Shirane** (2,162 metres, 7,093 feet) and **Kurohime** (2,053 metres, 6,735 feet). Nagano's two most popular ski resorts—**Naeba** and **Shiga Kogen** (*kogen* means 'plateau' or 'heights')—are to be found among these peaks, as are a number of fine hot springs, including **Jigokudani** (literally 'Hell Valley'), where two colonies of wild monkeys have their own bathing facilities and frequently invade the human spa too.

The other major city in Nagano prefecture is **Matsumoto** (population 192,000), which boasts a rare black-walled castle, originally built in 1504 and known as **Karasujo** (Castle of the Crow). Matsumoto is a good base from which to launch tours of **Lake Suwa** to the southeast and the majestic peaks and spas to the west which straddle the prefectural borders with Toyama and Gifu. These Northern Alps are part of yet another National Park, this time called **Chubu-Sangaku**, and include Mounts **Norikura** (3,026 metres, 9,928 feet), **Hotaka** (3,190 metres, 10,466 feet) and **Yari** (3,180 metres, 10,433 feet). Hidden among the eastern folds of the range and easily accessible by bus from Matsumoto is the picturesque **Kamikochi** valley, a favourite spot from which to appreciate the mountains' refreshing grandeur, and a starting point for several hiking trails along which the mountains' delights can be met at closer quarters. That such trails exist is due in no small part to the same hardy band of missionaries who lighted upon Karuizawa, in particular to an English missionary called Walter Weston, who pioneered the now immensely popular sport of mountain hiking in Japan. Before Rev. Weston, the more rugged countryside had been scrupulously avoided except by devout ascetics whereas, since Rev. Weston, Japanese calendar manufacturers have gone out of their way to include Alpine panoramas in calendars intended for distribution abroad in order to counter the impression, harboured by ignorant foreigners, that Japan is a backward, jungly nation like some of its unspeakable Asian neighbours.

It will be seen from this brief summary that Nagano's chief attractions are natural rather than historical or cultural. Short of a trip to Kyushu or Hokkaido (see pages 183 and 215), Nagano provides the visitor with his most convenient chance of escaping for a while from the relentless pressures of urban civilization and cultural must-sees to an area where the landscape is spectacular, the air invigorating, and the accommodation and recreation to be found in the dozens of spas, large and small, are almost entirely of the traditional kind. Nor nowadays do missionaries lurk in numbers sufficient to deny him these delights.

On the western side of the Northern Alps stands the city of **Takayama** (sometimes called Hida-Takayama, 'Hida' being the old name for this part of **Gifu** prefecture). Takayama (population 64,000) is architecturally one of the best preserved towns in Japan and, in addition to its picturesque rows of Edo- and Meiji-period houses and shops (lining streets laid out in a grid pattern like Kyoto's), it has several museums depicting local life and traditions, and a Folk Village (**Minzoku Mura**), to which a number of buildings from outlying rural areas have been brought and painstakingly reconstructed. Takayama's **Hie Shrine** also hosts (on 14 and 15 April) a spectacular annual festival, the **Sanno Matsuri**, during which large and elaborately decorated floats equipped with moving mechanical figures called *karakuri ningyo* are paraded through the streets.

Most of the population of Gifu prefecture is crowded into the flattish urbanized areas around the border with Aichi, while the northern reaches are either inaccessibly mountainous or solidly agricultural, harbouring small towns and villages that remain traditional in both appearance and outlook. The prefecture (originally the province of Mino) is famous for its Oribe ceramic ware (also called Mino ware), produced here from as early as the eighth century and gaining particular favour toward the end of the 16th century among connoisseurs of the tea ceremony. The small city of **Mino** (population 27,000) is also well known as a centre for the manufacture of hand-made paper (*washi*), the production technique for which has been designated a national treasure.

The prefectural capital is **Gifu** city (population 410,000), which stands on the **Nagara River**, whose urban reaches, together with those of the Kiso River at Inuyama in Aichi, are among the best-known places where the visitor can still view cormorant fishing (*ukai*), a tradition that goes back some 1,200 years. Though nowadays mounted purely for the sake of tourists, this event (staged nightly between mid-May and mid-October), in which trained, leashed cormorants dive by torchlight at the command of their regally aproned master, offers an impressive display of an almost vanished skill. Normally, sightseers board one of the many pleasure craft, mostly chartered by local hotels or ryokans, that follow the cormorant boats down river and which, whether the birds catch any *ayu* (sweetfish) or not, are always plentifully supplied with refreshment.

Due west of Gifu city, not far from the boundary with Shiga, lies the site of the famous barrier gate at **Sekigahara**, a name for history buffs to conjure with, since it was near here, in 1600, that one of the most decisive and significant battles of Japanese history was fought, when Ieyasu defeated the forces brought against him by Hideyoshi's son and former chief minister, and so removed the final obstacle standing between himself and the establishment of his family's two-and-a-half centuries of absolute power.

Aichi is a ferociously industrialized prefecture, on a par with Kanagawa and boasting a higher gross annual value in manufactured goods than either Osaka or Tokyo. This is because some of Japan's leading export-oriented manufacturers have their principal plants here, notably Toyota, the second largest automobile maker in the world, which, not content with a mere plant, has its own city, **Toyota City**, whose population of 282,000 makes it the third largest city in the prefecture. Honda, Suzuki and Yamaha also have their chief factories nearby.

Near **Inuyama** (population 65,000), already mentioned in connection with cormorant fishing, the **Kiso River** offers the prospect of rapids-shooting. As the mountains to the northeast are called the 'Japan Alps', so the river here is called the 'Japan Rhine'. Not far away, there is **Meiji Mura** (Meiji Village), a collection of about 50 late 19th- and early 20th-century buildings and other memorabilia from around the country (including the facade and lobby of Frank Lloyd Wright's 1922 Imperial Hotel from Tokyo), so admired for having survived a century or less that they have been transported here and reassembled brick by brick. Inuyama itself has Japan's oldest existing castle, built in 1440 and not yet rechristened Neuschwanstein.

The best that can be said for the prefectural capital, **Nagoya** (population 2.1 million, the fourth largest city in Japan), is that it is comparatively easy to find one's way around it, since it was almost completely refashioned on a grid pattern following the massive destruction it suffered during the war, and that it is attempting to soften its reputation as a focal point for the prefecture's grim heavy industries by encouraging such so-called 'clean' industries as fine ceramics (for use as electronic and computer components), into which the Japan Fine Ceramics Centre, based in Nagoya, is currently

(Preceding page) Matsuyama castle. Since the donjon was so vulnerable to fire, defence strategy relied on halting the attacker at the outermost walls.

pumping a great deal of cash. To polish its forward-looking image further Nagoya is preparing to stage a world fair called 'Design Expo '89'.

Still, Nagoya is a city that most visitors, whether they arrive in '89 or not, are likely to want to spend about as much time in as the bullet train does on its way from Tokyo to Kyoto (60 seconds). True, the city contains the **Atsuta Shrine**, founded in the third century, rebuilt in 1955, the repository of the Sacred Sword which forms a third of the imperial regalia (the other two-thirds, the Mirror and Jewel, are in the Ise Shrine and the Imperial Palace, respectively). And there is a feudal castle here, just as there is at Osaka (though this one was rebuilt 28 years later than Osaka's, in 1959, and is therefore less venerable, though it, too, is equipped with a convenient post-feudal elevator). If you are touring Chubu and southern Kansai, Nagoya is the perfect springboard for visits to Takayama or to Ise and the Kii Peninsula (see pages 103 and 106). Otherwise follow the example of the train.

The Japan Sea Back

Niigata city (population 458,000), the capital of **Niigata** prefecture, is the terminus of the Joetsu Shinkansen bullet train from Ueno, and thus the easiest point of access to the Japan Sea coast for the visitor from Tokyo. This Shinkansen line was inaugurated in 1982 and owes its existence almost entirely to the personal dynamism and influence of former Prime Minister Tanaka Kakuei, whose constituency was in Niigata prefecture, and whose energy in opening up this traditionally backward region to modern development ensured that his former constituents remained fiercely loyal to Tanaka through all the calamities that subsequently befell him—bribery scandal, forced resignation, court proceedings, prison sentence, stroke, and the dissolution of his political faction. Tanaka's notorious money politics and his long undisputed role of 'kingmaker' in the government are an extraordinarily clear testament to the ingrained feudalism that can flourish under a purportedly democratic system. Equally, Tanaka's own commitment to the region where his strongest support was centred is a clear example of the abiding spirit of *noblesse oblige*.

The area was a late starter, but in the last two or three decades Niigata and other cities along the coast have suffered the ravages of hectic industrialization as well as of natural disasters. In June 1964, a major submarine earthquake that triggered a five-metre-high *tsunami* destroyed between a quarter and a third of all the ferroconcrete structures in Niigata city, which is why so many of the taller buildings look conspicuously new. These urban ravages do not matter much, however, because the visitor to the region will not want to spend a lot of time in its cities, and the stretches of rugged coast between them, and the mountains of the Snow Country that tower inland, still offer the undeveloped out-of-the-wayness for which the

Back of Japan is famous.

The visitor with time and a desire to exploit this out-of-the-wayness to the full might consider a trip to **Sado** island, easily accessible by either conventional ferry or hydrofoil from Niigata. The Japanese often complain (though there is sometimes an element of boastfulness in the complaint) about their *shimaguni konjo* (islanders' complex), by which they mainly mean the insular cast of thought that comes from being entirely surrounded by ocean. The consequences of this 'complex' have been many—notably, the forced closure of the country under the Tokugawas, and at all other periods the impulse simultaneously to distrust, admire, resist and possess anything and everything that comes from abroad. Because Japan is itself an island nation, a trip to one of its many small offshore islands can provide the visitor with a remarkable insight into the preoccupations of the Japanese national character, since such islands are by their very nature microcosms of the whole.

Excepting Okinawa, which for much of its history was an independent kingdom, **Sado** (population 86,000) is the largest of Japan's offshore islands and thus the fifth largest island of the archipelago. It was for centuries an island of exile. The Emperor Juntoku was sent there in 1221, after a doomed attempt to overthrow the military regents, and remained there until his death. The politically ambitious priest Mongaku, for a while a protégé of Yoritomo's, was sent there in 1199 following an abortive plot against Juntoku's father. The irascible Nichiren was sent there in 1271 and spent two years on the island suffering from chronic diarrhoea. The founder of the Noh theatre, Zeami Motokiyo, was sent there in 1434 having angered the shogun for reasons no one has properly ascertained. And during the 17th and 18th centuries the island's extensive gold mine was worked by a large, grim colony of convicts whose life expectancy in the narrow choking tunnels under **Kinzan** (The Golden Mountain) was pitifully short.

Most of the island's historical sites are in some way related to these exiles. Part of the gold mine outside the town of **Aikawa** (which at the height of its 18th-century prosperity had a population of 100,000 and now has less than one-sixth of that) has been turned into a museum. Juntoku's reputedly haunted grave stands just outside **Mano**, where Nichiren's hut can also be seen in the grounds of **Myoshoji** temple. But Sado's main attractions are its rugged coast, its quiet country lifestyle, its mournful folk songs, and the neglected air of a place that has not suffered the ruination of an economic miracle. The principal town is **Ryotsu** (population 21,000), where the ferry docks. Here the visitor might take a bus to the government lodging house on **Mount Donden**, from where he can obtain a breathtaking view over the island, and next morning, if he is feeling hardy, hike down to the opposite coast through meadows, woods, and along the rough beds of old mountain streams.

(Preceding page)Anecoic test chamber at Nissan's Research and Development Centre.

Back on the mainland and away from the coast, the most notable spa and skiing resort in Niigata is **Yuzawa**, also called Echigo-Yuzawa, 'Echigo' being an old name for the province. It is conveniently situated on the express line from Ueno just beyond the long tunnel by means of which the train burrows under the prefectural border with Gunma.

Toyama city (population 305,000), the prefectural capital of **Toyama**, has a distinctly more prosperous air than does any part of Niigata, and this air infects the whole small prefecture. The city has been known since the 17th century for the manufacture of patent Chinese-style medicines called *kampoyaku* (Chinese concoctions) and visits can be arranged to the factory of the largest manufacturer, Kokando.

Mount Tateyama (3,015 metres or 9,892 feet) in the east of the prefecture, one of the northernmost peaks of the Northern Alps and a part of the Jo-Shinetsu-Kogen National Park, is regarded as sacred, not because of a particular sectarian affiliation as at Mount Minobu (see page 138), but, like Fuji, because of divine qualities that are perceived as inherent in the mountain itself. Below the southeastern slope of the mountain stands the massive **Kurobe Dam**, which has formed its own scenic lake, and lower down the **Kurobe River** is the lovely **Kurobe Gorge**, most easily reached via the town of **Unazuki** from **Kurobe** city. Along the private railway line that links Kurobe city with its gorge lie several small and picturesque hot springs.

Between the towns of **Tateyama** and **Omachi** in Niigata prefecture a scenic Alpine Route, not open to private vehicles, takes the visitor by means of bus, trolly bus and cable car through a series of tunnels, up slopes and over plateaus that offer breathtaking views of the surrounding mountains. The route passes the Kurobe Dam, and the journey can be broken overnight at **Murodo**. Otherwise the trip, in either direction, takes an entire day.

Toyama is a prefecture of towering peaks, lakes and gorges, ruggedly beautiful in summer and autumn and buried by deep snows throughout the long winter. Along the upper reaches of the **Shokawa River**, beyond the **Shokawa Gorge**, lies one of the many remote areas said to have been settled by the defeated Heike after their scattered flight following the battle of Dannoura in 1185 (see page 165). These areas are understandably hard of access, and this one is no exception. Its claim to settlement by the Heike is made unusually convincing by the name of the village, not far from the Gifu border, where the settlement seems to have centred. The village is called **Taira**, which was another name for the Heike clan. (**Taira** is written with a single ideogram meaning 'peace', and was the family name used by individuals of the clan, like Taira no Kyomori. The same ideogram can also be pronounced *hei*. It is, for example, the *hei* in **Heiankyo**, 'Capital of Tranquillity', the old name for Kyoto. *Heike* consists of this ideogram plus a second that means simply 'house' or 'family'.)

The capital of **Ishikawa** prefecture is the historic city of **Kanazawa** (population 418,000), one of the major centres of tourism along this stretch of the Japan Sea coast. The old name for Ishikawa prefecture was **Kaga** (see page 29), and, with an annual tax assessment of a million *koku* (one *koku* was the amount of rice needed to feed a samurai retainer for a year), it was the richest of all Japan's feudal fiefs, a fact which greatly increased the power and prestige of Kaga's most famous lord, Maeda Toshiie, whose spirit feeds off Kanazawa like a succubus. Toshiie was not a native of the region, and was appointed to the fief by his patron, Nobunaga, in 1583; so the degree of pride taken in him by Kanazawa's citizens must be counted a further testament to his outstanding abilities as a leader.

The building of **Kanazawa Castle** began with Toshiie's arrival. The donjon disappeared in the great fire of 1881, but the massive walls survive, as does a later version of the **Ishikawa-mon** gate, itself burnt down in the mid-18th century and rebuilt in 1788.

However, Kanazawa's main tourist magnet is **Kenrokuen** garden, the largest and best-known of the 'Three Most Beautiful Landscape Gardens' in Japan (the others are Mito's Kairakuen, see page 60, and Okayama's Korakuen, see page 163). Kenrokuen was laid out in its present form in 1819 by the 12th Lord Maeda, Narinaga, who also placed the much-fussed-over stone lantern called **Kotojitoro** (Lantern of the Koto Bridge) beside **Kasumigaike**, the garden's 'Pond of Mist'. The lantern is so called because its base is held to resemble in shape the bridge used for raising and separating the strings of a horizontal harp (*koto*). In fact, the entire park is much fussed over, and visitors in search of a simple stroll through attractive surroundings may well find this modest ambition frustrated by the streams of tourists and their bullhorn-wielding guides who crowd the narrow paths from morning till night.

Still, Kanazawa has other attractions, many of them to be found in its atmospheric back streets, and the city's ongoing attempts to encourage tourism have occasionally taken a happier form than the noisy exploitation at Kenrokuen; notably, the provision of maps and signboards to facilitate leisurely walking tours.

North of Kanazawa the rugged **Noto Peninsula** juts out into the Japan Sea, providing the visitor who wants to experience the rural out-of-the-wayness of this region with the same sort of opportunities presented by Sado island. The small city of **Wajima** (population 33,000) is noted for its lacquerware, and the peninsula as a whole is famous for a virile form of folk drumming in which the drummers wear colourful and hideously carved demon masks.

(Preceding page) Rice harvest in Fukushima prefecture. The smallness and inaccessibility of many paddies ensure that most farming operations continue to be performed by hand.

South of Kanazawa, on the coast near the city of **Komatsu** (population 104,000), where Kanazawa's airport is located, stands the site of the **Ataka** barrier gate, by far the most celebrated of the old checkpoints owing to its association with the flight of Yoshitsune and his quick-witted retainer, Benkei, in 1187. The ruse by which they succeeded in getting through the barrier is the subject of the Noh play *Ataka* and of the Kabuki play, *Kanjincho* (The Subscription List), which rivals in popularity the spirit-stirring *Chushingura* (see page 37). According to legend, Yoshitsune, on Benkei's advice, disguised himself as the party's bearer and, in full view of the barrier guards, Benkei beat him for his tardiness, an action unthinkable if the ostensible bearer were really Benkei's master. As with *Chushingura,* the play depicts the death-defying loyalty of a retainer for his lord, and this loyalty and the event that epitomized it are celebrated further in the small museum that stands on the beach near the barrier's original site.

In the extreme south of Ishikawa prefecture, near the border with Gifu, stands **Mount Hakusan** (2,702 metres, 8,865 feet), the centre of the **Hakusan National Park** and, like Tateyama, a peak regarded as sacred. Ishikawa prefecture is well supplied with hot-spring resorts, most of them sprawling and well developed. Among the better known are **Yuwaka**, southeast of Kanazawa, and **Yamanaka, Yamashiro, Awazu** and **Katayamazu**, which form a group around the little city of **Kaga** (population 65,000) near the prefectural border with Fukui. Near Yamashiro lies the small village of **Kutani**, famous since the 17th century for the colourfully-glazed pottery produced in the nearby kilns; pottery which has a clear affinity with the products of Arita in Kyushu, from whose potters the Kutani men learned their skills. Kutani ware is sold in most of the prefecture's souvenir shops.

The heavily indented coast of **Fukui** prefecture is attractive enough for it to have been designated a Quasi-National Park, although one part of it has earned its reputation for a grimmer reason. The Wakasa Bay area, particularly the city of **Tsuruga** (population 62,000), long a major port, is now Japan's most rapidly developing centre for atomic power, the newest of its 12 reactors having been completed in May 1987. These reactors together produce about 9.09 million kilowatts, which is slightly more than 35 percent of all atomic-generated power in Japan. A 1985 film, independently produced, called *Ikiteru Uchi ga Hana na no yo Shindara sore made yo To Sengan* (The While You're Alive Life is Like a Flower But When You're Dead You've Had It Party Manifesto) examined in a somewhat avant-garde fashion a persistent rumour that has dogged the Tsuruga atomic facilities: that the dangerous areas around the reactor cores are cleaned and maintained by unskilled labourers press-ganged into the work by criminal organizations, and that there have been several fatalities which, since the labourers are recruited precisely because they have no families or fixed addresses, have been hidden with swift efficiency. No hard proof that this appalling rumour is true has ever come to light, but it provides a vivid illustration of one of the reasons for Japan's alleged 'nuclear allergy' (see also pages 157–60).

The capital of the prefecture is **Fukui** city (population 241,000), traditionally famous for its silk industry but now more heavily committed to the production of man- rather than worm-made fibres. A short train ride east from Fukui brings the visitor to the gates of **Eiheiji**, one of the most beautiful and beautifully situated temples in Japan. Eiheiji is a temple of the Soto Zen sect, founded in 1246 by Dogen. Soto Zen differs slightly in emphasis from Rinzai Zen (see page 94) in that, whereas Rinzai tends to stress an intellectual discipline, Soto concentrates more on a strict physical regimen and on simple silent meditation. In many ways Dogen's writings and sayings encapsulate more perfectly than any others the elusive but distinct spirit of Zen. He believed that simply by sitting still and doing nothing a man could gain a profound understanding of the world around him and his part in it. He also believed, much as the early Shinto animists did, in a tangible life-force, comparable to a divinity, that inspired all nature:

> *The landscape of the mountains,*
> *The sound of streams—*
> *All are the body and voice of Buddha.*

Eiheiji attracts a large number of tourists, not all of them inclined to be as quiet and reverent as the temple and its teachings deserve. But the temple survives them with equanimity.

Hiroshima and The Chugoku Region
The Politics of Peace

Hiroshima (population 899,000), the commercial, administrative and industrial centre of the Chugoku region, is a pleasant city, pulsing with prosperity. Its roads and pavements are clean and airy, its shopping streets roofed to make fashionable arcades. The reconstructed donjon of its feudal castle, originally built in 1589, has been made the centre of a spacious park. Its professional baseball club, the Hiroshima Toyo Carp, has a fanatically devoted following not confined to the region, and is usually a strong contender for the Central League pennant, which it has won five times. These, however, are unlikely to be the associations uppermost in the visitor's mind.

You can play a game of word association with the names of cities that suffered large-scale destruction during the Second World War. Dresden: china. Coventry: cathedral. Berlin: wall. London: fog (this at least would be the response of very many Japanese people who are brought up to believe that the red-eyed British must grope blindly through the streets of their capital, alerted to the position of dangerous road junctions by the rattle of hansom cabs). Nagasaki: well, there are the martyrs if you are Catholic and Madame Butterfly if you are not. But Hiroshima leaves you little scope for the exercise of imagination, and such scope as it does leave the city authorities are particularly anxious to limit.

The authorities regard their city and its experience as a beacon lighting the world toward peace, and they have struggled to ensure that only one association should leap into the foreign mind, and into the malleable minds of Japanese youngsters. They have repeatedly mounted exhibitions abroad and invited important foreign dignitaries, such as former U.S. president Jimmy Carter and the late Swedish prime minister Olof Palme, to visit Hiroshima and say memorable things about the horrors of a nuclear holocaust and the necessity of avoiding one in the future. Their most frequented tourist site (nowadays an obligatory destination for many children on organized school trips) is the Peace Park which lies at the point marking the hypocentre of Hiroshima's atomic explosion. The Peace Park contains a Peace Memorial Museum, a Statue of a Prayer for Peace, a Flame of Peace, a Children's Peace Monument, a Peace Bell, and the road leading to it is called Peace Boulevard. One cannot be long in Hiroshima before one starts counting the occurrences of the word *heiwa* (peace) in its landmarks and tourist literature.

Nor can one be long in the Peace Park and its museum without noting a number of unsettling circumstances, chief of which, perhaps, is the complete absence of any sense of historical context. It is as though the bomb fell on Hiroshima, figuratively as well as literally, out of the blue. Nowhere is there any suggestion that it might have been triggered by past actions. Nowhere is there the least sign that any other nation or race might have suffered comparable wartime tragedies. This includes the Korean victims of the atomic bombing, estimated at around 20,000, who were in Hiroshima in August 1945 because they had been conscripted into the Japanese army or to work as forced labour in the munitions factories and docks. The city authorities have in fact resisted attempts by Korean lobbies in Japan to erect a monument to these victims in the Peace Park, although one now stands elsewhere. Some years ago Arnold Toynbee's granddaughter, Polly, was invited to visit Japan by the Sokagakkai, a lay Buddhist organization (see page 75) whose leader, Ikeda Daisaku, had published a series of tape-recorded 'dialogues' with Polly's famous grandfather. Polly was taken to the Hiroshima Peace Park and appears to have experienced there some of these potential discomforts. Later, she complained in a British newspaper that 'Hiroshima is the shrine to Japanese innocence', drawing attention to the fact that we are shown there, in great and disturbing detail, what terrible things the world did to Japan, but we are nowhere given any inkling of what Japan might have done to anyone else. I don't imagine Polly will be invited again.

Sympathy, even more than respect, is the attitude most required by Japan of her international partners and competitors, and one finds it solicited over and over again in the incessant reiterations of how 'small' Japan is, how 'misunderstood', how lacking in raw materials, how bent under the weight of its island complex and so on. Hiroshima, of course, provides sympathy seekers with a field day and, in a certain mood, one can stroll round the Peace Park, looking up at the Japanese flag flying from its tall pole (wondering why, if the park is dedicated to *world* peace, no other nations' flags are in evidence), itching to exclaim at the top of one's voice that feeling sorry for yourself is not the same as deploring the disasters of war, and that encouraging tourists to feel sorry for you (and foreign dignitaries to express their sorrow in public) is not the same as working for world peace.

Nonetheless, it is impossible, and no doubt immoral, to gainsay the extent and reality of the suffering visited on the people of Hiroshima, most of them civilians. Some 200,000 are thought to have died in the bombing and in the years since from related causes, chiefly radiation-induced leukemia. If, by coincidence, 200,000 is also a common estimate of the number of Chinese people, mostly civilians, who were killed by the Japanese army within one month of its entry into Nanking, let that stand recorded too, but let it not detract from the unspeakable horrors to which Hiroshima's museum, for all its want of context, provides soul-racking testimony.

When the Enola Gay, a specially equipped B29 bomber, took off from the small island of Tinian in the Marianas early on the morning of 6 August, 1945, neither pilot nor crew knew for sure their destination. The possible targets had been narrowed to four—Nagasaki, Niigata, Kokura and

Hiroshima. The final selection was made on the grounds that Hiroshima, that summer morning, was enjoying the most cloudless sky. This meant that scientific observation of the bombing could proceed with little or no impediment. In fact one reason for Hiroshima's inclusion on the short list was its topography: it is surrounded on three sides by hills, and this, it was theorized, would not only enhance the bomb's destructiveness but would allow satisfyingly accurate measurements of its destructiveness to be made.

Though it regards itself today as a beacon of peace, Hiroshima was, for much of its modern history, a city embroiled in military adventures. During the Sino-Japanese war of 1894–5, for example, the Imperial Army Headquarters was located neither in Tokyo nor in the old capital of Kyoto recently vacated by the emperor, but in Hiroshima. The Emperor Meiji, then commander-in-chief of his nation's forces, spent the duration of the war at Hiroshima Castle attending personally to its direction. The castle and practically everything within four kilometres (2.5 miles) of it were completely destroyed by the Enola Gay's four-ton payload.

Those who have sought to defend the atomic bombing have usually argued that it saved more lives than it took. If the Allies had landed in force on the beaches of mainland Japan before the signing of an article of surrender, they insist, casualties on both sides, including Japanese civilians, would have been far higher than they were at Hiroshima, and they cite the grim example of the battle for Okinawa (see page 210) to support their case. Had the Japanese succeeded in developing the atomic bomb before the United States (in fact, there was an active programme of development), the Japanese authorities would not have hesitated to sanction its use. What was wanted was an unmistakable demonstration that the war was lost for Japan in order to encourage the so-far reluctant Japanese government to steel itself for the inevitable capitulation.

These arguments have been hotly opposed. If a mere demonstration was necessary, why was it not conducted over the ocean instead of over a densely populated city where the bulk of casualties were certain to be civilian? Even assuming that the bombing of Hiroshima was unavoidable, can the same be said of Nagasaki, where, three days later, a repeat demonstration sealed the deaths of another 140,000? Besides, it has been claimed, mediation efforts were already under way and the Japanese government had itself put out peace feelers through a neutral party. All that was needed was patience and a little time.

With the benefit of hindsight, the arguments on both sides have grown more and more plausible as they have settled into the bleak realm of academic debate. Nowadays, though these historical questions remain important, they have been superseded in many minds by broader-ranging ones, such as: what constitutes a crime against humanity? If Auschwitz was such a crime, what about Dresden? If Nanking or the Bataan Death March,

Young members of an ultra-rightest group at their mecca, the Yasukuni Shrine in Tokyo, on National Foundation Day.

what about Hiroshima or the secret bombing of Cambodia? A pressing problem, for Japan at least, is the carefully selective way in which the horrors of war are taught, remembered, commemorated and deplored. Mention of 13 December 1937 (the date of the Japanese army's rapacious entry into Nanking) will elicit a look of blank incomprehension from the majority of Japanese people—indeed most will not even be able to name the year of that calamity—whereas 6 August is burned indelibly into the collective self-condoling consciousness. Perhaps that is only to be expected, but is it, therefore, less regrettable?

Personally, I think that a tour of Hiroshima's museum should be high on the itinerary of as many visitors to Japan as can be persuaded to go there. But I also think that those visitors will do well to equip themselves before they go, through a judicious amount of reading and thought, with the perspective necessary to a balanced appraisal of the things that they will see there.

Hiroshima's single most famous monument to the bombing stands just outside the Peace Park, at its northeast corner. This is the ruined **Atomic Bomb Dome**, the skeletal remains of the Industrial Promotion Hall left standing in the condition in which it was found in the aftermath. It is all the more eloquent for the prosperity and newness that gleam and bustle all around it. It has been calculated that the bomb exploded some 570 metres (1,870 feet) in the air about 160 metres (325 feet) southwest of this dome at 8.15 a.m. Similarly eloquent (much more so than the mediocre statuary) is the stone chest in the park that contains the names of all those who have died from bomb-related causes and is inscribed with these words addressed to their spirits, 'Sleep in peace: the error will not be repeated'. Most eloquent of all are the strings of tiny coloured folded paper cranes that festoon the **Children's Peace Monument**, and which are made and hung here as prayers for peace mostly by visiting school parties. Each year on 6 August a commemorative ceremony is held in the park.

In Hiroshima Prefecture

Except along its heavily industrialized coast Hiroshima is a green, rolling prefecture rising to its highest and most rugged points at its borders. Near the border with Okayama in the east lies the **Taishakukyo Gorge** and near the border with Yamaguchi in the west the **Sandankyo Gorge**, both picturesque and surrounded by attractive countryside.

But the chief tourist destination outside the prefectural capital is the small island of **Itsukushima**, also called **Miyajima** (population 3,300), which lies a short distance by ferry from the shore some 20 kilometres (12.5 miles) west of Hiroshima city, and is one of the 'Three Most Beautiful Scenic Views' in Japan (together with Amanohashidate, see page 99, and Matsushima, page 120). Miyajima means 'shrine island' and its chief attraction is the **Itsukushima Shrine**, founded at the beginning of the ninth century.

Particularly famous is the *torii* gate, erected in 1875, the largest such gate in Japan. Visitors to other shrines will have noticed how the precincts of most are entered through such a gate as this, serving to mark an imaginary boundary between the mundane and the worshipful. Here, this line has been drawn some 160 metres (325 feet) out from the shore, emphasizing the sanctity not only of the treadable land but of the untreadable sea. The gate also serves as a thought-provoking reminder that all three of Japan's 'Most Beautiful Scenic Views'—this, the sandbar and the pine-clad islands—depend for their beauty on being surrounded, like Japan itself, by water. In fact, the main shrine buildings stand on stilted platforms over the sea so that, when the tide rises, the whole edifice appears to float. In the past no births or deaths were permitted to occur on Itsukushima, both being regarded as conditions of impurity, and there is still no graveyard or crematorium there, the dead being ferried to the mainland and the returning mourners ritually purified before disembarking again on the island. Like Nara Park, Itsukushima and the precincts of its shrine are known for the deer that wander tamely about them.

The Rest of the Chugoku Region

All of Honshu west of the Kinki region is called **Chugoku** (Middle Country), not to be confused with Chubu, the Middle Region dealt with in the last chapter, nor with China, the Japanese word for which is also 'Chugoku', written, confusingly enough, with the same two ideograms. Since Chugoku consists so clearly of the western extremity of the main island, it seems oddly named; but the explanation must lie in the fact that it spans the gap between Kyushu, where the first Yamato Japanese settlements are thought to have been located, and the Nara basin, where the first Yamato state was born. The 'middle' region between these focal points must at some time have been crossed by a considerable migration.

In addition to Hiroshima, Chugoku consists of the four prefectures of **Okayama, Yamaguchi, Shimane** and **Tottori**. In some ways it is a microcosm of the entire island of Honshu. The southern coast, washed by the once-romantic Inland Sea, is heavily industrialized and the bulk of the population of the region lives in its cities. The northern coast, like the rest of the Japan Sea side of Honshu, is relatively unspoiled and still primarily agricultural. In the centre is a spinal chain of mountains which, while not so high and forbidding as those of middle or northern Honshu, are rugged enough to have deterred much large-scale settlement, and the only inland cities of major importance in the region are Tsuyama, in Okayama prefecture, and Yamaguchi city, which has the smallest population of any prefectural capital in Japan.

So far as tourism goes, the Chugoku region is relatively underdeveloped, most sightseers tending to pass straight through it on their way to Kyushu.

But its rolling countryside is very pleasant, its climate, except on the Japan Sea coast in winter, comparatively mild, and it offers the visitor several destinations of historical and cultural significance; among them the Izumo Taisha Shrine, second only in importance to the Grand Shrine of Ise, the pottery towns of Hagi and Bizen, and the lovely old willow-lined walks and buildings in the city of Kurashiki.

Okayama city (population 546,000), the capital of **Okayama** prefecture, contains the third of the 'Three Most Beautiful Landscape Gardens' of Japan, **Korakuen**, completed in 1700 (for the others see Kairakuen, page 60, and Kenrokuen, page 151). Some 9 kilometres (6 miles) west of the city stands the **Kibitsu Shrine**, whose present buildings, picturesquely sited on a hill, date from 1425. And about 26 kilometres (16 miles) east of Okayama stands the small city of **Bizen** (population 33,000), which has given its name to the famous iron-pigmented pottery produced in the neighbouring kilns.

But the chief tourist centre of the prefecture is the city of **Kurashiki** (population 410,000), which contains museums of local history, archaeology, folkcraft and pottery, and an art gallery (the **Ohara Gallery**) which boasts a world-famous collection of French Impressionist paintings. The folkcraft and archaeology museums are housed in distinctive black-and-white, feudal-era buildings that were once storehouses or granaries. (The *kura* in Kurashiki means 'storehouse'; the same *kura* as in Kamakura.) There are other old, well-preserved buildings in Kurashiki, almost all of them located, like the museums, on or near the city's pleasant willow-lined canal, the environs of which offer an unusually restful place in which to stroll and browse, or take a sightseeing tour by rickshaw. Kurashiki is also the Honshu terminus for road and rail traffic across the 37.3-kilometre (23-mile) set of bridges called collectively **Seto Ohashi** (Great Bridge of Seto, 'Seto' being a name for the Inland Sea area). The other terminus is Sakaide city in Kagawa prefecture (see page 181). The bridges, opened in April 1988, form one of three land routes connecting Honshu with Shikoku, diminishing even further the romantic associations which the now crowded and smoky Inland Sea could once lay claim to.

The chief city of **Yamaguchi** prefecture is not the small prefectural capital but the heavily industrial port of **Shimonoseki** (population 269,000) at the extreme western tip of Honshu, connected to the island of Kyushu by tunnel, bridge and ferry. When the **Kanmon Bridge** first opened in 1973 it was available to pedestrians and ranked as the largest suspension bridge in the Orient. Nowadays it is neither, pedestrians having been banned from the bridge because too many of them jumped off it, and the Korean construction company, Hyundai, having since built a longer road link between the island of Penang and Butterworth in West Malaysia. However, the water that flows

Emotion: as obligatory at a Japanese wedding feast as cold lobster thermidor.

under the Kanmon Bridge retains its deep historical significances, the chief of these being that it was here, in the Straits of **Dannoura** in 1185, that the Heike were finally defeated by the Genji, heralding the movement of real power from imperial Kyoto to the Kanto region which laid the foundation for much subsequent Japanese history. It was also here, in these narrow straits, that a pivotal event occurred in the process leading to the Meiji Restoration of 1868. Yamaguchi prefecture was the home of the warlike and xenophobic Choshu clan, who were among the prime movers in the struggle to topple the Tokugawa shogunate. Angered at what they considered to be a conciliatory attitude toward foreign powers on the part of the shogunate, the Choshu shore batteries in Shimonoseki took it upon themselves to open fire on foreign ships passing through the straits. This happened in 1863. In 1864 a combined expedition of American, Dutch, British and French warships bombarded the batteries and the Choshu forts, forcing the shogunate to intervene against the unrepentant clan, a move which was to spark an alliance between the Choshu and Satsuma fiefs that eventually brought the Tokugawas tumbling down. This small military engagement is still known in Yamaguchi as the *Bakan Senso* (Bakan War), *Bakan* (literally, 'horse barrier') being an old name for the straits and neighbouring shores.

Whether or not that name contains a clue to the migration of mounted tribes from the Korean Peninsula to Kyushu, and then eastward into Honshu, which some historians postulate must have happened in pre-Yamato times, has to remain a matter of conjecture. The city's chief shrine, too, has an equestrian reference in its name. This is the **Akama Shrine** ('Akamagaseki'—'Red-Horse Barrier'—being yet another old name for the region), and its precincts contain the small Buddhist temple of **Amidaji**, well known to readers of Lafcadio Hearn's ghost stories, or to fans of Kobayashi Masaki's 1964 film version of them, *Kwaidan,* as the temple in which the ghosts of the drowned Heike forced Hoichi, a blind lute player, to entertain them with his powerful rendition of the tale of the defeat at Dannoura. When the priest of the temple attempted to protect Hoichi from the ghosts by writing holy sutras all over his body, the ghosts wrenched his ears off, these having been left unprotected by the careless priest. In itself, Amidaji is hardly worth a visit but, for those alive to its associations, it is a sombre and moving place in which to spend an hour meditating on the tragic vision with which the Heike saga inspired subsequent generations of poets, playwrights and painters, since its tiny burial ground contains the green, crumbling graves of 14 of the drowned warriors.

There is a regular boat service between Shimonoseki and the South Korean port of Pusan.

The Japan Sea coast of Yamaguchi prefecture is mostly unspoiled and the area centering on the island of **Omishima**, which is joined by a bridge to the mainland, is especially pleasant. Just east of Omishima is the old castle town of **Hagi** (population 54,000), best known for its kilns which have been producing pottery here since the early 17th century. The castle has vanished except for its ruined foundations which, as often, have become the centrepiece of a park; but the pottery industry continues to flourish, and its delicately glazed ceremonial tea bowls are especially prized.

Inland, the principal focus of tourism in Yamaguchi is the karst plateau to the northwest of the prefectural capital, under which sprawls one of the largest stalactite caves in the world. The **Akiyoshidai** plateau is now a Quasi-National Park, and the **Shuhodo** cave features not only pools, waterfalls, streams and limestone pillars in shapes reminiscent of natural objects, but a convenient post-Palaeolithic elevator for visitors not feeling prehistoric enough to regain the surface on foot. **Yamaguchi** city (population 115,000) is a good base from which to explore the area, particularly since it contains the sleepy hot spring spa of **Yuda**. The city's most conspicuous religious edifice is the ferroconcrete Roman Catholic cathedral built in 1950 to commemorate the brief residence in 1551 of Saint Francis Xavier, the pioneering Spanish missionary who was the first to attempt the somewhat thankless task of persuading the refractory Japanese of the existence of a higher deity than those from which they claimed descent. Being themselves a chosen people, what use had they for a God who had committed the catastrophic error of fathering His son upon some other race?

Besides, Japanese people who felt themselves succumbing to Xavier's persuasions needed only to have their attention directed to the **Izumo Taisha Shrine** in neighbouring **Shimane** prefecture for sanity and refractoriness to come pouring back. Izumo is reputedly the oldest shrine in Japan; its records indicate that it was founded in mythological times, and for much of its history it was subject to the same ritual reconstruction as continues at Ise. Most of the present structures were rebuilt in the late 19th century. The Honden, or main shrine, however, dates from 1744, when it was reconstructed for the 24th time, and it is built in the oldest architectural style known in Japan, the most easily recognizable features of which are the huge crossbeams called *chigi* and the fact that the building is designed to be entered end-on rather than through one of the longer sides. The shrine is dedicated to the male deity Okuninushi no Mikoto, whose earthly palace is said to have stood on this spot, and who is credited with having instructed the Japanese in the arts of farming, fishing, medicine, and the raising of silk worms. As at Ise, the innermost and holiest part of the shrine is surrounded by a fence, and access is thereby denied. The expatriate author and journalist manqué, Lafcadio Hearn, who lived for a while in nearby Matsue city, visited the shrine and appears from what he subsequently wrote to have been under the impression that he had been permitted to enter the holy of holies at Izumo ('... I stood before the shrine of the Great Deity of Kitzuki, as the first

Occidental to whom that privilege had been accorded ...'), whereas he in fact got no further than the second storey of a gatehouse that partly overlooks the inner sanctum, and to which, in more recent times, the Soviet ambassador and the present author have also been admitted. Hearn wrote, 'This is the Shrine of the Father of a Race; this is the symbolic centre of a nation's reverence for its past.' And although, except for the sex of the progenitor, that description more properly applies to Ise, Hearn's sprinkled capitals plainly testify to the awe with which Izumo inspired him. According to local legend, thousands of gods from all over the country congregate at Izumo each October for their annual conference, which is why October is known throughout the rest of Japan as *Kannazuki* (Month Without Gods).

Matsue (population 135,000) is the prefectural capital of **Shimane**, and is closely associated in many Japanese minds with the aforementioned Hearn, storyteller and dreamer, half Irish, half Greek, with one good eye, who settled down to work there as a high school teacher in 1890. Hearn married a local woman in December of that year and clearly planned to live in Matsue for a long time; but the Japan Sea winter proved too much for his delicate health and, after little more than a year there, he moved to Kyushu, then to Kobe, where he took Japanese citizenship, changing his name to Koizumi Yakumo, and subsequently to Tokyo, where he died in 1904. That so few Westerners have ever heard of Lafcadio Hearn, let alone read his writings, is a real puzzle to most Japanese people, for whom his name is a household word, and among whom he is widely regarded as a pillar of English letters. Partly this reflects the incorrigible possessiveness of the Japanese, and partly their taste, where Western art is concerned, for tail-end Romantics and russet-tinted *fin-de-siècle* gloom. (The same taste stands revealed in the unshakable conviction that Millet's *Angelus* is one of the great monuments of Western painting and Sarasate's *Zigeunerweisen* one of the world's great pieces of violin music.) Hearn's house, still lived in, can be visited at the risk of some acerbic remarks from the irascible old owner, and a small museum dedicated to his life and work stands next door.

Matsue also has a well-preserved feudal castle, whose present donjon dates from 1642, and is a good base from which to explore **Lake Shinji**, Izumo Taisha, and the coastal area of the Shimane Peninsula around **Mihonoseki**, which is part of the **Daisen-Oki National Park**.

Sakaiminato in Tottori prefecture is the embarkation point for visits to the attractively distant **Oki** islands (population 30,000), the main port of which, **Saigo**, lies some 70 kilometres (43.5 miles) from the mainland, out in the Japan Sea. The islands are also a part of the Daisen-Oki National Park and, like Sado (see page147), have historically been places of exile. Among the highest ranking exiles to Oki were the Emperors Gotoba and Godaigo, both banished for their attempts to wrest power from the military government in Kamakura. Like Sado too, the islands are a place which Japan's economic

The torii gate at Itsukushima.

miracle has uncaringly passed by, and afford a rugged but peaceful refuge from the clang and clatter of modern urban life. A traditional form of bull-fighting, called *togyu,* is preserved there: not man against bull, but bull against bull; and the visitor fortunate enough to be present at one of the major events in the bull-fight calendar will see the animals paraded about, pampered, dressed and ranked like champion sumo wrestlers. The sport survives only in remote parts of Japan, including rural Okinawa.

The third section of the Daisen-Oki National Park stretches from **Mount Daisen** (1,711 metres or 5,613 feet) in **Tottori** prefecture south to straddle the prefectural boundary between Tottori and Okayama. Daisen is one more Something-or-Other Fuji, this time 'Hoki-Fuji', 'Hoki' being an old name for the region, and the mountain has good camping sites and ski slopes, as well as the remains of an eighth-century temple. East of Daisen lie the well-known hot-spring resorts of **Sekigane** and **Misasa**. Tottori is especially well provided with hot springs, and the coastal spas of **Kaike** and **Iwami** offer more interesting and relaxing overnight stays than do any of the larger towns. East of the rather dull prefectural capital, **Tottori** city (population 131,000), lie the **Tottori Sand Dunes** *(sakyu),* which occupy some 16 kilometres (10 miles) of the shoreline and are particularly striking since the rest of this coast, especially that part of it incorporated in the Sanin Kaigan National Park (see also page 111), which begins here and stretches east across the width of Hyogo, is noted for its pine-clad shoulders and undulating cliffs and fjords— not the sort of landscape where one would expect to find a sizeable chunk of what could easily pass for the Sahara desert. No doubt its un-Japaneseness accounts for the presence of the camels, whose services have been secured by entrepreneurs of the dunes, to supply visitors with rides and the material for exotic souvenir photographs.

The Inland Sea and Shikoku
This Side of Paradise

For the modern Japanese, the Inland Sea has become a paradigm of lost innocence. Kawabata Yasunari once remarked that, following the humiliation of defeat and surrender, Japanese authors of the postwar period had no choice but to write elegies; and a significant number of those elegies—in book and on film—have focussed on the islands of the Inland Sea. How much pastoral 'innocence' the area possessed in prewar times depends on the rosiness of the spectacles through which you view it. During the feudal period the Inland Sea islands were notorious as the haunts of pirates. Like most rural areas, the islands suffered from chronic poverty and crippling disease and these drawbacks to country life were magnified by the extra isolation with which the surrounding sea had burdened them. With the beginnings of industrialization the great ports along the southern coast of the Chugoku region—Tokuyama, Iwakuni, Hiroshima, Kure, Fukuyama and so on, none of which was opened to foreign trade in the way that Yokohama and Kobe were—launched themselves on a furious round of military and mercantile shipbuilding and related activities that continued ever clangier and smokier until August 1945, when they were silenced long enough for the elegies to begin.

The attractions of the Inland Sea islands to the urban Japanese imagination are complex. At one level, they simply partake in the same pastoral Never-Never-Land fiction that has shed its fairy light on Tohoku and transformed *kokeshi* into collectable souvenirs (see page 120). At a deeper level, because the sea is *inland* it belongs safely and exclusively to Japan in a way that the surrounding seas do not. All other seas are chasms, and to cross them, even from one Japanese island to another, is to be plucked up by the roots.

There are two ways of looking at islands; islands are either fortresses or dungeons. Throughout most of their history, the British took the fortress view of their country and regarded the encompassing sea both as a moat defensive and as a royal road to wealth and empire. But the Japanese have usually taken the dungeon view, hence the repeated stress on their being burdened with an island complex. Their consensus has always been that the surrounding sea weakens, not strengthens them, and it was never regarded as a royal road but as a discouraging obstacle to the full enjoyment of civilization and power. The Japanese were not great seagoers as the British were, and to them the sea was an adversary, never an ally.

The Inland Sea was the one glorious exception. By surrounding it, they tamed it and made it theirs. Thus its islands, far more than the offshore islands of exile like Sado and Oki, are protected microcosms of the whole, and the Inland Sea, contained and womblike, is the seminal fluid by which they live. It is as though the entire area were the model for a wholly imaginary universe in which Japan is perfectly self-contained, self-bounded and self-made.

The neutral observer might be forgiven for concluding that such spoliation as this paradise has suffered in modern times is due not so much to defeat and foreign occupation as to the greed of home-grown industrialists who have rarely hesitated to sacrifice fairyland on the altar of progress. One of the lessons of history, surely, is that innocence is less often lost than squandered. It is not so much the islands that have suffered as the seminal fluid that surrounds them. The red tides that wash through it—the result of the effluvia pumped into it from Osaka Bay and all points west—the massed shipping that clogs it, the bridges that span it, the smog that shrouds it, the oil spilled into it... Kawabata was right: we live in a time of elegies, and the Inland Sea provides the aptest of subjects.

But for all that, if the weather is fine and the wind is in the right direction (i.e. towards, not from, Osaka Bay) the islands of the Inland Sea can still afford a glimpse or two of what has to pass in our tarnished century for something like paradise. As an older expatriate writer on Japan once remarked to me in a tone of friendly chastisement: it is the difference between seeing that the cup is still half full and seeing only that it is half empty.

The Inland Sea (**Setonaikai**) is that body of water sandwiched between Honshu in the north and Shikoku in the south; and the 750 or so inhabited islands that dot it are variously administered by six prefectures—Hyogo, Okayama, Kagawa, Ehime, Hiroshima and Yamaguchi—but for once it seems sensible to ignore the prefectural boundaries and to treat the area of the Inland Sea as an indivisible unit. In 1934 the area was designated the **Setonaikai National Park**.

Two of the islands have already been described: Awajishima, the largest (see page 111), and Itsukushima, the most visited (see page 160). The next largest and most visited is **Shodoshima** (population 41,000), at the centre of which stand the picturesque **Kankakei** peaks and gorge, the peaks rising to 816 metres (2,677 feet). But Shodoshima's chief claim on the visitor's attention is its round of 88 pilgrim sites, associated with the prolific ninth-century temple-builder, Kobo Daishi (the posthumous name for Kukai), and revered in a minor way by the Shingon sect which he founded. Kobo Daishi may have visited Shodoshima round about 808–9, although, quite uncharacteristically, he seems not to have founded any temples there. Most of the present pilgrim sites—temples, grottoes and small monuments—were established by Shingon priests in 1686 in imitation of the 88 temples on neighbouring Shikoku, which Kobo Daishi definitely did either visit or found and which form today the best known and most devoutly followed pilgrim's

route in Japan (see page 174). Whether the Shingon priests of 1686 were motivated chiefly by piety or by an early revelation of the coming possibilities of the tourist industry is a matter for conjecture. But the unpretentious sites of Shodoshima—many in remote, out of the way corners of the island—provide the leisurely visitor with an ideal excuse for wandering off the beaten track, particularly if he can spare the four or five days needed to complete the entire circuit.

Omishima (population 12,000) is famous for its **Oyamazumi Shrine**, whose present Honden dates from 1378 and which is a repository for a collection of ancient and priceless suits of armour, comprising about 80 percent of all such suits that have been designated national treasures and which formerly belonged to, among other notables, Minamoto no Yoshitsune. On neighbouring **Ikuchijima** (population 13,000) stands a religious complex of another sort, **Kosanji** Temple, completed in 1946 by a devout island businessman-turned-Buddhist priest called Kanemoto Kozo in memory of his deceased mother. Mr Kanemoto was clearly not short of a few quid and had seen and been impressed by the Toshogu Shrine at Nikko. (In fact, his island temple is known locally as 'the Nikko of the West', and contains a full-colour replica of the Toshogu's famous gate, as well as smaller-scale replicas of about half a dozen other revered edifices from around the nation.) He can't have seen Disneyland because it didn't yet exist, although Tiger Balm Gardens, the other family monument that leaps to mind as an aesthetic progenitor, had been around since 1931. But Mr Kanemoto had been a sailor and may, therefore, have brought back to his treasured Inland Sea impressions of certain Chinese temples such as Kek Lok Si in Penang, which looks as though it has been constructed out of left-over bathroom tiles. So far as one can detect, Mr Kanemoto incorporated no left-over bathroom tiles into the construction of his deceased mother's temple, contenting himself for the most part with plywood, plaster and bright gloss paint, but one is left in no doubt that he certainly would have incorporated bathroom tiles if he had had any to spare.

There are scores of other islands in the Inland Sea less visited and worth visiting, those that lack glittery religious kitsch being generally the more rewarding. Perhaps the best way of seeing the Inland Sea and its islands is to take long ferry rides between well-separated destinations (like Osaka or Kobe in the east and Matsuyama or Beppu in the west, broken up by stops at, say, Takamatsu and Imabari to avoid too much nighttime travel). The disadvantage of this plan is that the large ferries call only at major ports and not at the smaller islands, but such a trip is leisurely enough for the visitor to take ample note of the remoter villages and harbours the ferries pass, and to ascertain from the pursers or from a travel agent how best these may be reached during the stages of an even more leisurely return.

An Unbridgeable Remoteness?

As Nagasaki's bomb is the forgotten bomb compared with Hiroshima's, so Shikoku, the smallest of Japan's four main islands is, as far as tourism is concerned, the forgotten island. Hokkaido and Okinawa are far more distant from Honshu's urban centres and in many important ways quite unlike the rest of the country, but those are precisely the reasons why the tourist industry has been keen to open them up. Because their remoteness from Tokyo in flying time means a greater revenue for the airlines that serve them, they have been made the subjects of campaigns and package tours in a way that Shikoku never has and probably never will. Opinion is divided on the likely effect of the three sets of bridges that have just been completed, or are nearing completion, and which join Shikoku to Honshu. Some argue, as they did on behalf of the Tohoku Shinkansen, that the bridges will bring more tourism to the island and facilitate the siting of new industries there. Others argue, as they did against the Tohoku Shinkansen, that the bridges will merely accelerate the already steady migration of rural people, particularly young families, to the sprawling industrial conurbations of Osaka-Kobe, Nagoya and Tokyo-Yokohama, where 46 percent of the total population of Japan now lives.

Whatever the case, most of Shikoku is likely to remain for the foreseeable future an out-of-the-way destination with an out-of-the-way destination's rewards. The main urban centres, including all four of the island's prefectural capitals, are situated on or very near the coast. The northern coast, washed by the Inland Sea, is the most industrially developed part of the island. The southern coast is mainly unspoiled and the stretch between Cape Ashizuri and Uwajima, with its coral formations and subtropical vegetation, is now a National Park. Inland, Shikoku is extremely rugged, there being no major towns or extensive highways and limited access by rail. The areas around the island's two highest peaks, Mounts Tsurugi in the east and Ishizuchi in the west, are virtual wildernesses.

The most conspicuous visitors to Shikoku are devout, wealthy or leisured members of the Shingon sect of Buddhism following the island's famous pilgrims' route round the 88 temples built by, or otherwise associated with, the sect's founder, Kobo Daishi. Dressed all in white and equipped with identical sets of rosary beads and walking staffs, they are unmistakable. In feudal times the route (which extends over some 1,200 kilometres or 740 miles, and usually occupies between three and four months if undertaken entirely on foot) was especially popular with beggars and outcasts such as those suffering from leprosy and other shunned diseases. Nowadays it is popular with pensioners who make the round of the temples in air-conditioned buses equipped with a contraption like an umbrella stand just inside the automatic door to contain their pilgrims' staffs. These they recover solemnly when filing off the bus at the gate of each temple, since one can no more claim to be a pilgrim without a staff than one can claim to be an alpinist without a tartan shirt and a pair of herringbone knickerbockers.

It is also essential (since a part of the ritual) that the temples be visited in the correct order. Of the four prefectures in Shikoku, Tokushima contains temples 1–23, Kochi temples 24–39, Ehime temples 40–65 and Kagawa temples 66–88.

The prefectural capital of **Tokushima** is **Tokushima** city (population 249,000), nationally famous as the home of the **Awa Odori**, a form of Bon dance which, instead of being performed in circles round a central tower as most Bon dances are, is a true processional, and during the four nights of 12–15 August occupies long cordoned-off stretches of the city's main roads and some of its back alleys. 'Awa' is the old name for this part of Shikoku and the dance originated as a celebration of the completion of Tokushima castle in 1586. Nowadays it offers one more glaring example of how the nature and purpose of large-city Bon festivals have altered in postwar times from reaffirmation of local identity to floodlit, carefully orchestrated spectacle with amplified commentaries and busloads of paying spectators. Much of the dancing is performed competitively in front of grandstands erected for the purpose, to which an admission fee is charged. There are reduced rates for dead ancestors.

Little remains of the castle, but such as does remain has been transformed into an amusement park and zoological garden. Otherwise the city's chief attractions cluster round **Otaki Hill**, where there is a cable car, a prefectural museum, a **Peace Memorial Pagoda**, erected in 1958 and supposed to contain a small quantity of the Buddha's ashes, and several monuments commemorating the residence in the city of Wenceslau de Moraes, a Portuguese diplomat, for a time vice-consul in Osaka, who spent some 30 years in Japan, the last 14 of them in Tokushima. Moraes is much less celebrated than his contemporary Japanophile and expatriate, Lafcadio Hearn (see page 167), although he too wrote a great deal about his adopted country, married a local woman, and made a lot more headway with the language than Hearn did.

The little city of **Naruto** (population 63,000), some 15 kilometres (9.25 miles) north of Tokushima and the terminus for the set of bridges that now links Shikoku to Honshu via Awajishima (see page 111), has given its name to the narrow strait on which it stands and to the famous whirlpools created by the fast currents and resulting differences in water level that characterize the straits. The whirlpools can often be viewed from the ferries that ply between Awajishima and Shikoku or from the sightseeing boats that exist for the purpose of viewing them.

Hanami: *cherry-blossom viewing in Tokyo. The yellow crates and aluminium cans contain beer; the blue-labelled jars contain sake.*

Mount Tsurugi (1,955 metres or 6,414 feet), in the rugged inland reaches of the prefecture, is the centre of a Quasi-National Park.

The prefectural capital of **Kochi** is **Kochi** city (population 301,000), the pleasantest, most hospitable and most relaxed of Shikoku's prefectural capitals, and the most interesting on account of certain unique traditions, among which dog fighting and the breeding of spectacularly long-tailed cocks are the best-known. Dog fighting (*token*) is still a recognized sport in the prefecture and, since most forms of gambling are officially outlawed in Japan, is a magnet for the activities of the tough *yakuza* gangs for which Kochi is a traditional haven. Demonstrations of dog fighting can be seen several times daily in the amusement area at **Katsurahama** beach, just south of the city. The city itself has an elegant castle, originally constructed in 1603 and partly rebuilt in 1748. But its traditional heart, like the heart of old Edo, was a bridge—the nowadays unprepossessing **Harimayabashi** across which trams clang, but which retains a certain romantic association through the nationwide popularity of Kochi's most famous folk song. The song tells the story of a love-struck Buddhist priest who bought his love an expensive ornamental hairpin in one of the shops near the bridge that specialized in items for the elegant and warmly hospitable women of the city (something else for which Kochi has a well-deserved and enduring reputation). The purchase caused a scandal, the lovers were arrested, arraigned on charges of public immorality, banished from the city in opposite directions, and were apparently never reunited. Today, in Kochi's souvenir shops, you can buy small wooden dolls representing the lovers: the priest looking decidedly smug as he clasps the hairpin to his bosom, standing beside his mistress who is dressed, mysteriously enough, in the habit of a Buddhist nun, so prompting the question to what possible use she could have put a hairpin.

Kochi prefecture was in feudal times the province of Tosa, whose leaders, together with those of Satsuma (nowadays Kagoshima, see page 202) and Choshu (nowadays Yamaguchi, see page 166), were prominent in the struggle that led to the downfall of the Tokugawa shogunate and the restoration of power to the Emperor Meiji. The best known Tosa hero was Sakamoto Ryoma, who was assassinated at the age of 31, one year before the restoration was carried through, and to whom thus accrues all the melancholy adulation due a man who exerted himself in a cause he was never to see succeed—a favourite qualification for heroism among the Japanese. There is a statue of Ryoma looking suitably doomed-but-determined at Katsurahama beach.

The most prominent landmarks on the Kochi coast are its two sharp capes, **Muroto** in the east and **Ashizuri** in the west. Muroto is the unhappy recipient of the brunt of frequent fierce storms and is famous for its battered lighthouse. Ashizuri is less famous for its lighthouse than for its reputation as

(Preceding page) A 'love hotel' near Hakone. The rooms, equipped and decorated to satisfy a variety of jaded tastes, are rented by the hour.

a favoured spot for romantically-motivated suicides. The local chapter of the Salvation Army has placed at strategic points on top of the cliffs noticeboards bearing the simple message, *Chotto Matte Kudasai* (Please Wait a Moment). At the neck of the promontory that terminates in Cape Ashizuri is the small city of **Tosa-Shimizu** (population 24,000), which likes to pride itself on possessing a certain cosmopolitanism owing to the fact that it was the birthplace of Nakahama ('John') Manjiro who, as a result of having been shipwrecked and rescued by an American whaling ship, became in 1842 the first Japanese person to visit the United States, where he lived for almost a decade. When the American Commodore Matthew C. Perry arrived in Japan in 1853 to demand the opening of its ports to foreign vessels (an event that, quite as much as the doings of the Tosa, Satsuma and Choshu clans, signified the end of Tokugawa isolation and, eventually, of Tokugawa rule), John Manjiro was drummed into service as Perry's interpreter, a role that has ensured him a dubious—or at least ambiguous—reputation, so far as Japanese posterity is concerned.

The coast to the northwest of Tosa-Shimizu, now the **Ashizuri-Uwakai National Park** is deservedly famous for its picturesque bays and rocky cliffs that poke through the rich layer of subtropical vegetation. Scuba divers in particular favour the area, but the unusually warm climate of Kochi prefecture makes the beaches and many small inlets of this coast favourite destinations for ordinary bathers too. Kochi is so warm, and its rainfall so heavy, that farmers in some parts of the prefecture are able to harvest rice twice a year.

The capital of **Ehime** prefecture is **Matsuyama** (population 402,000), the largest city on the island, whose petrochemical plants and coastal industrial zone spread a gloomy pall about it. The gloom is partly relieved by the fact that Shikoku's best-known hot-spring resort, **Dogo**, lies in the city's northern suburbs. Matsuyama is also famous for its very well-preserved castle, dating from 1603.

Like Mount Tsurugi in Tokushima prefecture, **Mount Ishizuchi** (1,981 metres or 6,500 feet) is the centre of a Quasi-National park, most easily reached from Matsuyama. Ishizuchi is the highest peak in Shikoku and (it comes as something of a surprise to learn since the mountains of Kyushu are far more famous) the highest in the whole of western Japan. Just south of the peak lies the **Omogokeikyo Gorge**, with its waterfalls, cliffs and unspoiled woods.

Like Kochi, Ehime has its share of odd animal-related traditions, such as cormorant fishing (*ukai*) in the city of **Ozu** (population 39,000) and bull fighting (*togyu*) in the city of **Uwajima** (population 72,000), though these practices survive more famously elsewhere (see pages 142 and 168). Both these cities have small but notable architectural monuments: Uwajima a castle dating from 1665, Ozu an elegant feudal-era cottage with garden and teahouse called **Garyusanso** (Villa of the Hill of the Prostrate Dragon), though the cities are eclipsed in this department too by the little town of **Uchiko**, some 15 kilometres (9 miles) northeast of Ozu, which has a street, **Yokaichi**, in which is preserved an entire row of fine houses and shops from the feudal and early modern periods. Uchiko is a quiet little town, completely off the tourist route. In fact, outside of Matsuyama, Ehime prefecture as a whole is not much frequented by sightseers, though its warm climate and strong agricultural base (it is one of Japan's chief fruit-growing areas, famous for its mandarin oranges) make it a pleasant enough choice for visitors in search of rural relaxations.

Kagawa is the smallest of Shikoku's four prefectures (and the second smallest in all Japan), but its location at the southern boundary of the narrowest stretch of the Inland Sea and in the corner of Shikoku closest to the great industrial sprawl of southern Kansai has given it an economic and commercial stature that belies its size. The prefectural capital, **Takamatsu** (population 317,000) was, before the bridges were constructed, the main gateway to the island and the first Shikoku port to feature a regular ferry connection with Honshu. It remains to be seen how the bridges and the faster-growing industries of Matsuyama will affect the city's commercial standing.

As were all the other prefectural capitals of Shikoku, Takamatsu was a castle town, though little remains of the castle but its site, now a city park. Though not one of the 'Three Most Beautiful Landscape Gardens' of Japan, **Ritsurin** garden is the city's chief sightseeing attraction. Like the famous trio, it was originally laid out as the grounds of a private villa belonging to the lords of the region, in this case the Matsudairas (who, like the Matsudairas of Aizu, were relatives and strong supporters of the Tokugawa shoguns). **Yashima**, on the coast just beyond the eastern suburbs of the city, was the site of several battles in the long struggle between the Genji and Heike clans, the last of which immediately preceded the final downfall of the Heike at Dannoura in 1185 (see page 165).

Outside Takamatsu, the chief magnet for visitors to Kagawa prefecture is the **Kotohiragu Shrine**, sometimes called the **Kompira Shrine**, founded in the early 11th century. Its precincts and chief buildings are laid out on the steeply sloping side of Mount Zozu and connected by long flights of stone steps. Five kilometres to the north stands **Zentsuji**, the 77th of the 88 temples on Kobo Daishi's pilgrims' route, but particularly venerated since it both marks the place where Kobo Daishi was born and acts as the headquarters of the Shingon sect which he founded. On the coast north of Zentsuji lies the city of **Sakaide** (population 66,000), the Shikoku terminus for one of the three sets of bridges that join the island to Honshu.

Kyushu

Pioneers and Persecutors

Visitors with limited time to spare who are anxious to get away from Honshu at least once during their stay in Japan, but who are not especially attracted by the extreme rurality of, say, Sado or Oki or the interior of Shikoku, are probably best off making for Kyushu, the southernmost and third largest of Japan's four main islands. Kyushu is a favoured destination among Japanese travellers for pleasure, too. The air route between Tokyo and Fukuoka, the capital of the island's richest and most developed prefecture, is the second busiest in the country (after Tokyo–Osaka). In 1975 the Shinkansen bullet train, which had previously run only between Tokyo and Osaka, and then (after 1972) between Tokyo and Okayama, was extended to reach Hakata (in Fukuoka city), and now links Tokyo with Kyushu in six hours. Japan's most famous hot-spring resort, its most spectacularly active volcanoes, one of the largest caldera craters on earth, a subtropical coastline with many unspoiled stretches, four National Parks, totally empty hills and woodland, and a modern tendency to site 'clean' industries rather than pollution-prone heavy industries on the island are among Kyushu's attractions.

It is likely that the first prehistoric settlements founded by the ancestors of the Yamato tribes were situated in Kyushu. Where these ancestors came from remains a matter for conjecture. In the remote past northern Kyushu was linked with the Korean peninsula by a land bridge, facilitating the movement of flora and fauna from the continent into the archipelago, and the narrow straits that succeeded this bridge may well have been crossed in later centuries by human migrants from as far away as Mongolia. If, as is also probable, some of the tribes who eventually settled down to become Japanese made their way, via the Ryukyu islands, from the Malay archipelago and the South Seas, then Kyushu was almost certainly their first Japanese port of call. Some of the earliest creation myths and myths dealing with the mischievous behaviour of the founding gods are associated with locations in central Kyushu, and the associations are perpetuated there by the continuing performance of Kagura and other dances at shrines and local festivals.

In more recent times, Kyushu was the first port of call of Saint Francis Xavier and the Christian evangelists who followed him in the 16th and early 17th centuries, the first Westerners to reach and settle in Japan. Certain of the lords of Kyushu were happy to embrace the Christian faith because the inducements to conversion included such useful gifts as arquebuses. Eventually, the Christians were blamed, as in Nero's Rome, for stirring up troubles against the authorities, with the result that Christianity was banned and its converts and preachers cruelly persecuted throughout the Edo period, the most famous of these persecutions taking place in Kyushu.

However, Christianity survived underground and, when the persecutions ceased at the time of the Meiji Restoration, a surprising number of active Christian cells resurfaced, particularly in and around Nagasaki, where they had been most viciously suppressed. Today, Kyushu has a higher proportion of practising Christians than any other part of Japan, though still not significantly high for a country evangelized since the mid-1500s.

Throughout the period of enforced seclusion under the Tokugawas, Kyushu contained the only foreign settlement permitted in Japan, the tiny Dutch and Chinese trading post at Nagasaki, through which, seclusion notwithstanding, a surprisingly active two-way trade was carried on. With the beginning of the modern age, northern Kyushu's extensive coal fields came in for heavy exploitation. Immediately prior to and during the Second World War these areas saw a large influx of forced labour from Korea, then a Japanese possession, mainly to work the mines. Mining continued just as actively during the hectic struggle to reestablish a viable industrial base following defeat and the severe economic depression of the immediate postwar period. The worst mining disaster in Japanese history occurred at Mitsui's Miike mine, straddling the border between Fukuoka and Kumamoto, in 1963 when an explosion killed 458 people. The case for compensating the victims' families is still dragging wearily through the Japanese courts. And in the 1950s and '60s the city of Minamata on the coast of Kumamoto prefecture became a focus of attention throughout the industrialized world as an example of the terrible price to be paid in human terms for the discharge of poisonous industrial wastes into the environment.

But if, during the decades that preceded and immediately followed the last war, Kyushu provided grim examples of the things that can go badly wrong when industrialization proceeds at too frantic a pace, it has more often provided models that the rest of the country has fallen over itself to adopt. The encouragement of foreign trade and the acceptance of artefacts, ideas and residents from the West were pioneered in Kyushu. One forward-looking Kyushu lord in the mid-19th century was almost single-handedly responsible for the introduction into Japan of Morse code and the subsequent development of telegraphy, the building of Japan's first steam-powered warship, the setting up of the first gas lamps in Japan, the establishment of Japan's first Western-style textile looms, glass and munitions factories, and he still found time to design *Hinomaru,* which remains Japan's national flag. That this energetic lord's clan was at the forefront of the movement to topple the Tokugawa shogunate and the floundering feudal system of which it was the pinnacle is hardly surprising. It is a move entirely in keeping with Kyushu's pioneering tradition.

Kyushu is home to about 12 percent of the total Japanese population. The interior is ruggedly mountainous, but more accessible than that of Shikoku owing to the tourist industry's success in placing some of the island's more famous landmarks—Mounts Aso and Kirishima, for example—high on many people's lists of attractive leisure destinations. Both of those peaks are the centres of their own National Parks, while two more National Parks have been created to highlight the splendours of Kyushu's heavily indented west coast and the islands that lie offshore.

In general, the further south you go in Kyushu the more dependent life becomes on the traditional industries of agriculture and fishing. The seven prefectures that make up the island are **Fukuoka, Saga, Oita, Nagasaki, Kumamoto, Miyazaki** and **Kagoshima**. The climate of Kyushu is warm in summer and generally mild in winter, although Fukuoka, because it faces the Japan Sea whose bleakness still clings to it in these lower latitudes, has its share of snowfall and winter gales. Southern Kyushu lies bang in the path of many of the summer and autumn typhoons that blow up through the South China Sea, making flooding and landslides frequent hazards.

The capital of **Fukuoka** prefecture is **Fukuoka** city (population 1.1 million), the chief commercial and administrative centre for the entire island. Confusion arises in the minds of some visitors over the fact that the city's railway terminus is not called Fukuoka, but **Hakata**, while the airport, a ten-minute drive away, is not called Hakata but Fukuoka. Hakata is a mere ward in the modern city, but it was the name of the ancient port out of which the modern city developed and from which envoys travelled to China as far back as the seventh century. The name Fukuoka came into existence when the castle was built in 1601 and was applied to the area around the castle which was mainly settled by the warrior class. Hakata became the merchants' and artisans' quarter, and the name of the city's famous May festival is a reminder of the association between Hakata and trade. The **Hakata Dontaku**, like Tokyo's Sanja and Osaka's Tenjin festivals, was in origin a merchants' celebration. 'Dontaku' is said to derive from the Dutch word 'Zondag', meaning Sunday and thus, by extension, 'holiday'. The main event of the festival (3–4 May, the height of Golden Week) is a long procession of groups of dancing women who accompany their dance by tapping out the rhythm with wooden rice scoops.

Nothing remains of the castle but its ruined outer walls, now incorporated as usual into a park. The city's best-known craft is the manufacture of extremely lifelike painted clay dolls called *Hakata ningyo* (*ningyo* means doll), some of which fetch astronomically high prices. The best often depict women in gorgeously painted kimonos or actors from the Kabuki theatre, but the most popular dolls among souvenir buyers represent the rotund, grim-faced figure of a samurai called Mori Tahei, standing legs astride, a huge sake bowl in one hand and an ornate spear in the other. The Lord of Hiroshima bet the Lord of Fukuoka that none of his retainers could quaff the contents of this mammoth bowl in one swallow. Mori accepted the challenge,

(Preceding page) Aru Pachiino *as* Sukaafueisu *('Scarface'), a film about the* baiorensu *(violence) of the* Amerikan Doriimu.

succeeded famously, and received the spear as a prize. The event is also commemorated in Fukuoka's best-known folk song, *Kuroda Bushi,* which has become a favourite at weddings and other occasions where the mood calls for Mori-style quaffing. Quaffing in Fukuoka tends to centre on the district called **Nakazu**, and an especially pleasant feature is the open-air stalls (*yatai*) which serve simple food and drink throughout the year. They operate only at night and are mostly to be found within sight of the bridges that link Nakazu to both banks of the river surrounding it and turning this famous pleasure spot into an island.

In the northeast corner of Fukuoka prefecture lies the sprawling city of **Kita Kyushu**, literally 'North Kyushu' (population 1.1 million), concocted by bureaucrats in 1963 out of five small neighbouring industrial cities, including **Moji**, the largest international port in Kyushu, **Kokura**, one of the proposed targets of the first atomic bomb, and **Yawata**, the home of Japan's biggest steel works. The distinction of being the largest city in Kyushu see-saws back and forth between Fukuoka and Kita Kyushu as their population figures fluctuate. Kita Kyushu is joined to Shimonoseki in Honshu by means of the Kanmon Bridge (see page 163) and the Kanmon rail and pedestrian tunnels. Largest or not, the city has little to offer the non-industrial sightseer.

In the southeast of the prefecture, near the border with Oita, stands the village of **Koishiwara**, famous as a centre for the production of folk pottery and comparable, in this regard, with Mashiko in Tochigi prefecture (see page 58). Virtually the whole village is given over to the production of pots and, although a waterwheel is preserved as a tourist attraction, most of the clay is now electrically ground, the glazes chemical, and kilns oil- or gas-fired.

Saga is a mainly rice-producing prefecture and its capital, **Saga** city (population 164,000) is one of the smallest and least industrialized prefectural capitals in Japan. The two most popular destinations for visitors to the prefecture are the city of **Karatsu** (population 78,000) and the little town of **Arita** (population 15,000), both famous for their ceramics. Like the well-known street leading to Kiyomizudera in Kyoto (see page 86), Karatsu was settled by Korean potters brought back to Japan following the military campaigns in Korea during the late 16th century, and it owes its success as a pottery centre to the skills they preserved and passed on. Arita also owes its fame to a naturalized Korean potter who built a kiln there in the early 17th century. The best Karatsu ware is of an unpretentious, single-glaze type highly favoured for tea ceremony bowls. Arita ware stands at the extreme opposite end of the ceramic spectrum, being a colourful enamelled porcelain similar to Kutani ware (see page 154), which is essentially a copy of it.

The principal tourist destination in **Oita** prefecture is the coastal city of

Beppu (population 136,000), Japan's chief mecca for hot-spring enthusiasts. Beppu is the most famous hot-spring resort in the country and has suffered a consequent degree of commercial spoliation. The city boasts eight different spas, containing together more than 3,000 springs, each known for its particular curative properties. The spas vary widely in character so that, although the city as a whole has been vigorously developed, it is still possible for the connoisseur or the visitor with sufficient time and energy to locate odd corners and traditional-style inns where development has been kept within acceptable bounds. The main tourist attractions are the *jigoku* (hells), the points where thermal water issues in bubbling milky-white or muddy-brown fountains from the ground at temperatures that reach boiling point. Mud and sand baths are available in addition to the usual facilities, and the enervating pastime of wending one's way from hell to purgatory to hell again with frequent stops at the city's multitudinous bars is enjoyed by an estimated 12 million enthusiasts annually.

Some 15 kilometres (9.5 miles) east of Beppu is the prefectural capital, **Oita** city (population 360,000), a pleasant enough place but with little to detain the sightseer. In the north of the prefecture stands the small city of **Usa** (population 52,000), the site of the **Usa Hachiman** shrine, the headquarters of a branch of Shinto to which belong the estimated 25,000 or so Hachiman shrines scattered throughout Japan. Hachiman is a protective deity variously identified as the god of war, as a bodhisattva whose special duty is the guardianship of Todaiji temple in Nara, and as the spirit of the legendary Emperor Ojin. His warlike aspect caused him to be adopted as the family deity of the Minamoto or Genji clan, but his shrines are more usually associated with such peaceful pursuits as the protection of small fishing harbours. Founded in 571, the Usa Hachiman shrine was the first to be dedicated to this deity and is accorded only slightly less reverence than is Izumo Taisha (see page 166).

Besides Beppu, Oita prefecture is comparatively rich in hot springs. At **Yufuin** spa, in the shadow of **Mount Yufu** (at 1,584 metres or 5,197 feet, yet another Something-or-Other Fuji, this time 'Bungo-Fuji', 'Bungo' being the old name for the province), an annual week-long film festival is held each summer (the dates vary) with showings of brand new, classic and obscure pieces from the Japanese cinematic repertoire. The festival is usually attended by celebrities from the film world who, instead of preening themselves for the cameras as at better known festivals, give quasi-intelligent talks and seminars for the benefit of the conspicuously young film buffs who attend.

In much of Kyushu, particularly the southern half, the traditional tipple is not sake but *shochu,* a clear, rather bitter-tasting liquor, sometimes compared to vodka, distilled from whatever raw material is cheapest and most conveniently to hand, the commonest being sweet potatoes, barley, millet and sugarcane. The millet and sugarcane varieties, found mainly in Okinawa and

Lavatories, Baths and Other Headaches

Guidebooks to European countries tend to assume that Asian travellers possess sufficient common sense and adaptability not to be thrown into confusion by having to lift a Western-style lavatory seat or keep their shoes on in a house. Guidebooks to Asian countries for Western travellers tend to assume the opposite—that their readers are all potential oafs and dimwits—so thay go out of their way to supply long lists of cultural do's and don'ts. Authors of guides to Thailand, for example, warn readers that they must not pat Thais on the head since the consequences could be unpleasant. They do not seem to have pondered the possible consequences to an Asian tourist in Great Britain of going about patting, say, Scotsmen on the head.

George Bernard Shaw refused to take his shoes off when visiting Japanese houses. The consequences, presumably, were that he made few friends, was hardly ever invited out, and was considered an insufferable boor. Shoes are removed in the entrance hall (*genkan*) of a Japanese house or inn and the host or inn staff supplies the guest with slippers for use indoors. But even slippers are not normally worn when walking on *tatami* (the straw covering of Japanese-style floors, more like large inlaid tiles than mats), nor are these indoor slippers worn in lavatories, where a different pair of slippers or clogs is customarily provided.

Western-style lavatories are nowadays very common in Japan, but they have not supplanted the traditional Japanese lavatory which is much lower, requiring the user to squat, not sit. This is healthy, since the user's behind does not touch any lavatory surface and remains inelegantly poised in the air. It is also unhealthy since the traditional lavatory has a cess pit, not a flush, so the user's nasal membranes can suffer unlooked for assaults. It is also a considerable hardship for the elderly, heavily pregnant or infirm.

The main Western complaint about the lavatories found in Japanese restaurants is that they are shared by both sexes. This has never seemed an inconvenience to me; all that is required is a knock on the door before entering. Much more inconvenient is the complete absence of hand towels. You are presumably expected to wipe your hands on your hair (unless, of course, you are Thai).

Do not wash or shampoo yourself in a Japanese bath. Wash before you get into the bath, either under a shower or by emptying small plastic buckets (supplied) of water over your body. Once in the tub, you are obliged to do nothing except sit there and enjoy the heat. Since no soap is ever brought into a tub, and since the bather is (in theory) scrubbed before he gets in, the water remains clean enough to be shared by whole families or even whole neighbourhoods—though water at public baths (*sento*) is constantly replenished from running taps. If you are bathing communally, do not force Japanese people's heads under the water since the consequences could be unpleasant. Do not do this to Scotsmen either.

the Amami islands, are called *awamori* and are far and away the most potent, some types having an alcohol content as high as 80 percent proof. The potato variety (*imo-jochu*), widely drunk in and around Kagoshima, is well known for its strong smell and long lurking presence the morning after. Both these forms are traditionally favoured by manual labourers and have never been widely popular outside their immediate localities. But in recent years the mildest form of shochu, made from barley or other grain (*mugi*), has become fashionable with the young as a base for various mixed drinks (such as shochu and lemon or shochu and soda) and popular among office workers who drink it diluted with either hot water or water and ice, much as they drink whisky. For a while, in the early 1980s, shochu looked set to eclipse sake in nationwide popularity and to replace whisky as the bottled drink most commonly 'kept' by regular customers in the bars they frequent (the 'bottle keep' system is explained on page 231). The height of the shochu boom seems now to have passed, but the mild-tasting and almost completely odourless grain shochu produced in Oita and Miyazaki prefectures remains a favourite among the diehards.

The city of **Nagasaki** (population 447,000), the capital of **Nagasaki** prefecture, was the target of the world's second atomic bomb attack at 11.02 a.m. on 9 August 1945, when almost the entire city was destroyed and an estimated 140,000 people killed outright or doomed to die of bomb-related causes in the decades that followed. The Nagasaki bomb was larger and slightly heavier than the bomb dropped on Hiroshima three days earlier, and packed a much greater explosive power (the equivalent of 22 kilotons of TNT as opposed to 13), though the destructive effect was not so great as at Hiroshima owing to Nagasaki's irregular and hilly topography. Like Hiroshima, Nagasaki was chosen as a target because it was a major naval base and shipbuilding centre. In fact, at the time of the bombing, the Nagasaki shipyards were the largest privately-owned shipyards in Japan. Like Hiroshima, the city has also commemorated the bombing by building a Peace Park near the hypocentre and decorating it with municipally inspired statuary. As at Hiroshima too, a single building stands as an eloquent reminder of the tragedy. At Hiroshima the building is the ruined Atomic Dome (see page 160) and at Nagasaki the **Urakami Catholic Cathedral**, with its grimly ironic symbolism: Christian target of a Christian bomb. The Atomic Dome has been left, conspicuously and accusingly, in its gutted state, while the cathedral, entirely destroyed in the bombing (before which it was the largest Christian church in the Far East), was completely rebuilt in ferroconcrete in 1959, and all trace of the holocaust expunged. In a way these two buildings seem perfectly to characterize the attitudes of their respective cities to the bombs: Hiroshima's to go on relentlessly reminding, Nagasaki's to plough under and forget.

A game centre in Tokyo: the nimble-fingered teenagers' alternative to T.V. and comic books.

In any case, the associations that Nagasaki has for the Western visitor are longer-standing and less one-track-minded than Hiroshima's. Christianity is, perhaps, the foremost of these. The area near the Urakami Catholic Cathedral was a centre of underground Christian activity during the Tokugawa persecutions. In **Oura**, the 19th-century foreigners' quarter, stands the city's other famous Christian church, built in 1865, a miraculous survivor of the bombing. Near Nagasaki Station lies **Nishizaka Park**, the site of the martyrdom of six foreign priests and 20 of their Japanese converts in 1597. The 26 were crucified (crucifixion being the usual method of execution for commoners during the feudal period) and, despite the official animosity toward Christianity, the place rapidly became a focus of pilgrimage owing to the miracles that were said to occur there. The 26 martyrs were canonized in 1962.

Nagasaki's other foreign associations are of a secular kind. The one Dutch and Chinese trading post that continued to operate throughout the period of national seclusion was situated on a tiny man-made island called **Dejima** in Nagasaki Bay. Little trace of this settlement remains, though there are plans to rebuild and restore it as a tourist attraction. In the meantime, tourists interested in Nagasaki's Dutch connection can visit **Oranda Mura** (Holland Village), not far outside the city, where they can see windmills, a replica of an old Dutch sailing ship, souvenir shops, museums, and specimens of real live foreigners kitted out with bonnets, clogs and pipes, bearing all the signs of having been shipped over from the Netherlands in ventilated crates. The city's other famous foreign landmark is the house of Thomas B. Glover, a Scottish engineer who came to Nagasaki in 1859 and founded an import-export business. The large and elegant **Glover Mansion**, now open to the public as a museum, stands on a prime residential site overlooking Nagasaki Bay, and credulous visitors are told that Madame Butterfly lived there (Glover, who married a Japanese woman, is sometimes said to have been the model for Puccini's Pinkerton). But, unlike Pinkerton, Glover never left Japan, and visitors to his lavish residence will have no difficulty seeing why. Another monument to Glover's enterprise stands out in the bay itself: the tiny, almost deserted island of **Takashima**, energetically developed as a coal mining centre under Glover's supervision and recently abandoned despite emotional protests from the miners and their families by its subsequent owners, Mitsubishi. The cheap ferroconcrete high-rise apartment blocks that were the miners' homes, and which crowd practically every square metre of space not occupied by slag heaps on the unhappy little island, now stand crumbling and empty.

Nagasaki's Chinese connections are evident in the **Chinatown** area with its numerous authentic restaurants, in the Chinese Ming-style Zen temple of **Sofukuji**, founded in 1629, and in the city's two main annual festivals, the **Okunchi** (8–9 October) which features a Chinese-style Dragon Dance and

the **Peiron** Dragon Boat races (the name is derived from the Chinese *P'a-lung,* meaning 'dragon') on the Sunday nearest 15 June.

Hilly and situated at the end of a long, almost landlocked bay, eminently accessible by sea (hence its foreign connections) and extremely tedious to reach by land, the city of Nagasaki is a microcosm of the heavily indented, fjorded prefecture of which it is the capital. Most of Nagasaki prefecture is made up of islands and peninsulas which are almost islands (the Japanese word for peninsula—*hanto,* literally 'half-island'—seems nowhere more explicit and appropriate than here).

The **Shimabara** Peninsula, in the centre of which stands **Mount Unzen** (1,359 metres or 4,459 feet) is famous for the rebellion that occurred there in 1637–8. The rebellion was a popular uprising inspired by chronic poverty and exorbitant taxation but, because both of the fiefs from which the rebels came had been nominally Christian before the total ban on Christianity enforced 23 years earlier, the shogunate found it convenient to blame Christian provocateurs for the uprising, a policy that enabled officialdom both to overlook the social inequities that were the actual cause and to redouble its religious persecutions. No popular rebellion in history, including that led by Spartacus, was ever suppressed more viciously. The entire rebel garrison of **Shimabara Castle** was slaughtered together with their woman and children, the dead eventually totalling some 37,000. The castle donjon was rebuilt in 1964 as a museum and monument to the unhappy early history of Christianity in a country that prides itself on its religious tolerance (by which it exclusively means the tolerance of Shinto for Buddhism and vice-versa). The area around Mount Unzen is one of four in Japan (Sakurajima in Kagoshima prefecture is another) that receive government funds to provide for possible evacuation in case of eruption and are required to carry out regular emergency and survival exercises. Unzen is very active and there are frequent earth tremors in the region, but this has not prevented its becoming the main showpiece of the **Unzen-Amakusa National Park**, which features several good hot-spring resorts, both in Shimabara and on the **Amakusa** islands (population 140,000), joined to the mainland south of the town of **Misumi** in Kumamoto prefecture via a set of bridges.

Nagasaki's other National Park is the **Saikai** (literally, 'West Coast') **National Park**, which includes the island of **Hirado** (population 28,000), also joined to the mainland by a bridge and which was the earliest part of Japan to be settled by foreigners (Dutch, English, Portuguese and Spanish, all of whom built trading posts and warehouses there in the mid-16th century). Further offshore lie the picturesque **Goto** islands (population 97,000), less bleak and rugged than the Oki islands (see page 167) and an ideal destination for fishermen or those wanting a complete respite from urbanity and the pressures or organized tourism. The islands are comparatively low-lying, which in itself is something of a relief after the mountainous terrain of most of Japan, and many of the villages still harbour small Christian churches underscoring the area's reputation as a centre for the faith.

The islands of **Iki** (population 40,000) and **Tsushima** (population 50,000), though administratively parts of Nagasaki prefecture, are best reached via Fukuoka, from where there is a regular ferry service. Lying in the narrowest straits between Japan and the continent, these islands have long served as stepping stones from mainland Asia. Iki is particularly interesting in that it is practically the last place in Japan to preserve a vigorous form of phallic worship. Phallus-shaped stones were once fairly common throughout the remoter parts of Japan, where they were set up as charms to promote fertility. In the small shrines of Iki the chief objects of worship are often small delicately-carved wood or stone phalluses, and in the island's annual festival, two huge papier-mâché constructions, one representing the female organ and the other the male, are manipulated in a manner that is explicit rather than suggestive. Tsushima is a great deal more rugged and sparsely populated than Iki, and foreign visitors disembarking from the ferry are sometimes questioned by local police who suspect that the island is one of the principal entry points for illegal immigrants from Korea. The police must know as well as everyone else that the ferry has come direct from Fukuoka, so pointing this out to them, though a natural reaction, cannot help but seem a trifle gratuitous.

The main tourist destination in **Kumamoto** prefecture is **Mount Aso** (1,592 metres or 5,223 feet), the centre of the **Aso-Kuju National Park** (**Kuju**—1,787 metres or 5,863 feet—is an extinct volcano in western Oita). Aso has five cones, one of which is still very active and last erupted in 1979. The landscape surrounding these cones is extremely arresting since the peaks of Aso stand in the centre of one of the largest caldera craters on earth, originally the mouth of a far more gigantic volcano, and the walls of this almost perfectly circular crater can be seen rearing up spectacularly from almost any point within it. The crater has a circumference of 80 kilometres (50 miles) and contains three separate townships as well as several hot-spring spas.

Due west of Aso stands the prefectural capital, **Kumamoto** city (population 526,000), famous for its very large feudal castle, built in 1607 and restored in 1960. The castle is remarkable not only for its size but in having been the last Japanese castle to undergo a medieval-style siege. This took place, incredibly enough, in 1877 (the year in which the English lawn tennis championships were first played at Wimbledon), when the castle was invested for 50 days by rebel forces from Kagoshima under the charismatic former Marshall of the Army and Counsellor of State, Saigo Takamori. Saigo had been commander of the army that had toppled the shogunate nine years

(Preceding page) Traditional foodstuffs—seaweed strips, sweet beans—on sale in Tokyo's shitamachi. The signs promise bargain prices.

earlier and his rebellion was sparked by exasperation at what he regarded as the self-serving, cowardly and pragmatic policies of the cabinet he had helped bring to power. Kumamoto was the first major battle of the six-month campaign. The castle withstood the siege (though the donjon was destroyed) and was eventually relieved by government reinforcements, whereupon Saigo withdrew and fought a famous rearguard action at **Tabaruzaka**, some 15 kilometres (9.5 miles) northwest of Kumamoto, where the battleground is preserved and a small museum commemorates the conflict. (For the final outcome of the rebellion, see page 202.)

The other great martial figure associated with Kumamoto is Miyamoto Musashi, lately famous as the author of *Gorin no Sho* (The Book of Five Rings), written in a mountain cave in the Kumamoto suburbs in 1643 and widely touted in the United States as an important key to the understanding of 20th-century Japanese business practices, a belief which vividly underscores both the extreme desperation and the extreme gullibility of the American business community. Musashi was a famous swordsman who, after helping the government slaughter tens of thousands of peasants, women and children at Shimabara (see page 194), took to teaching, writing and ink painting as well as to lopping off losers' heads (by his own reckoning the personal head count was 60). Musashi's cave is preserved as a monument to his selfless dedication to these various arts.

Inland, south of Aso, the country is wild and sparsely inhabited, and the region spanning the border between Kumamoto and Miyazaki prefectures is so hilly and remote and its population so depleted that it is sometimes called 'the Tibet of Japan'. Survival training for the elite corps of Japan's Ground Self-Defense Forces, though conducted in secret, is rumoured to take place here. Anyone wanting a genuine taste of traditional country life and a glimpse of its attendant hardships could do worse than spend some days in the villages of these hills. On the other hand, the Kumamoto coast has suffered a large degree of industrial disruption. At the small city of **Minamata** (population 37,000), between 1953 and 1960, the Chisso Corporation's discharge of untreated methyl-mercury effluent into the sea resulted in more than 300 deaths among people who had eaten fish caught near the plant's waste disposal facility. Fishing is still prohibited in the bay.

The main attractions of **Miyazaki** prefecture are its subtropical coast, for an exploration of which the prefectural capital, Miyazaki city, is well situated, the mountainous inland region centering on the town of Takachiho, which is the site of several ancient legends concerning the founding and earliest pseudo-history of the Japanese islands, and the Kirishima-Yaku National Park, which spans the border with Kagoshima.

Miyazaki city (population 265,000) is traditionally regarded as the site of the palace of Japan's legendary first emperor, Jimmu, underscoring both

Arts, Martial and Polite

Mishima Yukio was not alone in finding in the broad field of 'Japanese culture' two opposing strains, a dark and a light. The American cultural anthropologist, Ruth Benedict, called her 1946 study of Japanese society *The Chrysanthemum and the Sword,* a title that emphasised the two strains' distinct qualities: the first natural and delicate, the second uncompromising and violent.

The West has tended to take the violent strain more seriously. Japanese martial arts have a considerable following abroad. The most popular of them, judo, became an Olympic sport in 1964, and the corridors of Tokyo's *Kodokan,* the mecca of Japanese judo, still swarm with overseas practitioners (there seems to be no convenient English word for someone who practises judo —judoist, judo-man and judo-player all seem awkward, quite apart from the tendency of the last to equate an 'art' with a mere 'sport'). The popularity of *karate* (a form of kick boxing) is more recent. *Aikido,* a purely defensive art, is the most pleasing of all the martial arts to watch, possessing qualities that are dancelike. *Kendo,* fencing with bamboo swords, is less popular abroad, but widely taught in Japanese schools and attracting more and more women (whose traditional weapon was not the sword but the short-shafted, long-bladed halberd called *naginata*). *Kyudo* (archery) was the subject of one or two books by Western authors in the 1960s, which saw it as a practical embodiment of Zen. This meant, essentially, that an archer who failed to hit the target after repeated tries could declare his interest to be spiritual, and thus above such a mundane ambition.

The West has tended to view the gentler arts—flower-arrangement (*ikebana*) and so on—as elegant indulgences for affluent wives. The Japanese regard ikebana in much the same light, though the teaching and awarding of proficiency certificates is a multi-billion-yen industry. *Shuji* or *shodo* (brush calligraphy), is still considered a serious attainment. With the advent of Japanese-language word processors it may suffer a decline; although the electronic calculator has only marginally curtailed the widespread use of the abacus (*soroban*). The writing of traditional forms of poetry (such as the 17-syllable *haiku*) is widespread and encouraged on a national scale by newspaper competitions. Perhaps the most intriguing of the gentler arts to many Western visitors is the tea ceremony (*cha-no-yu*), with its immaculately contrived rigmaroles of politeness, its snobbish conventions, and its underlying assumption that life's troubles are easily dissipated if the sufferer is subjected to a rigorous enough formality. A Western (or Japanese) guest at a tea ceremony, who finds after half an hour of sitting with his legs tucked under him that he can only get up and walk at the risk of severely torn ligaments and the complete destruction of his host's paper screens as he staggers desperately into and through them, can be forgiven for wondering whether this gentle art belongs to the dark strain or the light.

Waiting to form up for the annual 'Procession of a Thousand Armed Men' under the cryptomeria trees at Nikko.

the mythological connections and the age of human settlement in the region. The **Miyazaki Shrine** stands today where the palace is imagined to have stood and is itself supposed to date from mythological times.

Takachiho (population 20,000) is accessible by rail or bus from the city of **Nobeoka**, and stands on a spectacular gorge said to have been formed by the erosion of lava from Mount Aso. The municipal authorities have spared no effort to attract visitors to this remote little town. They have erected signboards outside virtually all the shops announcing to the sightseer that he has arrived in 'the country of the gods' and commissioned a local artist to paint scenes from the sacred Kagura dances in bright gloss paint on many of the metal shop blinds. A selection of Kagura dances is performed at the **Takachiho Shrine** every evening of the year and admission tickets are available at the shrine's busy box office. Emperor Jimmu is supposed to have set out from this shrine on his journey to the Nara basin to found the nation of Japan, and at the nearby and much smaller **Kushifuru Shrine** the grandson of the Sun Goddess is supposed to have descended from heaven. But the most celebrated of Japan's god-legends is associated with the shrine at **Iwato** (often called *Ama no Iwato*, or Heavenly Iwato) some 8 kilometres (5 miles) away. Here the visitor can see a cave reputed to be the very one in which the Sun Goddess, Amaterasu Omikami, in a fit of pique at the riotous behaviour of her brother the Storm God, hid herself, thus plunging the earth into darkness. In an effort to encourage her reemergence, a bevy of minor gods and goddesses crowded round the entrance to the cave and one of the goddesses performed an obscene dance. Intrigued by the sounds of mirth that she could hear and wondering what caused them, the Sun Goddess poked her head out of the cave, found herself reflected in a mirror which the gods had cunningly hung on a tree, and Lo! the light of the world revived. The obscene dance of the minor goddess is considered the original of all dances connected with shrines and shrine festivals, and the mirror is the original sacred mirror that forms a part of the imperial regalia (see page 103).

Near the small city of **Saito** (population 38,000) on the coastal plain north of Miyazaki city stands a cluster of fifth- and sixth-century tombs, numbering more than 300, less than one-tenth of which have been excavated. The excavations, carried out between 1912 and 1917, uncovered large amounts of armour, weapons and tomb sculptures testifying once again to the importance of the region in early human history as well as in sacred fiction.

Mount Kirishima, the centre of the **Kirishima-Yaku National Park**, is a cluster of volcanic peaks, the highest of which rises to 1,700 metres (5,577 feet). This high point lies exactly on the border between Miyazaki and Kagoshima, but the chief focus of tourism, the **Ebino Plateau**, with its lakes, hot springs and inns, is on the Miyazaki side. The last major eruption of Kirishima occurred in 1959, making it the most dormant of the four main active Kyushu volcanoes (this, Unzen, Aso and

Sakurajima), or, looked at from a less rosy point of view, the one longest overdue. The lower slopes of the Kirishima group are especially well provided with hot springs.

Sakurajima (1,117 metres or 3,665 feet) is the opposite of overdue. Originally an island in Kagoshima Bay, it spewed out enough lava in an eruption in 1914 to join itself to the mainland, and has remained an intermittent menace. In recent years its regular emissions of ash have earned Sakurajima (once a picturesque symbol of the area's natural attractions: its name means 'Cherry Blossom Island') the unrelenting wrath of the residents of Kagoshima city on whose streets and houses the ash falls, sometimes to a depth of several inches. Local television stations advertise industrial vacuum cleaning equipment for hire, but the ash has already so badly damaged the local tourist industry (before the current spate of eruptions Kagoshima was a favourite honeymoon destination) that the advertisements seem only to perpetuate the communal gloom. That a natural symbol should turn so visibly against its promoters strikes many with the force of a betrayal.

Kagoshima city (population 505,000), the capital of the prefecture, stands opposite the sour volcano in the northeastern quarter of the Satsuma Peninsula. Like Choshu (Yamaguchi) and Tosa (Kochi), Satsuma was at the head of the movement that toppled the shogunate in 1868 and ushered in Japan's modern age. This was the fief ruled by the energetic Shimazu Nariakira (see page 184) and which produced the irrepressible Saigo Takamori (see page 198), whose doomed rebellion of 1877 ended here in his native city. Saigo made his last stand on **Shiroyama Hill**, a great mound of crumbling earth that towers above the city centre. His headquarters were a cave (carefully preserved) which he quit when the government bombardment grew too fierce to withstand and descended the hill with his 200 or so remaining followers. He was hit in the groin by a government sniper and immediately decapitated by a lieutenant so loyal that he buried Saigo's head separately from his body, causing the government troops a great deal of extra effort in locating and digging it up. Many of the city's chief monuments are connected with the Great Saigo. Shiroyama is nowadays a shrine to his memory. At its base is a stone tablet marking the spot where he died, and a statue of Saigo in his Marshall's uniform stands outside the city's art gallery. His grave stands between a museum dedicated to his life and exploits and a small Shinto shrine where he is worshipped as the chief deity. That a defeated rebel should find himself posthumously heaped with official honours may strike the visitor as strange but, even in disgrace and even by his enemies, Saigo was regarded as embodying all the most admirable qualities of the rapidly vanishing samurai spirit. He was totally uncompromising, brave to the point of lunacy, intensely nationalistic, and preferred death with honour to success through opportunist machination.

As the northernmost prefecture of Honshu, Aomori, is crisply divided into two peninsulas, so is this southernmost prefecture of mainland Japan, a similarity which attests to the founding gods' taste for elegant symmetry. The two prefectures share further similarities: they are both among those regularly reporting the lowest per capita incomes in the nation and they are both famous for the impenetrability of their rural dialects, in which the inhabitants take a certain pride. The combination of extreme rurality and a reputation for martial exploits has caused some residents of Kagoshima to refer to themselves as *imo-zamurai* (potato samurai), a charming expression which the foreign visitor is advised to eschew in casual conversation. The natives of Kagoshima take their history seriously. In 1863 seven British warships sailed into Kagoshima Bay to demand reparations for two Englishmen killed by Satsuma samurai for crossing the path of their lord's procession. Satsuma refused, whereupon the warships opened fire destroying a large part of the city. However, the British ships were quickly dispersed by a typhoon that struck the bay, leaving some 60 of their crew dead or injured and contributing enormously to the belief that Japan is fated to be preserved from foreign aggression by a Divine Wind (*kamikaze*), the name given to the fortuitous typhoons that twice sank Mongol invasion fleets poised off the north Kyushu coast in the 13th century as well as to the special attack force mustered in the closing stages of the Pacific War to mount suicide missions against American warships. The incident of the British bombardment, which lasted all of one hot August afternoon, is still referred to in Kagoshima as the *Satsu-ei Senso* (The Anglo-Satsuma War), and reference to it is not taken lightly.

The eastern fork of Kagoshima prefecture is the **Osumi** Peninsula, which boasts a rocket-launching facility owned by the University of Tokyo. The western fork is the more interesting **Satsuma** Peninsula, near the tip of which, in the shadow of the perfectly conical **Mount Kaimon** (922 metres or 3,025 feet), lies the hot-spring resort of **Ibusuki**, featuring thermal sand baths on the beach. The west coast of the peninsula has one of the best swimming beaches in mainland Japan in **Fukiagehama** as well as a noted centre for the production of black Satsuma pottery at the village of **Naeshirogawa**, where the first kiln was established (once again by a Korean potter) in 1604. The most easily recognizable products of the village are its elegant flat shochu-warmers.

The Satsuma lords were very keen on expanding their territory and all the long chain of islands lying between the southern tip of Kyushu and Taiwan was at one time under their control. Today the islands of Yakushima and Tanegashima, which lie comparatively close to the mainland, as well as the more distant Amami islands, still belong administratively to Kagoshima prefecture.

Young lady meets mendicant outside the Meiji Shrine.

Despite its being the rainiest spot in the entire country (up to 10,000 millimetres or 390 inches annually in the mountains), **Yakushima** (population 15,000) remains popular with honeymoon couples, and is part of the Kirishima-Yaku National Park. **Tanegashima** (population 44,000) also has a rocket-launching facility and is remembered as the place where firearms were first introduced into Japan (by stranded Portuguese in 1543). Both islands are warm with subtropical vegetation and list sugarcane among their more important agricultural products.

Until the early 17th century the Amami islands were not a part of Japan at all but, like modern Okinawa prefecture, a part of the independent Kingdom of the Ryukyus, and are dealt with in the next chapter.

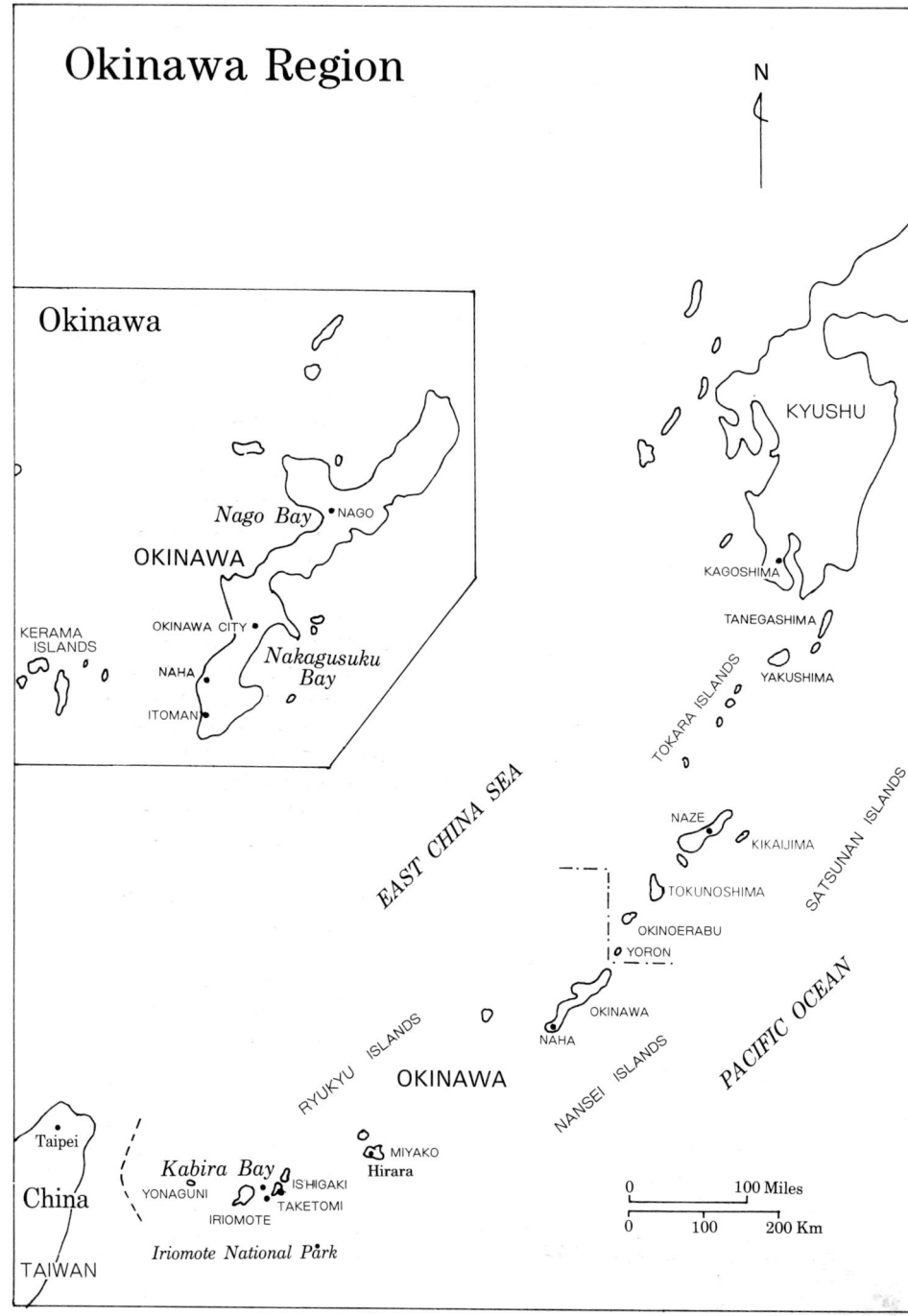

Okinawa and the Southern Islands
Invasion, Disruption, JALPAK

The history of the Ryukyu islands (comprising the four island groups of Amami, Okinawa, Miyako and Yaeyama) is a complex and depressing one. Until the beginning of the 17th century the islands were independent both of China (where they were known as *Liu-ch'iu*) and of Japan, though they had far stronger cultural and diplomatic ties with the continent. By the mid-16th century all four of the island groups were united under the rule of a single king whose capital was at Shuri, near today's prefectural capital of Naha on the main Okinawan island. The court at Shuri carried on an active trade with China, sent scholars to study there, and was so highly regarded by the Chinese emperor that he named Okinawa 'the land of propriety'. (By contrast, the representatives from mainland Japan were thought boorish in that they slighted the formalities and etiquette of the Chinese court—something the Okinawans apparently took very seriously—and were forever urging the ceremonially inclined Chinese to get on with the down-to-earth business of trade.)

In 1609 the Ryukyu islands were conquered by an expedition from Satsuma (present-day Kagoshima) and the court at Shuri was forced to declare itself a vassal state of the aggressively minded Satsuma lords. The Amami islands were directly assimilated into the Satsuma fief, but the other groups were permitted to maintain the fiction of autonomy together with their king and court, which somewhat confusingly both acquiesced in this arrangement and continued to send tribute to the emperor of China. A complicated system of triple sovereignty thus came into force: the ruler on the spot was the king at Shuri, but the de facto power was Satsuma while the ritual overlord was the Chinese emperor.

In 1879 the dispute between China and the new Meiji government of Japan over possession of the Ryukyus came to a head, and Japan settled this dispute, to its own satisfaction, by pensioning off the king, disbanding the court at Shuri, and declaring Okinawa a Japanese prefecture. China protested, and at first Japan offered to cede the Miyako and Yaeyama groups. But with Japan's victory in the Sino-Japanese war of 1894–5 all thought of appeasement ended and China was forced to relinquish its claim. Interestingly enough, though, Japan remains one of very few nations in the world today to maintain ongoing territorial disputes with every one of its immediate neighbours: with China and Taiwan it disputes possession of the Senkaku islands (*Tiao-yu-t'ai* in Chinese) which lie some 160 kilometres (99 miles) north of the Yaeyama group, with Korea it disputes possession of Takeshima (*Tokto* in Korean) which lies beyond the Oki islands off the coast of Shimane, and with the Soviet Union the group of islands off the northeast

(Preceding page) Coral reefs are among the 'un-Japanese' attractions of Okinawa's scattered islands.

coast of Hokkaido that were occupied by the Soviets at the end of the war (see page 214).

During the early modern period, the Japanese authorities made a number of half-hearted attempts to encourage settlement on the remoter Okinawan islands, but these attempts invariably ran up against the sound historical reasons for not settling them: poverty, squalor, malaria, cholera, hepatitis, famine, drought, typhoons, snake infestation (the *habu,* Japan's most poisonous snake, still infests large parts of rural Okinawa) and such a dearth of arable land and natural resources that on islands such as Iriomote in the Yaeyama group the Stone Age continued well into the 14th century.

Then came the Second World War, and the former 'land of propriety's' geographical location placed it squarely between the jaws of a terrible and unrelenting vice. In general terms, Japan's defensive strategy was to build a network of concentric fortified rings (much like the plan of a feudal Japanese castle) with the homeland at the centre and the outermost walls consisting of the far-flung occupied islands of the South Pacific and the Malay archipelago. The innermost wall of defence—the last to stand eventually between the Japanese mainland and the forces of invasion—was the Okinawan chain, with the result that one of the most destructive land battles of the war was fought on the main Okinawan island between April and July 1945. Altogether, a total of 50,000 American and 110,000 Japanese troops died on Okinawa, as did 150,000 Okinawan civilians caught in the crossfire. That one hears so much less about these noncombatant dead than one does about the victims of the Hiroshima bomb is presumably due to the fact that many of them were killed not by Americans but by Japanese.

Okinawa was governed directly by the United States until it reverted to Japan in 1972, prior to which Okinawan citizens were required by the Japanese government to carry alien registration certificates and special travel documents when visiting or living in mainland Japan. The legacy of this period, as well as of the general burden of the history of Okinawan suppression, is that, while not strictly speaking an ethnic minority, many Okinawans feel that they have suffered the same kinds of discrimination to which such minorities are often subjected. After reversion in 1972, the Japanese government made some loudly publicized attempts to boost Okinawa's depressed economy. These included a large 'Ocean Expo' in 1975, but the principal beneficiaries of the resulting influx of tourists were the concession-owners from the Japanese mainland who, once the event was over, packed up and went home, leaving the islanders little better off than before.

The Okinawan economy remains heavily dependent on the large American military bases located on the main island and the service industries that cater to them. About 10 percent of all the land in the prefecture is owned by, or leased to, U.S. forces and in some towns such as Koza (now bureaucratically renamed 'Okinawa City'), a large percentage of the population is made up of U.S. military personnel and their families. The bus between Naha and Koza (there is no railway on the island) ferries the visitor past long, depressing stretches of barbed-wire fence behind which native Okinawans are not permitted to venture, and towns such as Koza are run essentially as garrison economies, with bars staying open till the early hours, pawn shops flanking all the gates of the base, and the menus in restaurants and coffee shops printed in English and priced in dollars. Naturally enough, these circumstances have occasionally generated friction but, by and large, they are accepted by the islanders as the latest and not the heaviest link in a seemingly unending chain of foreign suzerainty. Besides which, as thoughtful Okinawans themselves remark, without the Americans a town like Koza would simply die.

The other great pillar of the Okinawan economy in modern times is tourism, and once again it is the airlines, packagers and agents on the Japanese mainland who continue to reap the greatest profits. Since reversion in 1972, a concerted effort to 'develop' Okinawa has resulted in a long series of promotion campaigns aimed mostly at honeymoon couples leery of Guam and at unmarried female college students who respond with unthinking alacrity to slogans such as 'Cinderella Summer'. Some shards of Cinderella's transparent slipper lie scattered about Okinawa's resort areas in much the same way that fairyland flutters over Tohoku and the Inland Sea, with package-tour operators anxious to ensure that midnight, in the form of historic and economic reality, never strikes. Mainly, it is Okinawa's subtropical beaches that are touted (the southernmost island of the Yaeyama group lies a bare one degree north of the Tropic of Cancer), but there is also, for the Japanese sightseer, an unmistakable *frisson* of foreignness about the islands that adds to their attraction. The Japanese spoken in Okinawa (variously described as a dialect and as a related but separate language), the climate, the flora, the food, the landscape, the music, the festivals, the architecture, the comparatively indolent lifestyle, all make Okinawa an exotic-but-still-comfortable destination for mainland holidaymakers, and definitely not a target for the visitor from abroad in search of something 'typically Japanese'.

Despite all historic and economic hardships, some aspects of Ryukyu culture remain vibrantly alive. Television has largely ironed out the many original differences of language so that 'Okinawan' as it was spoken a generation ago teeters on the verge of extinction, and the traditional architecture of the Ryukyus is nowadays so rare that in some places it is the subject of special preservation orders. But Okinawa has far more folk songs than any other Japanese prefecture and many of the islanders, including the young, can accompany themselves very competently on the short, snake skin-covered shamisen that is found only there. Festivals are wonderfully well preserved, particularly on the outlying islands, mainly because tourists are often resented. Old islanders have been known to snatch cameras from Japanese sightseers at rites still held by them to be sacred and expose rolls of Fujicolor to the island sun. Policemen have occasionally chided them for this out of deference to JALPAK, but the presence of outsiders at the islands' unpublicized folk festivals is more likely to be tolerated if their cameras stay in their bags.

The **Amami** islands, a part of Kagoshima prefecture, consist of **Oshima** (usually called Amami Oshima to distinguish it from the many other offshore 'Oshimas', a name that means simply 'large island') which has a population of 82,000, and the much smaller islands of **Kikaishima** (population 11,000), **Tokunoshima** (population 35,000), **Okinoerabu** (population 17,000) and **Yoron** (population 7,000). The only city in the group is **Naze** on Oshima, where more than half of the population of that island lives and which serves as the commercial and distribution centre for the sugarcane, pineapples and other exotic produce grown there. The Satsuma administration used some of the Amami islands as places of exile and imprisonment; Saigo Takamori himself (see pages 198 and 202) spent some time on Oshima, Tokunoshima and Okinoerabu during the brief period when he was out of favour with his lord, though within months of returning to Kagoshima he was serving as the Satsuma Secretary for War. All of these islands have good swimming beaches and no shortage of simple accommodation.

Okinawa proper consists of the main island, **Okinawa** (population 1.1 million) and the 20 or so very small offshore islands that surround it. The capital is **Naha** (population 296,000) where the airport and main ferry terminals for the entire prefecture are located. Little remains on the island from the prewar period, the devastation of 1945 having been almost total. The ruined gate of the old palace of **Shuri** was reconstructed in 1958 and attracts some sightseers, but the majority of visitors head straight for the beach resorts or for the simpler and more hospitable accommodation to be found in the rural parts of the island. The southern half of Okinawa is the more heavily urbanized and densely populated, while in the north of the island, beyond **Koza** (Okinawa City, population 95,000) near which stands the huge Kadena Air Base, the landscape is emptier of both people and barbed wire. The main city in the northern half is **Nago** (population 46,000) while, south of **Itoman** (population 42,000) at the extreme southern tip of the island, the site of some of the fiercest fighting of 1945 is now the 'Okinawa Former Battlefield Quasi-National Park'. In Koza the annual Bon festival takes the interesting form of a drum dance, called *Eisaa,* in which stand clearly revealed the cultural influences of the Asian continent.

The **Miyako** group consists of the main island, **Miyako** (population 33,000), and seven other very small islands. Like the Yaeyama group, the Miyako islands were spared wartime destruction and thus preserve more elements of traditional Okinawan culture (domestic architecture, for example) than does Okinawa itself. The chief port and centre of island life is the city of **Hirara**.

The **Yaeyama** group, in many ways the most interesting, consists of **Ishigaki** (population 40,000), **Iriomote** (population 1,500), **Taketomi** (population 300), **Yonaguni** (population 2,100) and several other small islands. Ishigaki boasts the only town of any size (Ishigaki city) and, as on Okinawa, the island's population is mainly concentrated in this small urban enclave in the south. The north is rugged and sparsely populated with some wonderfully unspoiled beaches, though **Kabira Bay** in the southwest is regarded as the most picturesque spot on the island. An ongoing controversy rages about the local administration's idiotic plan to build a new airport for tourists on top of one of the island's most beautiful stretches of coral. A short boat ride from Ishigaki lies the tiny coral island of Taketomi which preserves more or less intact an entire village built in the traditional Yaeyama manner: colourful tiled roofs, sharp coral walls, and Chinese-style screens in front of the main entrances. Iriomote is the second largest of all the Ryukyu islands but it is 90 percent primeval forest, the interior being entirely uninhabited and accessible only by two mangrove-banked rivers. In 1965 a species of wildcat (*yamaneko*), long thought extinct, was discovered to have survived in the island's impenetrable forests, since when Prince Philip of Britain has visited Iriomote in his capacity as President of the World Wildlife Fund and the island has been named a National Park. Its beaches offer wonderful bathing and the best coral reefs in Japan. Yonaguni is Japan's westernmost point and, lying almost within sight of Taiwan, is obviously Japanese only by dint of the vagaries of history. Some Yaeyama islanders continue to claim a closer racial connection with the indigenous people of Taiwan than with the Japanese of the mainland.

Hokkaido
The New Frontier

Like the Ryukyu islands, the island of Hokkaido was not fully incorporated into the Japanese homeland until towards the end of the 19th century. From the early 17th century there had been small Japanese settlements around the castle town of Matsumae in the extreme southwest of the island, but little attempt was made to push further north or east except by small bands of loggers and fishermen. Even in the 1880s the chief government office dealing with Hokkaido affairs was called the 'Office of Colonization' and the encouragement given by the government to settlers can be compared to the official enthusiasm with which the western United States was being opened up at the same time. The reasons for promoting development were similar too. Unlike the Ryukyus, Hokkaido was rich in natural resources, particularly timber and coal. Honshu was already perceived as being overcrowded and the opportunity to spread the population into this vast new space (Hokkaido is the second largest of Japan's islands) was seized with alacrity. There was also the question of deterring the Soviet Union from mounting any claims to the territory, the northern borders of which were still only loosely defined. The island of Sakhalin (in Japanese, *Karafuto*) is now Russian but was previously an object of dispute, joint settlement, and for a time split rule. It is clearly visible from the northern tip of Hokkaido, and Russian trappers had quite often crossed the straits from Sakhalin to Hokkaido during the late feudal period, though they had established no permanent settlements.

Such permanent settlements as existed in the island's interior belonged to the Ainu, Japan's indigenous people who are racially and culturally completely different from the Yamato tribes and their descendants. It is probable that the ancestors of the Ainu were the tribes (variously described as Ezo, Emeshi and Mishihase, meaning 'hairy people') against whom the Yamato, Nara and Kyoto courts mounted their genocidal campaigns aimed at bringing the whole of Honshu under their control. These tribes originally inhabited much of northern Honshu and, quite possibly, areas a lot further south if place names are a reliable indication: Mount Fuji's name, for example, is thought by some to derive from an Ainu word. By the close of the ninth century they had been driven out of Honshu and into Hokkaido (called Ezo until 1869), where they were left in comparative peace until fresh Japanese encroachments began during the rule of the Tokugawas, and then in earnest during the early modern period.

Today some 24,000 people identify themselves as Ainu, though few of these are pure blooded. Their traditions and culture are nothing like so spontaneously alive as those of the Ryukyu islanders, and continue to survive mainly as quaint entertainments trotted out on the occasion of specially concocted 'festivals'. The sight of this once dignified and solemn people dressed in their colourful appliqué robes performing dances and pretending to be 'at home' in picturesque huts doing picturesque things for the benefit of fee-paying tourists from Osaka can only sadden the thoughtful visitor conscious of the historical discrimination and suppression they have suffered. Buffalo Bill Cody's Wild West Show must have given similar pause to thoughtful Americans. Once in a while Ainu irritation flares, as it did briefly in 1986 following Prime Minister Nakasone's much-publicized remark to the effect that Japan's intellectual standards are superior to those of the United States because Japan is a 'monoracial' society. Ainu leaders on that occasion addressed a letter to Mr Nakasone in the Ainu language, to which the prime minister responded with even greater inanity by remarking that he possessed especially bushy eyebrows and so may well have Ainu blood in his own veins, a suggestion that merely added official sanction to a resented racial stereotype.

The visitor who goes to Hokkaido in search of Ainu culture, then, is doomed to disappointment. So, to some extent, is the visitor looking for 'the real Japan', since large-scale Japanese settlement of the island is so comparatively recent. Japanese visitors favour Hokkaido because, like the Ryukyus, it strikes them as in some ways 'un-Japanese', and package-tour advertisements have capitalized on this attraction by comparing it to Switzerland and Scotland. Hokkaido has no real rainy season, very little rice cultivation, few cherry trees (elsewhere a national symbol), no marked regional dialects, and in the winter months its northern coasts are grazed by distinctly un-Japanese icefloes. The natural splendour of its mountains, lakes, pastures, wetlands and wildlife reserves makes it an ideal destination for visitors primarily interested in The Great Outdoors, but Hokkaido should not figure high on the itinerary of anyone bent on getting a feel for Japanese society and culture as a whole. Such an ambition is far better satisfied in Honshu, Kyushu or Shikoku.

Much of Hokkaido in under deep snow for up to half the year making it a mecca for winter sports enthusiasts. Most visitors, however, favour the summer, when the much lower average temperatures (18–22°C or 64–71°F) provide a refreshing break from the enervating heat of western and central Honshu. Despite Hokkaido's sparse population (less than half that of Tokyo in an island the size of Austria), July and August can find its resort areas quite as crowded as many of those on the mainland. For all its size, Hokkaido is not divided into prefectures and remains a single administrative unit, with the capital at Sapporo. Its chief attractions are its six National Parks.

The city of **Sapporo** (population 1.4 million) was laid out as the seat of Hokkaido's colonial administration in 1869 on a checkerboard pattern similar to that of Kyoto or New York. In 1972 it was the site of the 11th Winter Olympic Games, the first ever held in Asia. Sapporo is a relatively clean,

modern city, with few items of historical interest, except for the red-brick, ivy-covered buildings of the old Sapporo Brewery (built in 1876), whose attractions have been massively increased by their being converted into the largest beer hall in Japan (the **Biiru-en**, where the beverages on the menu and the notices pointing the way to the lavatories are printed in German). Sapporo lies on the same latitude (43°N) as Milwaukee, the brewing capital of the United States, and likes to think of itself as belonging, with Milwaukee and Munich, to a sort of beer-producing holy trinity.

Older residents of Sapporo treasure fond memories of an avenue called **Tanuki-koji** (Badger Avenue), which in prewar days was the city's main entertainment quarter, famous throughout the island for its geisha, who found no difficulty in relieving patrons of the contents of their wallets with as much facility as the badger, an animal noted in folklore for its skill in that field. Today Tanuki-koji is a tame, roofed shopping-arcade indistinguishable from a thousand others, and the chief entertainment and tippling district has shifted to **Susukino**.

The city's agricultural college, founded in the same heady year as the brewery, is chiefly remembered for its first president, Dr William Smith Clark, who, during a sabbatical from his post at Massachusetts Agricultural College, was invited to advise the Japanese government on matters of education and spent nine months doing so at the new facility in Sapporo. He is mainly remembered for the parting remark he made to his students, many of whom he had converted to Christianity, 'Boys, be ambitious!', a remark that has echoed down the corridors of Japanese academic and social life and featured prominently in television advertisements for ballpoint pens.

Twenty-six kilometres (16 miles) southwest of Sapporo is the hot-spring resort of **Jozankei**, a convenient place for visitors to spend a night before proceeding further south to the lakes and volcanic peaks of the **Shikotsu-Toya National Park**. Of the two lakes that are the park's centrepieces, **Lake Shikotsu**, standing in the shadow of **Mount Eniwa** (1,320 metres or 4,331 feet), is the less commercially developed. It is the second deepest lake in Japan, after Lake Tazawa in Akita prefecture (see page 126). The small spa at **Marukoma** on the northern shore of the lake comprises one large traditional-style inn and several thermal baths including a small one situated on the rocky shore of the lake itself. **Lake Toya**, though a smaller body of water, has a much larger and more developed spa in **Toyako Onsen** (*onsen* means hot spring) on its southern shore. The spa lies just below the peak of **Mount Usu** (737 metres or 2,418 feet) and the entire town was evacuated during the summer tourist season of 1977 following the volcano's third major eruption this century. In fact, the area surrounding this lake is still at a dangerously active stage of seismological development. In 1910 an eruption of Usu resulted in the emergence of a new hill subsequently named **Meiji Shinzan** (New Mountain of the Meiji Era). In 1943–45 a much more violent spate of eruptions and upthrusts created the larger **Showa Shinzan** (408 metres or 1,339 feet; its name means New Mountain of the Showa Era).

On the sea coast southwest of Lake Toya stands the city of **Noboribetsu** (population 57,000), which contains Hokkaido's most famous hot-spring resort. Two more spas, **Shin** (New) **Noboribetsu** and **Karurusu** lie a few kilometres inland, and some 15 kilometres (9.5 miles) further east along the coast stands the 'Ainu' village at **Shiraoi**, established here in 1965, one of several such fabrications where, on the pretext of facilitating the 'study' of Ainu life and customs, souvenir shop owners can line their pockets.

Until March 1988 visitors who did not arrive in Hokkaido by air via Sapporo were likely to do so by ferry from Aomori to the port of Hakodate. However, the ferry service was discontinued with the opening of a rail link through the new **Seikan Tunnel** across the narrowest point of the Straits of Tsugaru, at 23.3 kilometres (14.5 miles) the longest undersea rail tunnel in the world.

Hakodate (population 320,000) was the largest city in Hokkaido until the great fire of 1934 caused many of its residents to move elsewhere, and it was the first major port opened to foreign commerce toward the end of the Edo period (in 1854, five years before the opening of Yokohama). Unlike Sapporo, which was a city from the moment of its carefully planned inception, Hakodate is simply a former fishing village that has grown to fill out its natural boundaries, these being the imposing **Mount Hakodate** (335 metres or 1,100 feet), which looms like a fortress over its well-sheltered harbour, and the sea that pounds both sides of the narrow peninsula on which the city stands. It is thus a more rewarding place than Sapporo to stroll in and explore for, besides being older (it was an established fishing port in the mid-1700s), it is full of the back alleys and odd straggling lanes that add life and interest to any city and which Sapporo conspicuously lacks.

The summit of Mount Hakodate is accessible by cable car and affords a wonderful view of the city, particularly at night. Otherwise the main sights are the various religious edifices, such as the Byzantine-style Greek Orthodox church, built near the foot of Mount Hakodate in 1862 and rebuilt in 1916, and the Trappist convent near neighbouring **Yunokawa** spa, where the city's favourite edible souvenirs, 'Trappist cookies', are manufactured by the contemplative butter-fingered inmates. Another tourist destination is the star-shaped **Goryokaku**, the first Western-style fort in Japan, completed in 1864 just in time to serve as the site of the last battle in the civil war that led to the restoration of the Emperor Meiji. Some 2,000 troops loyal to the fallen shogun occupied the fort in late 1868 and proclaimed Hokkaido (then still called Ezo) a republic, but they were besieged by the imperial army and surrendered in June 1869.

The little town of **Matsumae** (population 18,000) was the only feudal castle town in Hokkaido, having served as the seat of the Matsumae family from 1606 to 1869, during which period the whole southwest corner of the island was also known as Matsumae and was the only area open to Japanese settlement. The rest of the island was nominally recognized as Ainu territory, and settlement there was restricted until considerations of convenience and profitability began to outweigh those of justice and tolerance. The castle was restored in ferroconcrete in 1961.

Of Hokkaido's five remaining National Parks, those in the deep interior have most to offer the non-scientific visitor. **Daisetsuzan National Park** (the name means Great Snowy Mountains) is the largest inland National Park in Japan and lies in the exact centre of Hokkaido, the most convenient point of access being the city of **Asahikawa** (population 353,000). The park's chief attractions are its towering forested volcanoes, the tallest of which is **Mount Asahi** (2,290 metres or 7,513 feet), the highest mountain on the island. These mountains are a principal haunt of the Hokkaido brown bear, Japan's largest wild animal and, next to the Okinawan *habu,* its most dangerous. Bears are found throughout Hokkaido and northern Honshu, but the largest seem to congregate here. East of Mount Asahi, the upper reaches of the **Ishikari River** have carved out the spectacular **Sounkyo Gorge**, and **Sounkyo** spa at the centre of the gorge is the most popular resort for visitors planning to stay in the park overnight. There are several smaller hot-spring resorts scattered through the mountains.

The main attractions of the **Akan National Park** in eastern Hokkaido are its three lakes, which, unlike the slightly more southerly Lakes Shikotsu and Toya, are iced over in winter. The lakes are **Akan, Kutcharo** and **Mashu**, the water of this last reputedly having the greatest transparency of any lake in the world. Lake Akan is the home of a curious spherical water weed called *marimo,* which entrepreneurs have conjured into a tourist attraction. Mainly they have done this by selling small specimens of it in plastic containers so that you can take it home and watch it shrivel in the unsuitable environment of your goldfish bowl; but they have also devised an 'Ainu' ritual in which the weed is gathered, placed overnight on an altar and 'worshipped', the worship taking the convenient and lucrative form of dances and chants. This event takes place annually in October in the hot-spring resort of **Akan Kohan**, where there is an 'Ainu' village similar to that at Shiraoi (see page 218), except that, by some happy circumstance of Ainu lore, every building but one in the Akan Kohan village turns out to be a souvenir shop, the single exception being a 'house' equipped with spectators' benches and a box office, where you can watch traditionally garbed elders pretending that they live there. There is, however, nothing contrived about the beauty of the peaks and dense subarctic forests that surround the lakes, and if the real Ainu of old had little use for spherical water weeds, they at least knew the value of these.

Northeast of the lakes lies the **Shiretoko** Peninsula, nowadays the **Shiretoko National Park**. There is a hot-spring resort called **Rausu** at the

Thermal spring on the slope of Mount Asahi in Hokkaido's Daisetsuzan National Park.

foot of **Mount Rausu** (1,661 metres or 5,450 feet), but the park's main attractions are its coastal cliffs, best seen from a sightseeing boat, and its protected wildlife, which includes the rare sea eagle.

From the east coast of the peninsula the visitor will be able to see the slender island of **Kunashiri**. Further south, visible from the **Nemuro** peninsula, lies the small group of islands collectively called **Habomai**. And beyond these, stretching away northeast and forming the southernmost links of the Kurile chain, are the small island of **Shikotan** and the large island of **Etorofu**. All of these islands, previously Japanese territory, have been occupied by the Soviet Union since August 1945 and a campaign to demand their return is mounted spasmodically by the Japanese government. The campaign attracts little grass roots support, but the 'northern territorial issue' has complicated Japanese-Soviet affairs to the extent that, although relations were 'normalized' in 1956, no postwar peace treaty between the two nations has ever been signed. Japan continues to demand the return of 'its' islands, and the Soviet Union continues to insist that there is no outstanding 'territorial issue' to discuss.

Part of Japan's irritation with the status quo arises from the circumstances in which Russia invaded the islands. Russia did not declare war on Japan until after the bombing of Hiroshima and rushed its troops into the southern Kuriles a bare six days before Japan surrendered. Japan had previously enjoyed a treaty of neutrality with the Soviet Union and had in fact been attempting to obtain Russian mediation to end the war, so the sudden annexation of these northern islands must have seemed like the worst kind of betrayal. Alas, a sad but inescapable lesson of history is that nations which go to war for reasons that include territorial aggrandizement, and then proceed to lose the war, tend also to lose territory. Compared with the violence done to national boundaries in Europe following World War II, Japan was immensely fortunate. Had Russia been allowed to participate in the postwar occupation, there is a strong possibility that the whole of Hokkaido might have remained today under Soviet control. Once in a while, one wishes that Japan's much-touted struggle to achieve 'international-mindedness' would permit certain sections of the Japanese establishment to assess their country's status in the light of global realities.

The **Kushiro Marshland National Park** near the city of **Kushiro** on Hokkaido's southeast coast is Japan's newest National Park, opened in August 1987. It exists principally to provide a sanctuary for the sacred crane, a specially protected species. In Japan and China the crane is regarded as a symbol of felicity and often appears, together with the tortoise (symbolizing longevity) in designs intended for use at festive occasions. The **Rishiri-Rebun-Sarobetsu National Park** consists of the two offshore islands of Rishiri and Rebun and the coastal strip extending south from the windy city of **Wakkanai** (population 53,000), the northernmost city in Japan. This marshy plain, some 27 kilometres (17 miles) long, is famous in summer for its irises and rhododendrons. The two islands are topographically very different. **Rishiri** (population 12,000) is an extinct volcano rising straight out of the sea to a height of 1,719 metres (5,640 feet) and inhabited only along the coast; fishing is practically the only occupation. **Rebun** (population 5,900) is flatter, but even bleaker. It provides good hiking country in summer, particularly along the west coast where a rough hiking track is the only means of access, but there is little to see there except the grey Soya Straits and little to hear but the smack of the wind and the incessant barking of crows.

Helpful Information

Getting Around Japan

Most prefectural capitals and some other major cities are served by one or more of Japan's domestic airlines. ANA (All Nippon Airways—*Zennikku*) flies the main routes and TDA (Toa Domestic Airlines—*Toa Kokunai Koku*) duplicates many of these as well as serving smaller, remoter destinations. The national flag carrier, JAL (Japan Air Lines—*Nihon Koku*), flies major trunk routes such as those between Tokyo, Osaka, Fukuoka, Naha and Sapporo. SWAL (Southwest Air Lines—*Nansei Koku*) serves the Amami and Ryukyu islands. Tokyo's main domestic airport is Haneda, conveniently reached by monorail from Hamamatsucho Station. Japan's mountainous terrain has meant that many local airports have been built so far from the cities they serve that one can spend as long on the shuttle bus as one does on the plane. Domestic air transport in Japan is not cheap (a return trip from Tokyo to Okinawa is more expensive than a discount return to Hongkong).

Long-distance rail travel is not cheap either but, earthquakes permitting, it is extremely reliable. The *Tokaido Shinkansen* joins Tokyo to Fukuoka, calling at Nagoya, Kyoto, Osaka, Hiroshima, Okayama, Shimonoseki and other major cities on the way. The *Tohoku Shinkansen* joins Tokyo (Ueno) to Morioka via Sendai and other cities. The *Joetsu Shinkansen* joins Tokyo (Ueno) to Niigata. There are many other JR express services, not so rapid but equally punctual, and a fine array of local services, although unprofitable rural lines are forever being axed. Seats can be reserved on all expresses, and reservations can be made at travel agents and major JR stations. First class (Green Car) seats are available on most routes and non-smoking areas are being grudgingly expanded. Timetables (*jikokuhyo*) are issued monthly and available from book shops and station kiosks; they are in Japanese but can be worked through with a map, practice and God's benison. In addition to the JR network, there are some useful private lines, particularly in the Kinki region. Kyoto and Nara are more conveniently joined by the Kintetsu railway than by JR, and Nikko is more easily reached from Tokyo by the Tobu line, whose terminus is Asakusa.

Long-distance, air-conditioned buses are generally cheaper than express trains and overnight services can be a boon to the budget-conscious traveller. In daylight he should ensure that his bus is a regular one and not a sightseeing (*kanko*) bus, otherwise he will spend the journey being addressed non-stop through a microphone by a young lady in a stewardess's outfit who will babble to him, sing to him, and point out every passing tree to him: a delight if he is in the mood for it and a severe tribulation if it takes him unawares. Some cities, such as Tokyo, lend themselves to half-day, day or evening guided bus tours. Some cities, such as Nara, do not. The visitor who opts for a guided bus tour of Kyoto deserves the migraine it will give him.

(Preceding page) Disciplined commuters on the city-bound platform of Nakameguro station, Tokyo. Decorum lasts until the doors open.

Getting, and Not Getting Around Tokyo

Tokyo's taxi-drivers are nowadays mostly polite and helpful. You are not expected to tip taxi-drivers anywhere in Japan and some now equip their vehicles with *karaoke* tapes so that you can croon consoling ditties to yourself as the meter reduces you to penury. The trouble is that drivers frequently require you not only to tell them where you want to go, but to furnish them, in Japanese, with a detailed set of directions. This does not apply to major hotels and tourist destinations but a problem could occur if you got into a taxi in central Tokyo and gave the driver the address of a friend who lived out in the suburbs and whom you had never previously visited. This is not to say that it can't be done; only that it requires patience, a flexible time limit, a facility with sign language, and a repertoire of some two dozen consoling ditties.

The Tokyo subway and surface-rail systems are among the most efficient in the world. Surface railway lines either belong to JR East Japan (formerly part of the Japanese National Railways, which was denationalized and split into seven private corporations in 1987) or they have been privately owned from the beginning. There are 41 different JR East Japan lines, 23 private surface lines and 10 different subway lines in the Greater Tokyo area. The JR's Yamanote Line is a useful loop line linking the downtown business districts with the middle-class residential areas, taking in all of the major city terminuses. The Chuo Line is the main east-west route through the city, beginning at Tokyo Station and providing a rapid connection with the western suburbs. Otherwise, many of the lines seem arranged in so anarchic a fashion that one glance at a map showing all of them can induce Parkinson's disease. The problem is compounded by the difficulty of buying tickets (most ticket-vending machines have destinations written in Japanese only; a ticket bought on a private-line machine will be refused by a JR ticket collector etc.) and by the fact that many of even the largest Tokyo terminuses provide few signs in Roman script. A further problem—especially for families travelling with young children or for people suffering from physical disabilities—is the extreme crowdedness of most of the 74 lines throughout the day. During rush hours it often seems impossible that any more passengers could squeeze into the already chock-full compartments, but they do; and unless you begin your journey at the terminus, a seat is rare on most lines at any hour. One bright note is the cheerful colour-coding that has been adopted in painting JR trains (Yamanote=green, Chuo=orange, etc.), which allows the newcomer to recognize his train even when the platform is so congested that he can't get within three metres of the doors.

The Tokyo bus system is wonderfully arcane, and the newcomer is advised to train himself on the mandalas of the Shingon sect before attempting to tackle it.

Accommodation in Japan

Most cities, sizeable towns and major tourist resorts boast Western-style hotels. The rooms are likely to surprise the seasoned traveller by their smallness, but service is usually prompt and polite (tipping is never necessary but a 10 percent 'service charge' is added to the bill) and Western-style food is invariably available on the premises. 'International-class' hotels in major cities can be very expensive. In some surveys, Tokyo's Hotel Okura and Imperial Hotel rank as the priciest in the world.

'Business hotels' provide a cheap no-frills alternative. There is no room service, and often not even a coffee shop, but most are located very close to major railway stations or town centres so there is usually no shortage of restaurants in the vicinity. The rooms are barely large enough to contain a bed, but there is always a cubicle with shower, bath and Western-style lavatory. Business hotels are the best bet for budget-conscious travellers who either do not like Japanese food or do not wish to tie themselves down to fixed mealtimes.

A *ryokan* is a Japanese-style inn. The guest will use a tatami-matted room, to which his meals will be brought by a maid, and in which he will sleep on bedding (*futon*) which the maid will lay out. He will generally use a communal bath, although many ryokans now have rooms with bath and toilet attached, for which a higher rate is charged. Ryokans will expect to serve breakfast and dinner, and the guest has no say in the menu; but these fixed meals are a comparatively inexpensive way of experiencing 'full-course' Japanese cuisine without the bother of ordering separate items. Dinner is usually served quite early (6–7 o'clock), so if the guest finds everything totally unpalatable he still has time to slip out for a sandwich. You can opt to stay at a ryokan without being served meals, but the cost is only marginally less than for full board. A single guest will have a room to himself. A couple arriving together will normally be alloted the same room whatever their relationship. Four or more people arriving together may also find themselves sleeping in the same room. This is a saving in cost only for the ryokan, since bills are calculated per person, not per room.

A *minshuku* is a 'lodging house', in effect a no-frills ryokan. Some differ from ryokan hardly at all, except that the guest may be expected to lay out his own bedding. At others he will take his meals communally, often with the family who own the place. Minshuku are cheaper than ryokan and are mostly found in rural areas.

A *koku-minshuku-sha* is a government-operated lodging house, often found at popular tourist destinations. They are cheap, but vary in quality and must usually be booked well in advance.

A 'pension' is a Western-style minshuku, increasingly popular among the young, especially at ski resorts. Youth hostels are found at many tourist

(Preceding page) Western-style suburban development on the outskirts of Tokyo; a conspicuous absence of garden and garage. The architectural conformity is untypical of urban housing.

destinations, and guests may be encouraged to take part in enervating communal activities such as parlour games.

Eating Out

It is an article of faith among Japanese people that foreigners cannot enjoy their food. They firmly believe, for example, that they are the only nation in the world to eat raw fish; and foreign guests at a sushi shop will sometimes be the objects of gasps of awe punctuated by puzzled shakes of the head.

Sushi is bite-sized slabs of vinegared rice topped with slivers of raw fish or some other delicacy, dipped in soy sauce. Sushi shops are unique in that they rarely display their prices, so the master tends to charge what he likes. For this reason, even Japanese travellers are wary of blundering into unfamilar sushi shops. *Sashimi* is raw fish without the vinegared rice.

Unagi is grilled eel, an expensive and popular delicacy, especially in summer when its high calorie and vitamin content is regarded as a way of combating the deleterious effects of the heat. *Tempura,* said to be Portuguese in origin, is deep-fried food, usually fish, prawns and vegetables.

Sukiyaki (which, because it is a meat dish, is acknowledged to be edible by non-Japanese) is beef and vegetables cooked with soy sauce and sugar and dipped in a condiment consisting mainly of raw egg. It is a comparatively modern invention. So is *shabu-shabu,* wafer-thin strips of meat dipped briefly into boiling stock before eating. A humbler meat dish found throughout Japan is *tonkatsu,* pork cutlets.

Noodles come in a wide variety. *Soba* are thin noodles made from buckwheat, eaten in soup or fried Chinese-style (*yaki-soba*). *Udon* are thicker wheat-flour noodles and *somen* are ultra-thin noodles eaten cold in summer. *S*oba may also be served cold on a tray and dipped into flavoured sauce, in which case it is called *zaru-soba. Ramen* are thin noodles served in hot Chinese-style soup, very cheap and a staple of long-distance truck drivers.

Traditionally, resturants specialize in one or other of these types of food, but multi-purpose restaurants also exist, where the whole gamut, or most of it, is available. Lifelike plastic replicas helpfully occupy most of the window space. A useful word is *teishoku,* meaning a complete meal. For example, *sashimi teishoku* consists of a selection of raw fish with side dishes of pickles, boiled rice and bean-curd (*miso*) soup. Many restaurants also offer cheap set-course lunches. At Japanese-style restaurants these are also called *teishoku,* while at Western-style restaurants they are called *ranchi* (lunch). In the mornings, most coffee shops offer 'morning service', generally coffee, toast, a boiled egg and a tiny salad for little more than the price of a cup of coffee.

Western-style food outside of hotels and top-class restaurants tends to be stodgy. 'Chinese' food is cheap and very widely available, though few Chinese would recognize much of it, and at Korean barbeques (*yaki-niku*) the customer cooks his order of spiced meat on a gas- or charcoal heater brought to his table.

Drinking Out

A *bar* in Japan usually denotes a place where your drink will be poured for you by a 'hostess' who will sit beside you, flatter you, accept your offer of drinks in return, and charge you five times more than you ever dreamed of paying. At a *cabaret,* in return for the entire contents of your wallet, you will be permitted to grope the hostess under the table. A *karaoke* bar, nowadays a popular form of watering hole among salaried workers, may or may not be staffed by 'hostesses', but will certainly be equipped with a microphone and tapes of orchestral accompaniments (*karaoke* means 'empty orchestra') to which the customers sing. Many take this pastime very seriously and, even if you have no ear for Japanese ballads, you can gauge their talent by the loudness of the applause: the loudest applause invariably greets the most thoroughly tuneless performance. Modern karaoke bars have laser video discs instead of tapes and stages with spotlights and screens on which your image can be enjoyed not only by other patrons but by unsuspecting passers-by on the street above.

A *stand bar* or *snack* or *pub* will also often feature karaoke, but there will usually be no hostess, only a 'mama-san' who, except in dire circumstances (fire, theft, love at first sight), remains behind the counter, often barely large enough to seat six customers (the counter, not the mama-san). At such places you will be charged only for what you consume plus a small dish of food (rarely more than peanuts) which accompanies your first drink whether you want it or not, plus 10 percent government tax. Some places charge for each karaoke song, but if you are foreign-looking and not entirely tone deaf you may find yourself drinking at the other customers' expense for the rest of the evening or, if you choose to stay, your life.

Many places operate a 'bottle keep' system. This means that you buy a whole bottle of either whisky or shochu (see page 189), scrawl your name on it with a 'sign pen', preferably illegibly, and on future visits pay only a nominal charge for ice and water to mix with your drink until the bottle runs dry. If you are planning to frequent a place, this is an economical way of drinking as well as of securing the warm reception accorded a paid-up regular.

The safest, cheapest and most interesting choice of drinking spot for the curious visitor in a strange town who does not wish to exercise his vocal cords is an *akachochin* (literally, 'red lantern'), recognizable by that object's prominence above the door outside. There, you will be charged only for what

A geisha in traditional make-up.

you eat and drink. At some places you can eat a substantial meal of grilled fish or sticks of barbequed chicken (*yaki-tori*), an item so popular that many akachochin specialize in it. The atmosphere is often noisy and smoky and, whereas at a bar you go to flirt with a hostess and at a snack to talk to the mama-san, at a red-lantern place customers actually talk to each other; and you may find everything you have ever heard or read about Japanese reticence and politeness driven forever from your mind in the course of one heady night.

Hot Springs

Like most Asians, the Japanese have not traditionally shown a great deal of interest in the seaside as a place to go for rest and recreation; the extreme crowdedness of Japanese beaches on hot Sundays is a modern phenomenon (and still a strictly limited one since few Japanese will venture into the sea outside the month of August). Nor, before the last decades of the 19th century, did the Japanese show any interest in skiing, hiking or mountain climbing; all of those pastimes were introduced to them by energetic Europeans. Traditionally, when the Japanese (especially men) have wanted to relax, they have gone to one of the 20,000 or so thermal springs with which the earthquake- and eruption-ridden geology of the Japanese islands has blessed them, sometimes with their families and sometimes for a form of communal recreation to which their families would constitute a major hindrance.

Hot-spring spas (*onsen*) remain high on the list of favourite leisure destinations for Japanese people today, and it would be sad if the foreign visitor did not sample this hedonistic form of recreation at least once during his stay. There is no prefecture in Japan without hot springs and for many prefectures (such as Tottori, Oita and Akita), onsen are a major source of tourist revenue.

Some resorts consist almost entirely of large, garish Western-style hotels, where there are cabarets, nightclubs, theatres and 'geisha parties' (hot-spring geisha are neither as accomplished nor as hard-to-tumble as their famous Kyoto cousins and sexual adventures, discreet or otherwise, continue to be a factor in the popularity of onsen among all-male groups, though families with children can stay at the hotels in which these adventures occur and remain in complete and blissful ignorance of them).

At less ferociously developed resorts most of the inns are Japanese-style, often teetering on the banks of the river from whose bed the thermal spring erupts. Some are complete towns with numerous bars, restaurants and strip shows. Others may be little more than a cluster of traditonal buildings in a glade or on a mountainside. Some consist of a single inn.

One of the great attractions is the open-air bath (*rotenburo*), which is

almost always available to bathers of both sexes. Not all onsen hotels have *rotenburo,* and those that lack them tend to lavish extra care and expense on their inside baths, most of which are nowadays segregated though there is often a family bath (*kazoku-buro*) to get round this awkward and untraditional prudery.

Some onsen are famous for their curative properties and many of the guests are elderly or infirm. All onsen claim some health benefits, but the sheer relaxation they afford is reason enough for paying the somewhat higher rate that an onsen ryokan charges compared with other inns. The food is usually plentiful and meals and service are often of a higher standard than an ordinary rural ryokan might provide.

Language and Names

Many Japanese people are convinced that their language is 'the most difficult in the world', and refuse to believe that Westerners can speak it. Confronted with the increasingly common sight of Westerners speaking it quite competently, they exhibit a range of emotions including incredulity, revulsion and alarm. Their belief in the language's supreme difficulty was buttressed by early foreign missionaries who called it the 'devil's tongue' and it is a notion the Japanese cling to with a grip unshaken by empirical evidence.

Spoken Japanese is actually among the easiest of East Asian languages for a Westerner because it does not depend on tones. Nor do its sounds present significant difficulties to a speaker who can pronounce consonants roughly as in English and vowels roughly as in Italian. The main difficulties of spoken Japanese are its very large vocabulary and the importance of social propriety, but these are difficulties that English and other languages plainly share.

Written Japanese is another matter. The written language consists of ideograms (*kanji*), borrowed from the Chinese at about the same time as Buddhism, and two sets of 46 phonetic symbols called *kana* which were developed from simplified ideograms during the tenth century. One set, *hiragana,* is used for the grammatical parts of sentences (such as verb endings and particles) which have no equivalent in Chinese. The other, *katakana,* is used mainly for words of foreign (other than Chinese) origin, of which modern Japanese contains thousands. The chief difficulty, apart from the huge effort of memory required to master the system, is that, unlike in Chinese, a single *kanji* may have up to a dozen different pronunciations (though more often two or three), depending on its context and how it is combined with other *kanji* (see the note on *Taira* and *Heike,* page 150). This is, of course, as much a difficulty for the Japanese as it is for foreigners, particularly where names are concerned. At present, junior high school graduates are supposed to have learnt both *kana* syllabaries plus 1,945 *kanji.*

But this is nothing like enough to enable them to read, say, a sophisticated modern novel (Mishima used upwards of 5,000 *kanji*); and one is moved to ponder the often-heard boast that the Japanese are the most literate nation on earth. The only official standard for measuring 'literacy' is school attendance, which is clearly inadequate given both the limitations of compulsory education and the fact that you can take a horse to water without its doing much more than sipping.

All Japanese personal and place names 'mean' something. Former Prime Minister Tanaka's name means 'middle of the paddy', former Prime Minister Sato's name means 'helpful wisteria'. This sounds engagingly quaint, but these meanings impinge no more on the Japanese consciousness than the name 'Smith' conjures up pictures of people hammering anvils, or 'Oxford' calls to the minds of all who hear it a vision of cows wading across a river. In this book names appear in the Japanese order: family name before given name.

The Calendar, The Years and Public Holidays

Unlike some Asian communities, the Japanese abandoned the lunar calendar in 1873, and now calculate the dates of most festivals and all other annual observances by the Gregorian calendar imported from the West. This permits them to steal a march on the Chinese when it comes to New Year, since they have retained the 12 zodiacal animals—rat, ox, tiger, rabbit, dragon, snake, horse, ram, monkey, cock, dog and boar—but each ushers in the year over which it presides on 1 January instead of in February, when the lunar year normally begins.

There are two systems of counting years in Japan, used with about equal frequency. One is the Western system based on an unreliable estimate of when Jesus was born. The other counts years from the accession of each emperor. The present emperor, Hirohito, came to the throne in 1926. His reign is called the Showa (Enlightened Peace) era, 'Showa' being the name he will be known by after his death. Thus 1926 was the first year of Showa, or Showa 1. 1987 was Showa 62. 1900 was Meiji 33, 'Meiji' being the posthumous name of the present emperor's grandfather, who reigned from 1868 to 1911. 1912 to 1925 was the Taisho era, ruled over by the present emperor's father. Hirohito has reigned longer than any other emperor in Japanese history.

There are 12 annual public holidays in Japan. As in the West, 1 January is New Year's Day (*Ganjitsu*), the most important holiday of the year. 15 January is Adult's Day (*Seijin-no-hi*), when ceremonies are held for people who have reached the age of 20. 11 February is National Foundation Day (*Kenkoku Kinen-no-hi*), a day purporting to commemorate the accession of the mythological Emperor Jimmu. 21 March is the Spring Equinox

Sone Akemi fashion show, Tokyo.

(*Shunbun-no-hi*). 29 April is the Emperor's Birthday (*Tenno Tanjobi*). 3 May is Constitution Day (*Kenpo Kinenbi*), commemorating the enforcement of the American-drafted postwar constitution. 5 May is Children's Day (*Kodomo-no-hi*), the new name for the Boy's Festival when male children are pampered even more than usual and colourful carp streamers are flown by families blessed with them. There is a girls' equivalent (the *Hina-matsuri* or Dolls' Festival on 3 March) but it is not a public holiday. 15 September is Respect for the Aged Day (*Keiro-no-hi*). 23 September is the Autumn Equinox (*Shubun-no-hi*), a day for visiting and cleaning the graves of dead family members. 10 October is Sports Day (*Taiiku-no-hi*). 3 November is Culture Day (*Bunka-no-hi*) and 23 November is Labour Thanksgiving Day (*Kinro Kansha-no-hi*), the only day of the year on which many Japanese people will admit to being other than middle class.

Few offices open on these days, and all banks, post offices and similar facilities are closed, though rail and other forms of transport are unaffected. If a public holiday falls on a Sunday, the following Monday becomes a compensatory day off work.

Sources of Information

Detailed travel information can be obtained first-hand from English-speaking staff at the three Tourist Information Centre (TIC) branches, operated by the Japan National Tourist Organisation. The Tokyo branch is next to Yurakucho station at 6–6 Yurakucho 1-chome, Chiyoda-ku: tel. (03) 502 1461. The Kyoto branch is in the Kyoto Tower Building opposite Kyoto Station: tel. (075) 371 5649. The third branch is at Narita Airport: tel. (0476) 32 8711. They are open 9–5 Monday to Friday, 9–12 noon on Saturday and closed on Sunday. In addition to answering questions, they can supply you with enough timetables, handouts, maps, newsletters and free what's-on publications (such as *Tour Companion* and *Tokyo Weekender*) to fill several suitcases.

Tokyo Journal is a monthly English-language magazine containing very detailed information on current events, eating and drinking out, festivals etc. in Tokyo and the Kanto region. It costs 500 yen and is available from foreign-language bookshops and from many hotels. *Kansai Time Out* is a similar publication covering the Osaka, Kobe, Kyoto area.

Tourist information in English is also available over the telephone. In Tokyo you can contact English-speaking tourist advisers by ringing *Travel-Phone* at 502 1461. In Kyoto the number is 371 5649. A three-minute call costs 10 yen. Outside Tokyo and Kyoto the service is toll-free: call 0120 222800 for information about eastern Japan (Chubu to Hokkaido); 0120 444800 for information about western Japan (Kinki to Okinawa). In Tokyo you can hear recorded what's-on information by ringing 503 2911 (English) or 503 2926 (French).

All travel, hotel, ryokan, minshuku and other reservations can be made at any branch of JTB (Japan Travel Bureau), who also organize regional package tours. A variety of regional and period rail passes is available from JR booking offices or JTB. Most airports and major railway stations have information and reservation desks for local hotels and ryokans; ask for *ryokan annai* (ryokan information). You can, of course, walk into a ryokan or minshuku without a reservation and ask if they have a room, but at peak travel periods this is an unreliable method, besides which some innkeepers are still sufficiently thrown by the looming presence of foreigners in their entrance halls to pretend that they are full or closed, a nuisance that is usually (though not always) avoided by reserving through 'correct' channels. Still, it can be part of the delight of arriving in a strange Japanese town to wander through the streets making up your own mind about where you want to stay.

Tickets for theatres, concerts and cinemas can be obtained at *Playguide* desks, though the staff may not speak English. If you are at TIC in Yurakucho, the nearest Playguide is in the Mullion Building on the top floor of the Seibu Department Store; or you can stroll up to the Ginza 8-chome crossing, where you will find English speakers at *Ticket Pia* (tel. 571 1003).

Further Reading

The work of many of the better-known writers on Japanese society (Nakane Chie, Doi Takeo, former U.S. Ambassador Edwin Reischauer *et al*) is marred, in part, by their too ready acquiescence in the notion that the objects of their study are 'unique' and 'different' from the rest of humankind, and their assumption that generalizations like 'The Japanese' (or that even more chimerical entity, 'The West') are sensible and useful. These attitudes have been the bane of 'Japanology' ever since its inception, but Japanese studies today seem to be moving slowly away from such dehumanizing concerns toward an acceptance of the fact that this society is as full of conflicts, contradictions, idiosyncracies, inequities and sheer mess as most other social groups, and that the Japanese people themselves are human individuals, and not some species of consensus-worshipping extraterrestrial. From this point of view, the most valuable recent book on contemporary Japan is Ross Mouer and Yoshio Sugimoto's *Images of Japanese Society* (KPI), which sets out specifically to challenge the 'holistic' view, though its undisguised polemics will limit its appeal to some readers.

Two very good, and very different, books on rural Japanese society are Brian Moeran's *Okubo Diary* (Stanford University) and Junichi Saga's *Memories of Silk and Straw* (Kodansha International). The first is a British anthropologist's memoir of his stay in a tiny Kyushu village. The second is an oral history of a town in Ibaraki prefecture in which elderly people reminisce about pre-war life. Both help to dispel the cloying 'pastoral idyll' attitude toward the Japanese countryside so common among today's city dwellers.

Ian Buruma's *A Japanese Mirror* (Penguin) is an entertaining account of the preoccupations of modern Japanese popular culture. It deals with, among other things, the concept of the hero in Japanese society, a theme brilliantly expanded in Ivan Morris's *The Nobility of Failure* (Penguin), an exceptionally lucid book on those aspects of national character which 'The Japanese' most admire. For an equally lucid account of the cultural mainstream it is hard to better Sir George Sansom's *Japan: A Short Cultural History* (Tuttle), first published in 1931, revised in 1952, but not superseded. Readers seeking a brief historical introduction will benefit from Richard Storry's *A History of Modern Japan* (Penguin), which, its title notwithstanding, opens in prehistoric times. Roy Andrew Miller's *Japan's Modern Myth* (Weatherhill) is a stirringly iconoclastic book about the alleged difficulties and 'uniqueness' of the Japanese language. Several Japanese professors who specialize in detailing this uniqueness have boasted of hurling the book across the room in annoyance, so it needs no further recommendation.

My own *The Roads to Sata* (Penguin) is an account of a four-month journey I made on foot from the northernmost tip of Hokkaido to the southernmost tip of Kyushu, and of the encounters I had along the way.

General Index

Ago Bay　英虞湾　103
Aichi　愛知　135, 143
Aikawa　相川　147
Aizu-Wakamatsu　会津若松　114
Akaishi-dake, Mount　赤石岳　139
Akama Shrine　赤間神宮　165
Akan Kohan　阿寒湖畔　219
Akan, Lake　阿寒湖　219
Akan National Park　阿寒国立公園　219
Akasaka　赤坂　36, 50
Akashi　明石　110
Akashi Kaikyo Ohashi
　明石海峡大橋　110
Akihabara　秋葉原　33
Akita　秋田　114, 125, 126
Akiyoshidai　秋吉台　166
Ama no Iwato　天の岩戸　200
Amagi, Mount　天城山　135
Amakusa　天草　194
Amami　奄美　212
Amanohashidate　天橋立　99
Amidaji　阿弥寺　165
Aobajo　青葉城　120
Aoi Matsuri　葵祭　98
Aomori　青森　114, 128, 130
Arashiyama　嵐山　95
Arima　有馬　110
Arita　有田　188
Asahi, Mount　朝日山　219
Asahi-dake, Mount　朝日岳　118
Asahikawa　旭川　219
Asahiza　朝日座　101
Asakusa　浅草　32
Asakusa Kannon　浅草観音　32
Asakusabashi　浅草橋　33
Asama, Mount　浅間山　139
Ashizuri, Cape　足摺岬　177
Ashizuri-Uwakai National Park
　足摺宇和国立公園　180
Aso, Mount　阿蘇山　195
Aso-Kuju National Park
　阿蘇久住国立公園　195
Atami　熱海　135
Atomic Bomb Dome　原爆ドーム　160
Atsuta Shrine　熱田神宮　146

Awajishima　淡路島　111
Awazu　粟津　154
Axis Building　アクシス・ビル　44
Azabu　麻布　50
Azuma, Mount　吾妻山　117
Bandai, Mount　磐梯山　116
Bandai-Asahi National Park
　磐梯朝日国立公園　116
Beppu　別府　189
Bessho　別所　141
Biiru-en　ビール園　217
Biwa, Lake　琵琶湖　102
Boso Peninsula　房総半島　60
Bridgestone Museum of Art
　ブリジストン美術館　41
Chagu-Chagu Umakko
　チャグチャグ馬子　124
Chiba　千葉　51, 60
Chichibu-Tama National Park
　秩父多摩国立公園　55
Chichijima　父島　51
Children's Peace Monument
　原爆の子の像　160
Chion-in　知恩院　87
Chokai, Mount　鳥海山　118
Choshi　銚子　60
Chubu　中部　134
Chubu-Sangaku　中部山岳　141
Chugoku　中国　162-8
Chuguji　中宮寺　79
Chusonji　中尊寺　125
Chuzenji, Lake　中禅寺湖　59
Daibutsu　大仏　54
Daibutsuden　大仏殿　77
Daikakuji　大覚寺　95
Daisen, Mount　大山　168
Daisen-Oki National Park
　大山隠岐国立公園　167
Daisenin　大審院　94
Daisetsuzan National Park
　大雪山国立公園　219
Daitokuji　大徳寺　94
Dannoura　壇ノ浦　165
Dewa Sanzan　出羽三山　117
Disneyland　デイズニーランド　40

Dogo 道後 180
Dojoji 道成寺 107
Donden, Mount ドンデン山 147
Dotonbori 道頓堀 101
Ebino Plateau えびの高原 200
Ehime 愛媛 180
Eiheiji 永平寺 155
Emburi えんぶり 130
Engakuji 円覚寺 54
Eniwa, Mount 恵庭岳 217
Enryakuji 延暦寺 102
Entsuji 苔提寺 131
Etorofu 択捉 221
Foreigner's Cemetery 外人墓地 51
Fuji, Mount 富士山 137
Fuji-Hakone-Izu National Park
　富士箱根伊豆国立公園 55, 135
Fujiyoshida 富士吉田 138
Fukiagehama 吹上浜 203
Fukui 福共 154, 155
Fukuoka 福岡 185
Fukushima 福島 114
Futamigaura 二見浦 106
Garyusanso 臥龍山荘 181
Gassan, Mount 月山 117
Geku 外宮 103
Gifu 岐阜 135, 142
Ginkakuji 銀閣寺 87
Ginza 銀座 45
Gioji 祇王寺 95
Gion 祇園 84
Gion Matsuri 祇園祭 98
Glover Mansion グラバー家 192
Gobo 御坊 107
Goryokaku 五稜郭 218
Gosho 五所 91
Goshogake 後生掛 125
Gotenba 御殿場 137
Goto Islands 五島 194
Gunma 群馬 51, 55
Habomai 歯舞 221
Hachijojima 八丈島 50
Hachimantai Plateau 八幡平高原 125
Hachinohe 八戸 130
Hagi 萩 166
Haguro, Mount 羽黒山 117
Hahajima 母島 51
Hakata 博多 185
Hakata Dontaku 博多どんたく 185

Hakkoda, Mount 八甲田山 128
Hakodate 函館 218
Hakodate, Mount 函館山 218
Hakone 箱根 55
Hakusan, Mount 白山 154
Hakusan National Park
　白山国立公園 154
Hanagasa Matsuri 花笠祭り 118
Harajuku 原宿 36, 50
Haramachi 原町 117
Harimayabashi 播磨屋橋 177
Hasedera 長谷寺 54
Hayachine, Mount 早池峰山 125
Heian Shrine 平安神宮 82
Heiankyo 平安京 63, 150
Heijokyo 平城京 63
Hie Shrine 日枝神社 36, 142
Hiei, Mount 比叡山 102
Higashi Honganji 東本願寺 90
Higashiyama 東山 116
Hikone 彦根 102
Himeji 姫路 110
Hirado 平戸 194
Hiraizumi 平泉 124
Hirara 平良 213
Hirosaki 弘前 130
Hiroshima 広島 157
Hokkiji 法起寺 81
Hokokuji 法国寺 54
Hongu 本宮 107
Horinji 法輪寺 81
Horyuji 法隆寺 78
Hoshi 法師 55
Hotaka 穂高 141
Hyogo 兵庫 62, 110
Ibaraki 茨城 51, 59
Ibusuki 指宿 203
Idemitsu Gallery 出光美術館 41
Iimori Hill 飯盛山 116
Iki 壱岐 195
Ikuchijima 生口島 173
Imperial Palace 皇居 28
Inawashiro, Lake 猪苗代湖 116
Inubo, Cape 犬吠埼 60
Inuyama 犬山 143
Iojima 硫黄島 51
Iriomote 西表 213
Ise Jingu 伊勢神宮 103
Isetan 伊勢丹 44

Ishigaki　石垣　213
Ishikari River　石狩川　219
Ishikawa　石川　151
Ishikawa-mon　石川門　151
Ishizuchi, Mount　石鎚山　180
Itoman　糸満　212
Itsukushima　厳島　160
Itsukushima Shrine　厳島神社　160
Iwaki, Mount　岩木山　130
Iwaki Shrine　岩木神社　130
Iwami　岩美　168
Iwate　岩手　124, 125
Iwate, Mount　岩手山　124
Iwato　岩戸　200
Izu Islands　伊豆諸島　50
Izu Peninsula　伊豆半島　135
Izumo Taisha Shrine　出雲大社　166
Jakkoin　寂光院　98
Japan Science Museum
　日本科学技術館　41
Jidai Matsuri　時代祭　98
Jigokudani　地獄谷　141
Jo-Shinetsu Kogen National Park
　上信越高原国立公園　141
Jojakkoji　常寂光寺　95
Jozankei　定山渓　217
Kabira Bay　川平湾　213
Kabukicho　歌舞伎町　48
Kabukiza　歌舞伎座　39, 45
Kaga　加賀　151, 154
Kagawa　香川　181
Kagoshima　鹿児島　185, 202
Kaike　皆生　168
Kaimon, Mount　開聞岳　203
Kairakuen　偕楽園　60
Kakunodate　角館　126
Kamakura　鎌倉　53
Kamigamo Jinja　上賀茂神社　98
Kamikochi　上高地　141
Kanagawa　神奈川　51
Kanagi　金木　131
Kanazawa　金沢　151
Kanazawa Castle　金沢城　151
Kanda　神田　33
Kanda Matsuri　神田祭　32
Kanda River　神田川　29
Kankakei　寒霞渓　171
Kanmon Bridge　関門橋　163
Kanto Matsuri　竿灯祭り　126

Kappabashi　河童橋　33
Karasujo　鴉城　141
Karatsu　唐津　188
Karuizawa　軽井沢　139
Karurusu　カルルス　218
Kasamatsu Park　箱松公園　99
Kasuga Shrine　春日大社　73
Kasumigaike　霞が池　151
Kasumigaseki　霞ガ関　40
Kasumigaura, Lake　霞ケ浦　59
Katayamazu　片山津　154
Katsura Imperial Villa　桂離宮　91
Katsurahama　桂浜　177
Kawagoe　川越　55
Kawaguchi　川口　138
Kawaguchiko, Lake　河口湖　137
Kawaramachi　河原町　98
Kazuno　鹿角　125
Kegon Fall　華厳滝　59
Kenrokuen　兼六園　151
Kii Peninsula　紀伊半島　106
Kikaishima　喜界島　212
Kinkakuji　金閣寺　87
Kinkazan　金華山　122
Kinugawa　鬼怒川　58
Kinzan　金山　147
Kirishima, Mount　霧島山　200
Kirishima-Yaku National Park
　霧島屋久国立公園　200
Kiso River　木曽川　143
Kita Kyushu　北九州　188
Kiyomizudera　清水寺　86
Kobe　神戸　110
Kochi　高知　177
Kofu　甲府　138
Kofukuji　興福寺　71
Koishiwara　小石原　188
Kokedera　苔寺　95
Kokugikan　国技館　36
Kokura　小倉　188
Koma-ga-take, Mount　駒ケ岳　139
Komatsu　小松　154
Komoro　小諸　141
Kompira Shrine　金毘羅神社　181
Konjikido　金色堂　125
Korakuen (Okayama)　後楽園　163
Korakuen (Tokyo)　後楽園　41
Koryuji　広隆寺　84
Kotohiragu Shrine　金刀比羅宮　181

Koya, Mount　高野山　107
Koza　コザ　212
Kozujima　神津島　50
Kudan　九段　36
Kuju　久住　195
Kujukurihama　九十九里浜　60
Kumamoto　熊本　185, 195
Kumano　熊野　107
Kumano Shrines　熊野三社　107
Kunashiri　国後　221
Kuonji　久遠寺　138
Kuramae　蔵前　36
Kurashiki　倉敷　163
Kurobe　黒部　150
Kurobe Dam　黒部ダム　150
Kurobe Gorge　黒部峡谷　150
Kurobe River　黒部川　150
Kurohime, Mount　黒姫山　141
Kuroyu　黒湯　125
Kusatsu　草津　55
Kushiro　釧路　221
Kushiro Marshland National Park
　釧路国立公園　221
Kutani　九谷　154
Kutcharo, Lake　屈斜路湖　219
Kyoto　京都　62, 63, 81-99
La Foret　ラ・フォレ　44
Magoroku　孫六　125
Mano　真野　147
Marukoma　凡駒　217
Mashiko　益子　58
Mashu, Lake　摩周湖　219
Matsue　松江　167
Matsumae　松前　218
Matsumoto　松本　141
Matsushima　松島　120
Matsuyama　松山　180
Matsuzaka　松坂　102
Meiji Mura　明治村　143
Meiji Shinzan　明治新山　217
Meiji Shrine　明治神宮　36
Meoto Iwa　夫婦岩　106
Mie　三重　62, 102
Mihara, Mount　三原山　50
Mihonoseki　美保関　167
Mikurajima　御蔵島　50
Minakami　水上　55
Minamata　水俣　198

Minami Arupusu National Park
　南アルプス国立公園　139
Minamiza　南座　98
Mino　美濃　142
Minobu, Mount　身延山　138
Minzoku Mura　民族村　142
Miroku Bosatsu　弥勒菩薩　79, 84
Misumi　三角　194
Mito　水戸　60
Mitsukoshi　三越　33, 44
Miyagi　宮城　114, 120
Miyajima　宮島　160
Miyakejima　三宅島　50
Miyako　宮古　212
Miyazaki　宮崎　185, 198
Miyazaki Shrine　宮崎　200
Miyazu Bay　宮津湾　99
Mogami River　最上川　118
Moji　門司　188
Morioka　盛岡　124
Motomachi　元町　53
Motosu, Lake　本栖湖　138
Motsuji　毛越寺　125
Muroto　室戸　177
Myojin Shrine　明神（神田神社）　33
Myoshinji　妙心寺　94
Nachi Falls　那智滝　107
Naeba　苗場　141
Naeshirogawa　内白川　203
Nagano　長野　135, 139, 141
Nagara River　長良川　142
Nagasaki　長崎　185, 191
Nago　名護　212
Nagoya　名古屋　143
Naha　那覇　212
Naiku　内宮　103
Nakasendo　中山道　139
Nakazu　中津　188
Namahage　なまはげ　126
Nandaimon　南大門　77
Nara　奈良　62, 66
Nara National Museum
　奈良国立博物館　73
Narita　成田　60
Naruto　鳴門　175
Nasu　那須　58
National Diet Building
　国会議事堂　40

National Museum of Modern Art
　　国立近代美術館　41
National Museum of Western Art
　　国立西洋美術館　33
National Science Museum
　　国立科学博物館　33
Naze　名瀬　212
Nebuta Matsuri　ねぶた祭　130
Nemuro　根室　221
Nennokuchi　子ノ口　128
NHK Hall　NHKホール　41
NHK's Broadcasting Centre
　　NHK放送センター　41
Nigatsudo　二月堂　77
Nihonbashi　日本橋　33
Nihonbashi River　日本橋川　33
Niigata　新潟　146
Niijima　新島　50
Nijo Castle　二条城　90
Nikko　日光　59
Nikolai Cathedral　ニコライ堂　45
Ninnaji　仁和寺　86
Nippon Budokan　日本武道館　41
Nishi Honganji　西本願寺　90
Nishizaka Park　西坂公園　192
Nobeoka　延岡　200
Noboribetsu　登別　218
Norikura, Mount　乗鞍岳　141
Noto Peninsula　能登半島　151
O-mizutori　お水取り　77
Ochanomizu　お茶の水　29
Odate　大館　126
Oga Peninsula　男鹿半島　126
Ogasawara Islands　小笠原諸島　51
Ogasawara National Park
　　小笠原国立公園　51
Ohara　大原　95
Ohara Gallery　大原美術館　163
Oirase River　奥ス瀬川　128
Oita　大分　185, 188, 189
Okayama　岡山　162, 163
Oki　隠岐　167
Okinawa　沖縄　212
Okinoerabu　沖永良部　212
Omachi　大町　150
Omaru　大丸　58
Omishima　青海島　165, 173
Omogokeikyo Gorge　面河渓峡　180

Onioshidashi　鬼押出　141
Oranda Mura　オランダ村　192
Osaka　大阪　62, 101
Osaka Castle　大阪城　101
Oshika Peninsula　牡鹿半島　122
Oshima　大島　50, 212
Osorezan　恐山　131
Osumi　大隅　203
Oyamazumi Shrine　大山祇神社　173
Ozu　大洲　180
Parco　パルコ　44
Peace Memorial Pagoda
　　平和記念塔パゴダ　175
Pearl Island　パール島　103
Peiron　ペイロン　194
Pontocho　先斗町　98
Rausu　羅臼　219
Rausu, Mount　羅臼岳　221
Reiyukai　霊友会　44
Rikuchu Kaigan National Park
　　陸中海岸国立公園　125
Rishiri-Rebun-Sarobetsu National Park
　　利尻礼文サロベツ国立公園　221
Rissho Koseikai　立正佼成会　45
Ritsurin Park　栗林公園　181
Rokko, Mount　六甲山　110
Rokuonji　鹿苑寺　87
Ryoanji　龍安寺　90
Ryogóku　両国　36
Ryotsu　両津　147
Sado　佐渡　147
Saga　佐賀　185, 188
Sagi ike　鷺池　77
Saihoji　西芳寺　95
Saikai National Park　西海国立公園　194
Saiko, Lake　西湖　138
Sainokawara　賽の河原　131
Saitama　埼玉　51, 55
Sakaide　坂出　181
Sakaiminato　境港　167
Sakata　酒田　118
Sakuragicho　桜木町　53
Sakurajima　桜島　202
Sandankyo Gorge　三段峡　160
Sangatsudo　三月堂　77
Sanin Kaigan National Park
　　山陰海岸国立公園　111
Sanja Matsuri　三社祭　32

Sanjusangendo 三十三間堂 86
Sanno Matsuri 山王祭 32, 142
Sanzenin 三千院 95
Satsuma 薩摩 203
Seikan Tunnel 青函トンネル 218
Sekigahara 関ヶ原 143
Sekigane 関金 168
Sendai 仙台 120
Sengakuji 泉岳寺 37
Senjo-ga-take, Mount 仙丈ケ岳 139
Sensoji 浅草寺 32
Seto Ohashi 瀬戸大橋 163
Setonaikai 瀬戸内海 171
Setonaikai National Park
　瀬戸内海国立公園 171
Shiga 滋賀 62, 102
Shiga Kogen 志賀高原 141
Shikinejima 式根島 50
Shikotan 色丹 221
Shikotsu, Lake 支笏湖 217
Shikotsu-Toya National Park
　支笏洞爺国立公園 217
Shima 四万 55
Shimabara 島原 194
Shimabara Castle 島原城 194
Shimane 島根 167
Shimane Peninsula 島根半島 162, 166
Shimoda 下田 135
Shimogamo Jinja 下賀茂神社 98
Shimokita 下北 131
Shimonoseki 下関 163
Shin Noboribetsu 新登別 218
Shin-Kabukiza 新歌舞伎座 101
Shinagawa 品川 37
Shinbashi 新橋 45
Shingo 新郷 128
Shingu 新宮 107
Shinji, Lake 宍道湖 167
Shinjuku 新宿 48
Shinobazu Pond 不忍池 33
Shinshoji 新勝寺 60
Shiobara 塩原 58
Shiogama 塩竃 122
Shiomi-dake, Mount 塩見岳 139
Shirakawa 白河 114
Shirane, Mount 白根山 139, 141
Shiretoko 知床 219
Shiretoko National Park
　知床国立公園 219

Shiroishi 白石 120
Shiroyama 城山 202
Shitennoji 四天王寺 101
Shizuoka 静岡 135
Shodoshima 小豆島 171
Shoji, Lake 精進湖 138
Shokawa Gorge 庄川峡 150
Shokawa River 庄川 150
Shosenkyo Gorge 昇仙峡 138
Shosoin 正倉院 78
Showa Shinzan 昭和新山 218
Shugakuin Imperial Villa
　修学院離宮 91
Shuhodo 秋芳洞 166
Shuri 首里 212
Shuzenji 修善寺 135
Sofukuji 崇福寺 192
Soma Nomaoi 相馬野馬追い 117
Sotoyama 外山 124
Sounkyo Gorge 層雲峡 219
Sugimotoji 杉本寺 54
Suginami 杉並 45
Sumida River 隅田川 36
Susukino 薄野 217
Suwa, Lake 諏訪湖 141
Tabaruzaka 田原坂 198
Taiji 太地 110
Taira 平 150
Taishakukyo Gorge 帝釈峡 160
Takachiho 高千穂 200
Takachiho Shrine 高チ穂神社 200
Takamatsu 高松 181
Takashima 高島 192
Takayama 高山 142
Takebashi 竹橋 41
Taketomi 竹富 213
Tama Canal 玉川上水 29
Tamagawa 多摩川 125
Tanabata Matsuri 七夕 120
Tanegashima 種子島 203
Tanukikoji 狸小路 217
Tateyama 館山 150
Tateyama, Mount 立山 150
Tawaramachi 田原町 33
Tazawa, Lake 田沢湖 126
Tenjin Matsuri 天神発 101
Tenryuji 天龍寺 95
Toba 鳥羽 103
Tochigi 栃木 51, 58

Todaiji 東大寺 77	Usa Hachiman 宇佐入幡宮 189
Toei Eiga Mura 東映映画村 84	Usu, Mount 有珠山 217
Toi 土肥 135	Usui Pass 碓氷峠 139
Tokai 東海 60	Utsunomiya 宇都宮 58
Tokeiji 東慶寺 54	Uwajima 宇和島 180
Tokunoshima 徳え島 212	Wajima 輪島 151
Tokushima 徳島 175	Wakakusa, Mount 若草山 78
Tokyo Metropolitan Art Gallery 東京都美術館 33	Wakayama 若山 106, 107
Tokyo National Museum 東京国立博物館 33	Wakkanai 稚内 221
Tokyo Station 東京駅 40	Yaeyama 八重山 213
Tokyo Tower 東京タワー 40	Yakushima 屋久島 203
Tokyo University 東京大学 29	Yamadera 山寺 118
Tosa-Shimizu 土佐清水 180	Yamagata 山形 114, 117, 118
Toshima 豊島 50	Yamaguchi 山口 162, 163, 166
Toshodaiji 唐招提寺 70	Yamanaka, Lake 山中湖 138, 154
Toshogu Shrine 東照宮 59	Yamanashi 山梨 135, 138
Tottori 鳥取 162, 168	Yamashiro 山代 154
Tottori Sand Dunes 鳥取砂丘 168	Yanaka 谷中 36
Towada, Lake 十和田湖 128	Yari, Mount 槍ケ岳 141
Towada-Hachimantai National Park 十和田八幡平国立公園 125	Yasaka Shrine 八坂神社 84
	Yashima 屋島 181
Toya, Lake 洞爺湖 217	Yasukuni Shrine 靖国神社 36
Toyako Onsen 洞爺湖温泉 217	Yasumiya 休屋 128
Toyama 富山 150	Yatsu-ga-take, Mount 八ケ岳 139
Toyota City 豊田市 143	Yawata 八幡 188
Tsugaru 津軽 131	Yokaichi 八日市 181
Tsukiji 築地 33	Yokkaichi 四日市 102
Tsukiji Honganji 築地本願寺 45	Yokohama 横浜 51
Tsukuba 筑波 60	Yokokawa 横川 139
Tsurugajo 鶴ケ城 116	Yonaguni 与那国 213
Tsurugaoka Hachiman Shrine 鶴岡八幡宮 54	Yoron 与論 212
	Yoshino 吉野 81
Tsurugi, Mount 剣山 177	Yoshino-Kumano National Park 吉野熊野国立公園 81
Tsushima 対馬 195	Yoshiwara 吉原 32
Uchiko 内子 181	Yoyogi Park 代々木公園 50
Ueda 上田 141	Yuda 湯田 166
Ueno 上野 33	Yufu, Mount 由布岳 189
Umeda 梅田 101	Yufuin 油布院 189
Unazuki 宇奈月 150	Yunokawa 湯川 218
Unzen, Mount 雲仙岳 194	Yurakucho 有楽町 40, 45
Unzen-Amakusa National Park 雲仙天草国立公園 194	Yuwaku 湯涌 154
	Yuzawa 湯沢 150
Urakami Catholic Cathedral 浦上天主堂 191	Yuze 湯瀬 125
	Zao, Mount 蔵王山 120
Urayasu 浦安 40	Zenkoji 善光寺 141
Usa 宇佐 189	Zentsuji 善通寺 181
	Zuiganji 瑞巌寺 122

Index of People Mentioned

Antoku 安徳 (1178–1185), by traditional count the 81st emperor, ascended the throne at the age of three and was drowned, aged eight, at the sea battle of Dannoura.

Asano Naganori 長徳淺野 (1667–1701) was the provincial lord, immortalized as Enya Hangan Takasada in the Kabuki play *Chushingura*, who committed ritual suicide after being goaded into drawing his sword in the shogun's castle, and was famously avenged by his 47 loyal retainers.

Ashikaga Yoshimasa 足利義政 (1436–1490), the eighth Ashikaga shogun, ruled from 1449 to 1474, years marked by growing social unrest, the decline in the power of his family and the beginning of a long period of civil war. Yoshimasa had little interest in affairs of state and lavished his energies on artistic projects such as the building of the Silver Pavilion.

Ashikaga Yoshimitsu 足利義満 (1358–1408) was the third Ashikaga shogun, having succeeded his father at the age of 10. He was an energetic ruler who continued to revel in luxury and artistic refinement after retirement into the priesthood. These loves are exemplified in the Golden Pavilion, which he built.

Ashikaga Yoshinori 足利義教 (1394–1441), the sixth Ashikaga shogun, who ruled from 1429 to his death, was responsible for the downfall and exile of Zeami.

Benkei 弁慶 (?–1189) was the (perhaps legendary) retainer of Yoshitsune, whose prodigious wit, strength and fidelity to his lord are celebrated in the Kabuki play *Kanjincho*. In their last stand against the forces of Yoritomo, Benkei fought to the death in order to allow Yoshitsune time to commit suicide.

Blunden, Edmund Charles (1869–1974) was a British poet who lived and taught for long periods of his life in Japan and Hong Kong.

Clark, William Smith (1826–1886) was the American educator who advised the Japanese government on agricultural and educational matters during his tenure (1876–77) at the newly-opened agricultural college in Sapporo.

Date Masamune 伊達政宗 (1567–1636) was a warrior who, having supported Ieyasu at the Battle of Sekigahara, was rewarded with the fief of Sendai, which he developed and where he built his famous castle.

Dogen 道元 (1200–1253) was the founder of the Soto sect of Zen Buddhism and its head temple, Eiheiji. He was a prolific author whose writings stress the Buddha nature in all things and the importance of realizing this nature through insight into oneself and the world.

Ganjin 鑑眞 (688–763) was the Chinese Buddhist monk (properly called Chien

Chen) who founded Toshodaiji temple in Nara. He was blind when he reached Japan at the age of 66 and is said to have died in the full lotus position of meditation.

Gio 祇王 is the otherwise unknown lady who, according to the *Heike Monogatari* (Tale of the Heike), entered the convent now called Gioji at the age of 21 after losing the love of Kiyomori. The convent, originally called Ojoin, was renamed for her in 1895.

Glover, Thomas Blake (1838–1911), a Scotsman, established a trading firm in Nagasaki in 1859 and financially supported the anti-shogunate forces in the Meiji Restoration. In the 1860s he diversified into railways and mining, and went bankrupt in 1870.

Go-Daigo 後醍醐 (1287–1339), by traditional count the 96th emperor, reigned from 1318 to 1339. He was exiled to the Oki islands in 1332 for attempting to overthrow the Kamakura shogunate, but escaped the next year, when forces mustered by him defeated the shogun's army and restored Go-Daigo to power. The restoration was short-lived and he abdicated one day before he died, following the establishment of a new line of shoguns, the Ashikagas.

Go-Toba 後鳥羽 (1180–1239), by traditional count the 82nd emperor, reigned from the age of three until 1198. In 1221 he joined Juntoku, his son, in an uprising against the Kamakura shogunate as a result of which he was exiled to Oki.

Hamada Shoji 浜田庄司 (1894–1978) was Japan's most famous modern potter, who contributed hugely to the revival of interest in folk pottery. He was named a Living National Treasure in 1955.

Harris, Townsend (1804–1878) was the first U.S. consul general in Japan. He arrived in 1856 and succeeded in concluding a commercial treaty in 1858, one of the landmarks in Japan's at first reluctant opening to the West.

Hearn, Lafcadio (1850–1904) was an author and teacher intoxicated by the romantic view of Japan which he helped introduce to the late Victorian West. He lived in Japan from 1890 to his death. A selection of his writings about Japan has been published by Penguin.

Hirohito 裕仁 (1901–) is the present emperor of Japan (by traditional count the 124th) and, if one excepts the early fictions, the longest reigning sovereign in Japanese history. He came to the throne in 1926 and after his death will be known as *Showa*–also the name for the period in which he has reigned.

Hojo Tokimasa 北條時政 (1138–1215) was Yoritomo's father-in-law and first regent of the Kamakura shogunate, an office he held from 1203 to 1205.

Honen 法然 (1133–1212) was the Buddhist priest who founded the Jodo (Pure Land) sect, which advocates total reliance on the chanting of the *nembutsu* (the name of

Amida, the Compassionate Buddha) as the sole means of achieving grace.

Ikeda Daisaku 池田大作 (1928–) was the third president of Sokagakkai and the founder of its political party, Komeito. He retired as president in 1979 but remains the head of Sokagakkai International.

Ishida Mitsunari 石田三成 (1560–1600) was the most important of Hideyoshi's ministers and, after his master's death, led forces against Ieyasu, who defeated him in 1600 at the Battle of Sekigahara, following which he was captured and executed.

Ishikawa Jozan 石川文山 (1583–1672) was the Rinzai priest, Confucian scholar and Chinese-style poet who built the secluded Shisendo hermitage, to which he retired at the age of 58.

Jimmu 神武 (711 BC–585 BC!) was the legendary first emperor of Japan, who is supposed to have reigned from 660 BC until his death. The dates are wholly impossible and there is doubt that he even existed.

Juntoku 順徳 (1197–1242), by traditional count the 84th emperor, reigned from 1210 until his abdication in 1221 following an unsuccessful revolt against the Kamakura shogunate, as a result of which he was exiled to Sado, where he died.

Kammu 桓武 (737–806), traditionally the 50th emperor, reigned from 781 until his death. His mother was of Korean origin. He is best remembered for having established the capital at Heiankyo, later Kyoto.

Kawabata Yasunari 川端康成 (1899–1972), Japan's only Nobel laureate in literature, won the Prize in 1968. He was a lyrical and elegaic writer whose qualities are perhaps best seen in the novels *Yukiguni* (Snow Country) and *Senbazuru* (Thousand Cranes), both translated into English by Edward Seidensticker. His death in a gas-filled room of his apartment was perhaps suicide, perhaps misadventure.

Kenreimon-in 建礼門院 (1155–1213), the daughter of Kyomori, leapt into the sea with her son, the Emperor Antoku, when defeat for the Heike was assured at the Battle of Dannoura in 1185. The boy was drowned, but the mother was rescued and retired to the Jakkoin as a nun.

Kinmei 欽明 (509–571), traditionally the 29th emperor, reigned from 540 until his death. During his reign Buddhism was introduced into Japan from Korea.

Kira Yoshinaka 吉良義央 (1641–1703) is better known to posterity as Kono Moronao, the villain of the Kabuki play *Chushingura*. Kira goaded the young lord Asano Naganori into drawing his sword in the shogun's castle, for which offence Asano was sentenced to commit ritual suicide. Asano's 47 loyal retainers bided their time before assassinating Kira at his Edo residence and laying his severed head on their lord's grave.

Kobayashi Masaki 小林正樹 (1916–) is a film director, best-known for his anti-war trilogy *Ningen no Joken* (The Human Condition) and for *Seppuku* (Harakiri), which calls into question Japan's vaunted warrior ethic. His 1964 *Kwaidan* is a version of four tales by Lafcadio Hearn.

Kugyo 公暁 (1201–1219) was the priestly name taken by Yoritomo's grandson, whose own father, the shogun Yoriie, had been deposed by Yoritomo's second son, Sanetomo, in revenge for which Kugyo assassinated Sanetomo at the Tsurugaoka Hachiman Shrine in Kamakura in 1219 and was himself pursued and killed.

Kukai 空海 (774–835) is more widely known by his posthumous name, Kobo Daishi. He founded the Shingon sect of Buddhism and the monastery on Mount Koya, and was an unflagging builder of temples, including the 88 in Shikoku that form Japan's most famous pilgrim circuit. He is also credited with having invented the *kana* syllabary.

Kuninaka no Muraji Kimimaro 国中連公麻呂 (?–774), the grandson of a naturalised Korean official, was according to one source, 'the most eminent Nara-period sculptor of Buddhist images' and was responsible for casting the Great Buddha of Todaiji temple in Nara, despite which, no doubt because of his parentage, his name is absent from most Japanese guides and reference books.

Kurosawa Akira 黒澤明 (1910–) is Japan's best-known living film director, though his reputation has always seemed more secure abroad than at home. His most recent films are *Kagemusha* (The Shadow Warrior), about the circumstances surrounding the death of Takeda Shingen, and *Ran* (Conflict), a version of *King Lear*.

Leach, Bernard Howell (1887–1979) was an English potter who, with Hamada Shoji, introduced Japanese pottery and ceramic methods to the West. He was also instrumental in helping to revive an interest in the folk arts in Japan.

Maeda Toshiie 前田利家 (1538?–1599) was one of Nobunaga's principal vassal lords, who later fought on the side of Hideyoshi and was rewarded in 1583 with the fief of Kaga.

Matsuo Basho 松尾芭蕉 (1644–1694) was, and is, Japan's foremost haiku poet. He adopted the name Basho (Banana Tree) in 1681 after the tree that stood in his garden. His single most famous haiku is: *furuike ya/kawazu tobikomu/mizu no oto* ('An old pond/a frog jumps in/sound of water') and his best-known travel book, which contains many poems, is *Oku no Hosomichi*, translated into English by Yuasa Nobuyuki as *The Narrow Road to the Deep North*.

Meiji 明治 is the posthumous name of Mutsuhito (1852–1912), by traditional count the 122nd emperor of Japan, who reigned from 1867 until his death, a period also known as Meiji. The restoration of power to him in 1868 marked the end of the shogunate and the beginning of Japan's modern era. He was the present emperor's grandfather.

Mikimoto Kokichi 御木本幸吉 (1858–1954) was the father of Japan's cultured pearl industry. He succeeded in producing his first cultured pearl in 1893 and by 1911 had set up stores in London, the U.S.A. and China, establishing himself as the 'pearl king'.

Minamoto no Sanetomo 源実朝 (1192–1219) was Yoritomo's second son and the third Kamakura shogun, an office he assumed in 1203 at the age of 11. He was assassinated by his nephew, Kugyo, who blamed him for his father's death.

Minamoto no Yoritomo 源頼朝 (1147–1199) was the founder of the Kamakura shogunate (1192–1333), and one of the most ruthless and powerful warlords in Japanese history. Posterity's regard for him has been lessened by his jealous persecution of his charismatic younger brother, Yoshitsune.

Minamoto no Yoshitsune 源義経 (1159–1189), Yoritomo's half-brother, can claim to be Japan's chief tragic hero. He was hugely instrumental in the overthrow of the Heike, but soon after incurred the jealousy and suspicion of Yoritomo and was forced to flee from his brother's forces. He died surrounded by Yoritomo's warriors, after having first killed his wife and daughter.

Mishima Yukio 三島通庸 (1925–1970) was a prolific novelist, playwright and essayist, widely remembered for the histrionic ritual suicide he committed after leading members of his private army in occupying part of the headquarters of the Ground Self-Defence Forces and exhorting the personnel there to rise 'in defence of the emperor'. In his last years he made a cult of body-building and the martial arts and adopted extreme right-wing attitudes, but his novels are remarkable for their delicacy of observation and their rampant aestheticism. *Kinkakuji* (The Temple of the Golden Pavilion) has been translated into English by Ivan Morris.

Miyamoto Musashi 宮本武蔵 (1584–1645) was a master swordsman who developed the method of fighting with two swords, one long, one short. He was also a painter and calligrapher whose work is regarded as having been heavily influenced by Zen.

Mongaku 文覚 (dates uncertain) was a Buddhist priest and associate of Yoritomo's. He was exiled to Sado in 1199, having been implicated in a plot against the emperor.

Moraes, Wenceslau de (1854–1929) was a Portuguese naval officer, diplomat and author who spent much of his life in the East, at Macau and subsequently in Japan where he lived permanently from 1898 until his death.

Mukai Kyorai 向井去来 (1651–1704) was the poet, a disciple of Basho's, who lived in Saga, on the outskirts of Kyoto, in the rustic cottage called *Rakushisha* (Hut of Fallen Persimmons).

Nagako 艮子 (1903–), the eldest daughter of Prince Kuni no Miya Kunihiko, is the present empress of Japan, having married Hirohito, then crown prince, in 1924.

Nakahama (John) Manjiro 中浜万次郎 (1827–1898) was a fisherman from Kochi who was shipwrecked in 1841, rescued by an American whaler and invited by its captain to the U.S., where he lived until 1851, studying and working as a cooper, seaman and gold prospector. On his return to Japan he became the shogunate's chief interpreter.

Nakasone Yasuhiro 中曾根康弘 (1918–) was Japan's prime minister from 1982 to 1987. During his period in office he alternately impressed foreign governments with his much vaunted 'internationalism' and horrified them with gestures and words that were widely interpreted as racist, chauvanist and ultra-nationalistic.

Nichiren 日蓮 (1222–1282) founded the sect of Buddhism that bears his name, and which teaches that salvation can be achieved by repeatedly chanting the formula *namu myoho renge kyo* (I take refuge in the Lotus Sutra).

Nogi Maresuke 乃木希典 (1849–1912) was the general who led Japan's Third Army in the Russo-Japanese War of 1904–05 and is remembered as the victor of Port Arthur, though his 'strategy' of unrelenting frontal assault cost 56,000 Japanese casualties.

Noguchi Hideo 野口英世 (1876–1928) was a bacteriologist who isolated the causative agent of syphilis and, in 1918, began work on a vaccine for yellow fever. His trip to Africa, on which he died of yellow fever, was undertaken to confirm his results.

Oda Nobunaga 織田信長 (1534–1582) was the great unifier of Japan after a hundred years of civil war. Hideyoshi and Ieyasu were both originally his vassals and could never have wielded their subsequent power without the groundwork laid by Nobunaga's blend of brutality, ruthlessness and vision.

Ojin 応神 (201–310?) was, by traditional count, the 15th emperor and is supposed to have reigned from 270 to his death. More likely he was a provincial ruler of the 5th century. A keyhole-shaped mound near Osaka is believed to be his tomb.

Perry, Matthew Calbraith (1794–1858) was the U.S. commodore who arrived off the coast of Japan with his 'black ships' in 1853 and again in 1854, and pressured the shogun into signing the Treaty of Kanagawa, under which certain ports were opened to foreign commerce.

Saga 嵯峨 (786–842), by traditional count the 52nd emperor, was both an energetic statesman and an enthusiastic poet. He ruled from 809 to 823 and, after abdicating, retired to his suburban villa, now Daikakuji temple.

Saigo Takamori 西郷隆盛 (1827–1877) was the former Marshall and Counsellor of State who led the last armed rebellion against the Japanese government in 1877. He is still widely regarded as a paragon of old samurai virtues. His statue stands in Ueno Park.

Sakamoto Ryoma 坂本龍馬 (1836–1867) was one of the prime movers in the Meiji

Restoration of 1868, to which he contributed by helping cement a crucial alliance between the Choshu and Satsuma clans. He was assassinated by an agent of the increasingly desperate shogunate the year before it fell.

Shimazu Nariakira 島津斉彬 (1809–1858) was the energetic lord of Satsuma who embarked on an active programme of Westernization, including the building of factories producing weapons, gunpowder, glass, ceramics and chemicals.

Shinran 親鸞 (1173–1263) was the founder of the Jodo Shin (New Pure Land) sect of Buddhism, which maintains that simple faith is the only necessary prerequisite for salvation.

Shotoku 聖徳 (574–622), usually called Shotoku Taishi or Prince Shotoku, was a great regent, administrator and supporter of the spread of Buddhism, who is credited with having promulgated the Japanese nation's first constitution.

Suinin 垂仁 (70 BC–AD 70!), traditonally the 11th emperor, is supposed to have reigned from 31 BC until his death. His tomb is in Nara. Almost nothing is known about him, but he is credited with having founded the first shrine at Ise.

Suzuki Daisetz 鈴木大拙 (1870–1966) was the Buddhist scholar largely responsible for the popularity of Zen Buddhism in the West, where some 30 volumes by him have been published.

Taira no Kiyomori 平清盛 (1118–1181) was an ambitious and powerful warrior and statesman under whose influence Taira (Heike) power at court reached its zenith. During his lifetime he retained iron control of the state, placing his grandson, Antoku, on the throne in 1180, but after his death opposition to Heike hegemony grew and the family was finally overthrown in 1185.

Takeda Shingen 武田信玄 (1521–1573) was the famous lord of Kai, nowadays Yamanashi, whose warlike ambitions brought him into confrontation with Nobunaga and Ieyasu.

Tanaka Kakuei 田中角栄 (1918–) was Japan's prime minister from 1972 to 1974, when he was forced to resign amid allegations of financial misdealing. He was arrested in 1976, accused of having received bribes from the Lockheed Corporation while in office, and was eventually sentenced to prison, though a series of appeals has kept him at liberty.

Tokugawa Iemitsu 徳川家光 (1604–1651) was the third Tokugawa shogun, who intensified the persecution of Christians, suppressed the Shimabara rebellion and instituted the policy of *sakoku* (strict national seclusion). He ruled from 1623 to 1651.

Tokugawa Iesada 徳川家定 (1824–1858), the 13th Tokugawa shogun, ruled from 1853 to his death, and reluctantly concluded the commercial treaty with Townsend Harris that spelt the end of Japan's seclusion.

Tokugawa Ieyasu 徳川家康 (1542–1616) was the founder of the Tokugawa shogunate and ruled as its first shogun from 1603 to 1605. Building on the unifying work of Nobunaga and Hideyoshi, he instituted a period (the Edo period, 1603–1867) of comparative peace and stability. The Toshogu Shrine at Nikko is his mausoleum.

Tokugawa Yoshimune 徳川吉宗 (1684–1751) was the eighth Tokugawa shogun, under whom the first nationwide census was conducted. He ruled from 1716 to 1745.

Toyotomi Hideyori 豊臣秀頼 (1593–1615) was Hideyoshi's son, on whose behalf Ishida Mitsunari fought Ieyasu at Sekigahara. Hideyori survived until 1615 when, besieged by Ieyasu at Osaka Castle, he committed suicide.

Toyotomi Hideyoshi 豊臣秀吉 (1537–1598) was the warlord who completed Nobunaga's unification of Japan. He is remembered for his humble origins (his father was a foot soldier) and for his campaigns of foreign conquest in Korea, but his chief contribution to history is the groundwork he laid for the founding of the Tokugawa shogunate.

Weston, Walter (1861–1940) was a Church of England missionary who came to Japan in 1889 and helped popularise the sport of mountaineering.

Wright, Frank Lloyd (1867–1959) was the American architect who designed Tokyo's old Imperial Hotel and other buildings.

Yamamoto Isoroku 山本五十六 (1884–1943) was Commander-in-Chief of the Combined Fleet during World War II and the man who first proposed a surprise attack on Pearl Harbour, even though he believed that a war with America was ultimately unwinnable.

Yanagita Kunio 柳田国男 (1875–1962) was a bureaucrat, journalist and scholar who, from 1930, concentrated his full energies on establishing the discipline of Japanese folklore studies. His classic in the field, *Tono Monogatari* was published much earlier, in 1910, and has been translated into English by Robert Morse as *Legends of Tono*.

Zeami 世阿弥 (1363–1443) was a brilliant actor and dramatist who established the Noh theatre as a respected form. He was exiled to Sado in 1434, having perhaps refused to reveal the secret teachings of his art to his nephew, a protégé of the shogun's.

About the Author

Alan Booth was born in London in 1946. He has an honors degree from Birmingham University and did postgraduate research at the Shakespeare Institute. He won the Birmingham Post Prize for Poetry in 1967.

He came to Japan in 1970 and has walked the length of the country, a journey described in his 1985 *The Roads to Sata*. Kirkus Reviews called that book 'a wonderful work' and the author a 'literary stylist, sociologist, anthropologist and travel writer armed with a poet's vision.'

Alan Booth has won three PATA literary prizes, including Best Story (Any Language) in 1982. He is Japanese film critic for the *Asahi Evening News*, a regular contributor to the *Far Eastern Economic Review* and the *Times Literary Supplement*, among others.

Alan Booth lives in Tokyo with his wife, Sok-Chzeng, and daughter, Mirai.